SAFARI HOME

A Memoir of Africa

Lani van Ryzin Havens

D1739053

Illustrations and photos by the author

IDYLL RIVER HOUSE

For David

every step of the way

TABLE OF CONTENTS

FOREWARD

When David and I left for Africa in 1983 we left behind our newly blended family, six children, all in their early 20's just setting out in life, our parents were aging, each of us with our own share of family complexities. For my family there was the lingering pain following the collapse of my marriage to John, his revealing that he was gay, our separation, then divorce, the years of healing for all of us and the recognition that we would remain a family that cared about each other no matter how the structure might look to others. John, so supportive when I met David, so proud of me when I finished my PhD in Madison, such a faithful father to our four children, remained my dearest friend.

Over the five and a half years David and I worked in Kenya we spent most of our time on safari. Safari in Kiswahili means a journey, any kind of journey that takes you away from home, not just a wildlife expedition. Our safari took us across Kenya documenting, filming, and evaluating the impact of development assistance on grassroots communities. I soon learned that Africans are storytellers, wonderful oral historians and the rhythm of their words, the depth of meaning they reveal is spellbinding. I also learned there is no one face of Africa, no one story to be told, no one storyteller. I was equally captivated by what I learned from squatter women, nomadic leaders, British settlers, Kenyan scholars, NGO and church workers. I have included a number of these stories just as they were told, others I created from strings of stories we heard from the people we met, all woven together with our own unfolding safari in Africa.

Given the poor state of communications coupled with my roots in journalism, I wrote lengthy family letters on our experiences as much for my own needs as for those we left behind. Also, not quite severing my academic roots, I was called on to evaluate various humanitarian assistance programs from a grassroots perspective and wrote numerous articles sharing what insights we were gleaning in the fine art of relief and development support across cultures. Each harrowing journey, each new village brought a new insight. Each song of welcome, each celebration shared told a story to be saved and treasured.

4

The names and titles of some of the names and organizations mentioned here have been altered in concern for continuing political risks and the longevity of memories.

IT WAS ALL BECAUSE OF THE DALAI LAMA

The Dalai Lama was coming to the University of Wisconsin in Madison to do a *Kalichakra,* a meditative retreat and initiation into Buddhism. I heard about it soon after I had completed a course in transcendental meditation which was soon after I had decided not to be a Catholic which was soon after John left me and the children saying he was gay which threw my life into a cold downward spiral.

It was like falling into an abyss that had no bottom. I insisted we both go into counseling convinced I could save him. Then came therapy groups on my own, plunging into a master's degree, still falling, that cold lost feeling of falling. While completing my research for my doctorate, I was simultaneously trying out psychics to discover what lay ahead which is where, eventually, the Dalai Lama comes in.

I had gone to New York during a teaching break at the university to visit a close friend of John's, a dear soul we had both been close to as undergraduates, literally a member of our wedding party. It was another of my attempts to put past pieces together to figure out the future, this time with someone who knew us both. I wrestled with the reality that I would always love John, feeling somehow he would always love me but how was that even feasible.

While in New York trying to distract myself so life could go on I wandered through an exhibit of Aztec pottery spending hours soaking in exquisite primitive forms baked in earth. Since I was doing pottery and clay sculpture at the time it was easy to get lost in the simplicity and primal beauty of it all. I bought the exhibition publication mesmerized by the magnificent piece on the cover.

Back home a few days later I was sitting in the sun on our deck absorbing the Aztec images once again paging through the brochure. I was killing time, waiting to leave for my appointment to see a psychic, wondering if I was being totally ridiculous and should just cancel. His name had been given to me by a colleague before I left for New York. She had a friend doing graduate work in parapsychology who had been documenting his uncanny abilities. He was visiting from India, only in town for a few days. Feeling totally absurd I called. He never asked my name. Write down on a piece of paper what you want to know was his only instruction on the phone. I did, then sat there in the sun with my Aztec pottery booklet waiting for my appointment and my future to appear.

I felt totally the fool when I rang the doorbell at a stranger's home. What in the world was I thinking? I had been absorbed for the past month rechecking my data for my dissertation, hardened by the scientific method, now here I was seeking answers from a psychic recommended by a friend of a friend. As I turned in retreat a thin middle-aged Asian man opened the door, nodded, no introductions, and led me to a back screened porch. He motioned toward a chair and sat opposite me, his kindly unhurried motions calming my racing heart. I handed him my folded piece of paper, a bit rumpled and sweaty. He held it covering it with both hands, not opening it, just looking at me.

7

The silence seemed endless before he spoke. "I am having a difficult time reading you just now," he said. "You are completely covered in images of what looks like ancient pottery. Aztec perhaps?"

I broke out in a sweat, shivering. My hands went clammy. Obviously aware of my reaction he asked me to take deep breaths, blow out slowly. I breathed in, deeply, pursing my lips to blow out as slowly as I could, always the over-achiever even now. He never set the paper down, never read my scrawled questions, what lies ahead for me, will, will I ever stop falling, will I ever meet someone to share my life with again? A few more deep breaths, blow out slowly.

The pause seemed endless before his words, slow and simple, floated out. You will marry a man named John, I see three children.

I felt a cold rush. "But I am, I was married to a man named John. We have — four children," I blurted out.

His silence was painful. Then, "Protect your children."

My whole body tightened. "I had twins, my first born, two sons, then a daughter, then another son."

"Ah. Yes, three birthings, that is what I am seeing, three birthings, that explains it." He seemed to be exhaling his words. "Your children are fine. They are all fine."

I blew out slowly again, my clammy clutching hands tightening their grip on the arms of the wicker chair.

I had to break into another of his long nodding silences. "I'm searching for a position. I need to make decisions, soon, where to go, but I'm feeling so alone that...." I couldn't finish. This whole thing was beginning to feel frightening. The urge to leave was rapidly growing but I also felt frozen in place.

He sat there nodding then a quiet stream of words fell into the space. "You will meet someone you've been with before in several previous lives. You'll relate to each other on so many different levels. You will even work together, yes, I see you working together."

8

I felt my heart beating in rhythm now with every syllable he spoke.

"Meditate, you will see his face. His name will come to you, soon. When you are quiet and still, gather the light within you. Let it rise up and float out of the top of your head. Watch where it goes. Follow it. You will know the path ahead."

That night I wrote down the experience in my journal. It all seemed somewhere between miraculous and ridiculous. Nevertheless, I sat bolt upright in bed and followed his instructions. Meditate, gather the light, send it upwards.

At the time with the kids' band practicing in the rec room just beneath my bedroom, it was a challenge. The phone had been ringing incessantly while the band thumped on.

"It's David, he can't make it." Someone had finally picked up the phone.

David was their drummer. More guitars booming out, phone ringing again.

"David, again. His mom said OK. He's on his way."

Back to my white light energy, rising up, letting it float, follow it. My energy floated across the golf course at the end of our road and plopped straight down on the shores of Lake Mendota. I had been considering teaching options in faraway places, a university in the south Pacific another in coastal Maine, picturesque places where I could paint and write. However, it was evident I wasn't getting any farther than the end of our road even though I gave my floating light a suggestion for faraway places. I tried again, each attempt plummeting down shortly after takeoff on the shores of the nearby lake.

That night sometime in the twilight just before sleep a face abruptly came into focus, kindly eyes, a smile rimmed with a beard, tousled hair, clear then foggy, again the name David echoing from the band below.

The experience floated in and out of focus over the next several months as I was completing my research, exploring the link between human behavior and the environments we design for people. My studies incorporated architectural planning and design, so my obvious next step should have been to search out schools of architecture where this had become a required course, but other forces were rising to the forefront — keeping my family together above all else, my abiding ache in losing John, wanting to still have him in our lives, yearning to do something with my own life that mattered, something that pushed me beyond my familiar path.

I had grown up listening to my dad's stories of his life in Hawaii, serving as navigator for the Bishop Museum collecting artifacts from uncharted islands, racing an old yawl in transpacific races from the California coast back to Honolulu. His father's ship caught in a cyclone off the coast of Australia, ten days in a life raft before being rescued, later finding his way to Hawaii and becoming a sea captain. Sailing had been in our family's blood for generations, a key part of my growing up years, and since childhood my fantasies had been on writing, painting and sailing. My undergraduate degree was in journalism and art and now with more degrees in hand, I was trying to hang onto the pieces of my life, questioning whether I even wanted to continue with this academic path.

It was one of my children's band friends who mentioned in passing that the Dalai Lama was coming to Madison. His words came like a bolt. I immediately tracked down the details. The Dalai Lama would be conducting a Kalachakra, an initiation into Buddhism. To be eligible to participate you had to attend a course at the University Buddhist Center. I immediately signed up. I was searching for new roots. If the Catholic church had no room in the pews for John, then there was no room for me or our children. Meditation had brought me into a new state of being that was both spiritually exhilarating and frightening at the same time finally realizing how deep my need for spiritual understanding was. I was driven to pursue this opportunity.

The Buddhist Center was located in a house just across the golf course from our house on the road that hugged the shores of Lake Mendota. The first session of the class included a reception with a spread of

Tibetan food, artifacts and music that certainly signaled I was in a specific cultural milieu. Many wore Indian or Nepalese shawls, still looking like a gathering of graduate students you might find anywhere in Madison.

"Welcome." A smiling sandy haired man held out a tray, cups of aromatic tea. His name was Jim, an architect. He lived directly across the street from the Center, son of a protestant minister and long-time member of this Buddhist community. We chatted for quite a while with the hum of conversations surrounding us, Jim talking about the excitement of the Dalai Lama's visit, asking about my coursework in architecture, me sharing my excitement about the Kalachakra, my difficult personal situation being newly divorced, my job search dilemma.

"But what do you really, really want to do next?" It was evident he was a good listener of what lay between the lines.

"I'd really like to live on a sailboat and write and illustrate kids' books." I heard myself say it but it sounded as though it were someone else talking. I had published a number of young adult books but had never really given any conscious thought of doing that as a life plan.

His eyes widened with his smile. "I'm going to introduce you to my housemate, David," he said above the chatter. "But not until we finish this project we're working on together." His smile grew even wider. "Once he meets you, I won't see him again."

A gong sounded and I followed the crowd into a chapel-like room, my heart beating wildly. David?

For the next several months I attended the sessions, sitting on an embroidered cushion on the floor, meditating with a roomful of strangers, the peaceful drone of chanting words everyone there seemed to know but I didn't understand, lectures on the power of love, the power of silence, visualizing peace in our souls, the oneness of our being, the path to enlightenment. My tea break chats with Jim were part of the calm I was beginning to feel.

The final training session ran longer than expected so I didn't stay for the informal chat afterwards. I pulled cautiously out of the Center's parking area between high banks of fresh snow. As I turned onto the narrow lake road a man stepped out between snow mounds and crossed right in front of me. I braked. When our eyes met a rush went through me. It was the face I had seen in my meditation. I had no doubt. The kindly eyes, the tousled hair, the beard, it all came vividly back. For a moment I couldn't move. I waved him on. Everything shifted into a slow paced pre-scripted reality.

When I got home, I called Jim's house. A voice much deeper than Jim's answered. After giving my name I asked, "Is this — David? Did you just cross the road in front of the Buddhist Center?"

He was. He had.

"I think we are supposed to meet," was all I could think of saying.

Jim had told him about me, he had come over to the Center for coffee hour hoping to find me there but I had already left so he was heading back to their house directly across the road on the shores of Lake Mendota. I invited them both over that afternoon.

I had just baked bread and laid it out with some homemade marmalade. David declared marmalade was one of his absolute favorites. The three of us talked, uncanny connections collecting in the air until it was almost dark.

As we were about to say our farewells, I mentioned I had an appointment in Milwaukee the next day, an interview for a position at the UW school of architecture. I was not looking forward to the two-hour drive each way given the snow. David's smile turned quizzical. He had a winterization training workshop to conduct in Milwaukee the next day, part of the state's poverty program where he worked. He could drive me there. At this point we had both ceased to be amazed.

We drove to Milwaukee the next morning, life stories softly tumbling back and forth like the beat of the windshield wipers against the snow, the slow unveiling of our inner selves, his reluctance to follow his family's push for him to go to seminary vying with his greater

12

reluctance to get drafted into the Vietnam War. He had been an active war protestor and soon realized the potential power of wearing a collar to protests so seminary became his path to changing the world. While at a boring meeting of church leaders at his assigned student church he began fearing the confines of a minister's life. He glanced at the headlines of a newspaper lying on the chair next to him. Batista Flees Cuba. The last revolution there will ever be was the thought running through his head, so he left the meeting, borrowed his roommate's Leica camera, hitchhiked to Miami and got on a flight to Cuba. Posing as a photojournalist he was assigned to a group of soldiers policing order in the old city as Castro was preparing to enter Havana.

Images swirled in my head as he spoke. His marriage, the uphill battle of trying to save someone from themselves, his obvious love of parenting his two daughters, his drive to nurture in them a deep caring for others coupled with a sense of playfulness, his own sense of the same. His years with Cesar Chavez in the beginning days of the farmworker movement, getting squirted with mustard at the Kresge's sit-in then dragged out into the streets, the march on Selma, his work with the Civil Rights Movement, putting his wife through law school, the painful decision to separate, all painted a portrait of this man next to me. The turns in our lives felt so different yet parallel, aspirations, perspectives, shared thinking on every conceivable topic.

My interview at the Architecture Department went better than expected. His workshop went smoothly, though once again the pain of poverty in a wealthy society was a jolt. On the trip home our conversation flowed with a comfort level I wasn't prepared for as though we had always been together and were just catching up. Here sat David, here he was nearly a year after I had seen his face, heard his name echoing from the band below. His story was new to me but he was not. I didn't know what to feel. The long anticipation I had experienced was the one piece of me I couldn't share with him, the quiet Asian psychic, the rumpled questions I had handed him. Not yet. Not in the pauses as we watched the snow blanket the road ahead.

Barely aware of time on that drive I made the decision to accept the teaching position in architecture. Jim was right. He lost his housemate. David and I never separated from that day on.

The Dalai Lama's arrival created a great stir in Madison. The *Kalichakra* would be the first he had conducted outside of Tibet or Nepal. The *stupa* Jim had designed, a swooping roofed structure with elegantly painted trim work, was built in the countryside outside of Madison, a sacred place to memorialize the event. Nearby a great white tent had been erected with a platform set with pillows and chairs draped with colorful fabrics.

I saw the Dalai Lama for the first time at the welcoming reception, an unpretentious figure with an overwhelming presence, one shoulder draped in a golden saffron throw the other bare revealing the biceps of an athlete. He greeted each of us swirling around him, the magnetism of wanting to be in his sphere was overwhelming. His smile spoke volumes when he looked me straight in the eye, laughing joyfully. Monks in ruby and saffron robes were everywhere, trays loaded with teacups carried high, the gaggle of exuberant voices filling the air. The thrill of just being there was surging through me mingling with this distinct reluctance, almost a fear of getting caught up in the spiraling enthusiasm of the crowd around me. I had been having strange feelings throughout the months of preparation sitting on that cushion listening to the chanting of those around me. They all knew the words; they knew what they meant. But for me the language was music but not meaning.

John and I had sold the house that was our children's childhood home, the house I had designed, soaring ceilings, windows to the sky, memories in every corner. I bought an old prairie style house in the middle of farmland on the outskirts of Madison to shorten my commute to the Milwaukee campus.

By whatever happenstance the farmhouse was close to the rolling hills where the Kalachakra was unfolding. The *stupa* sat elegantly on a rise near the huge tent with fluttering banners as I parked nearby on that first morning. I entered the tent with the others, the droning of long horns filling the air, gongs sounding, dancing monks in elaborate robes and head pieces twirling in exuberance, spiraling down the aisle, other monks of every age in humble saffron and ruby robes filling the platform at the front, seemingly floating into place. This was truly a spiritual celebration, ecstatic joy, so unlike the somber solemnities of my Catholic memories.

I'm not sure how I ended up in the front so close to the Dalai Lama that his presence was palpable, the platform for the *mandala* next to him. The painting would emerge as monks hovering in a circle shoulder to shoulder were tapping sand into place creating an ancient depiction of the pathway to enlightenment that would guide our meditation.

Nothing seemed to happen in sequence. Everything was bound together as one place in time, the joy-filled words of the Dalai Lama, the droning chants, the powerful silence of so many meditating together under one tent, the fragrance of mint tea. Somewhere between sleep and hyper awareness I floated into a space I had never been. Kindness, love, no word fit nor mattered. Time was irrelevant. At day's end monks gave each of us a stalk of wheat. Take it home, the Dalai Lama said softly, place it under your mattress. I don't remember driving home.

David had dinner waiting, quietly waiting, but words were hard to choose. I placed my wheat under our mattress that night collapsing into sleep and a vivid, tangible dream. I was in a magnificent parade riding an elephant, my soft saffron veils and pink scarves fluttering around me so that sometimes I was seeing the throngs in the street through different hues. We were parading past huge ancient buildings with deep balconies, people in festive attire cheering us on as our procession made its way around the massive square, banners fluttering half blocking the view ahead as my slow-moving pachyderm patiently put one foot in front of the other propelling me through time.

I felt still in a stupor the next morning as David drove me back. Everything at the Kalachakra appeared the same as when I had left the day before, stalk of wheat in hand, but I felt profoundly altered, the dream inhabiting me as though it were the true reality and all of this around me was surreal. David had peered over his coffee cup that morning as I shared my dream, sensing my state, offering so casually to drive me to the Kalachakra, to wait for me parking in the shade of a roadside tree. He had a good book, not to worry. Where had this amazing man come from? Was he surreal too?

Inside the tent people were crowding around the *mandala* platform, murmuring voices rising and falling as those in front gently made room for others to see what the monks had painted with sand while we slept. I inched my way forward and held back a gasp. A procession of elephants, ancient buildings surrounding a square, the same deep balconies, saffron and pink images glowing in perfect detail in the sands, everything was there as vividly as I had seen it. I'm not sure how long I stared at what was already etched in my memory before I made my way to a chair. The brochure for the *Kalachakra* was on the chair, the cover showed a vibrant image of the *mandala,* elephants with their riders, figures with scarves blowing across faces, parading the streets.

The remaining days of the *Kalachakra* are woven together in one piece of memory. Only the exquisite *mandala* remained in its own memory space saturating into my mind's eye. On the final day I held my breath when, in one moment, the *mandala* was ceremoniously brushed away as scattered sand by the monks. Nothing in this life is permanent. We are all on the path to enlightenment. This tangible earth is only for now, for this part of our path. We will ultimately brush it all away. We will ultimately reach the divine.

David was waiting for me in the shade of the tree his book flopped over his face.

"Home?" he asked when I slid onto the seat beside him.

"Yes. Home."

GOOSE GRATITUDE

I think it was David's childhood memories of his sister's geese that inspired us to buy that big old house in the country. David's father died when he was ten and in those growing up years, he often spent weekends with his older sister Eleanor and her husband George. They lived on a lime green hill in a rambling country house with an enormous front porch and the family sat on the lawn while the dogs chased the geese and the geese chased the dogs and there was pastoral bliss. I detected gradual embellishments in the images that had grown over the years but who was I to challenge a childhood remembrance.

We were at a farmers' market the week before we were to move into our own rambling country house on a lime green hill when David spotted a stand selling goose grease. Where there's goose grease there's geese he rationalized, and while I bought rhubarb jam and potted herbs, he bought a box of goslings. Six in all. We did not question what we were going to do with them in town for the coming week while we packed nor the complications of moving them to the country. It all seemed inevitable, given the childhood dream, and in a way, it was.

We did not get off to a great start as goose raisers. When we woke the next morning, we discovered all of the goslings had escaped from the chicken-wire pen David put up in the backyard. Packing was abandoned as we scoured our suburban neighborhood without success. How far could a gaggle of goslings go? In desperation we called the police. It seemed the pinnacle of absurdity to report missing geese to the police but they took the description down in all seriousness and in a half hour a kindly officer called back. The goslings had been spotted by a patrol car heading toward the golf course not far away. With baskets in hand we raced out on our first of many goose chases.

For the remainder of the week the goslings squawked away in the dining room in a cut down cardboard refrigerator box as I said my goodbyes to our family home. I had designed the house with its soaring shed roofs, tall windows capturing light from every angle, built into the hill with a bridge walkway leading down from the street to the small courtyard. John and I raised our four children here in this unique community attached to the UW campus, and now it overflowed with memories as moving day arrived. John had moved on to Columbia University and it was evident we were both trying to weave together how to be an extended family. Gregg, Garrett and Jeanne Claire followed him there to start college. Chris had one more year of high school, a gift to have him with me for at least this year. My hesitant attempts at dating had been interspersed with meeting John for lunch somewhere familiar, conversations on how we were each doing, how the kids were dealing with everything, John always encouraging me to reach out, apologizing for the pain he had caused me, everyone, me of course crying through it all, saying we'd all be fine. It was a calming relief when he and David met for the first time, John later telling me he really liked David, he was happy for me. He looked wistful, glassy eyed saying that. I never did understand, yet leaving the house that day I felt as though I could be happy for me too.

Now with a back seat loaded with goslings David and I headed to the country, an old prairie style house sitting on its own lime green hill awaiting us. David built a secure goose pen before we even unloaded our bed. Under the shade of a giant elm with a carpet of lush grass it looked strong enough to house a badger. But security was not the problem this time. In the morning four of the goslings were lying on their backs, feet up to the sky. We were never quite sure what did them in but the dwindling of the ranks was in retrospect a blessing in disguise.

Our two dogs took to the countryside with genetic grace, Mr. Blue, an Australian Blue Shepherd, gangly and exuberant, and Kimmer, our elderly Cairn terrier who ruled the roost. They loved being off-leash and stuck together as a twosome exploring their new turf those first few days while we were unpacking. In the midst of the final unpacking the phone rang, it was our neighbor asking if our dogs were with us. Someone had spotted a small dog by the side of the road apparently hit by a car. A larger dog was guarding it and wouldn't let anyone approach. We ran outside calling. No sign of Kimmer or Mr. Blue.

I found the old afghan I had crocheted. It had years of history on our family couch with the kids trying to tug it away from Kimmer who loved to scramble it into a heap then sleep on top of it. David raced off in the car while I stayed watch in case our fears were mistaken and the dogs would return. An hour or so later David returned carrying Kimmer's body wrapped in the afghan. Mr. Blue slouched to the ground.

Quiet tears streaming down my face we dug her grave next to a large smooth boulder near the house. It would be her gravestone. I wrapped her in the afghan she loved and placed her in the ground. Mr. Blue lay in the grass nearby, head resting on paws watching our every move. When David tapped in the last bit of earth we stood there together. She was the dog of my children's childhood, the dog who loved to roll in dead Alewives on the shores of Lake Michigan at my parents' summer home, the comfort dog who read our sadness and joys. She was Toto when my four children dressed as the characters from the Wizard of Oz in our village 4th of July parade. When we added Mr. Blue to our family, she harassed him into family norms never relinquishing her position of first dog, never leaving his side nor he hers.

As we turned to take the shovels back to the barn Mr. Blue suddenly leapt to his feet on high alert, head turning in every direction as though he was trying to spot something. He bolted off sniffing the ground around Kimmer's grave circling it in increasingly larger circles as he sniffed, running, seemingly on the trail of something. His speed increased as his circles grew now circling the house then the entire yard at a frantic gallop. It proved useless trying to waylay him. All we could do was watch until exhausted he collapsed on the porch. He stayed out there, nose pointing out toward the grave for the next three or four days. We couldn't coax him in at night. He didn't want to eat. Eventually he came inside sticking close to our side as we unpacked the last boxes.

Life was changing for all of us. Though we lavished affection on the remaining pair of goslings it was the lawn tractor that won their hearts. Somehow its bulging posterior and pointed nose and the way it charged up and down the lawn must have reminded them of Mother. Once they had imprinted with it there was little we could do. Every time we tried to mow our lime green lawn the goslings ran frantically after Mother screeching pathetically. When we paused to make sure we hadn't unwittingly chopped their wing feathers they scurried underneath taking shelter next to her whirling blades. The grass grew long on our lime green hill that summer and the lawn tractor ceased whirling, ensconced near the lilac bush giving shelter to her goslings.

Mr. Blue however did not take to the geese and vice versa as David's fond memories had suggested. The *Kalachakra* had left me with a new surge of energy coupled with an internal calm. In between renovation projects we dealt with brief dog-goose skirmishes as we pressed on digging out a much too large basin as a goose pond. We edged it with rocks, fern and tiger lilies. It was beautiful, nostalgic even though the overhanging mulberry tree was destined to seasonally turn the pond into a purple vat.

In the evening we sat on our lime green hill and watched as the geese chased Mr. Blue and he snapped back making it evident that there was no pastoral charm in their relationship. As the geese grew the battles grew ranging from cold to hot wars with nips and hissing and soon we were not excluded from the skirmishes.

Our quiet strolls through the rolling oak wood hills had by now turned into challenge matches. Before setting out I learned to case the position of the geese. Leaving by the farthest door I slipped out as

20

noiselessly as possible avoiding crunching leaves. It is amazing how noisy long grass can be, but there was no such thing as a clean escape. Suddenly from behind a bush there'd be the flutter of feathers. With heads down and wings outstretched they charged, screeching in their frenzy. I became quite adept with a broom and never went out of the house without it. Still, it never quite felt pastoral strolling the hills with broom in hand, listening for a hiss in the bushes.

When winter and Wisconsin snows were not far off David converted a giant old dog house into a goose house. He stacked hay bales around the sides and over the top and rigged a large light bulb inside for warmth. Alas, the geese never liked it. They huddled under their tractor mother which we eventually draped with a tarp while the snows made a mountain of them all. Determined, broom in hand, I tried coaxing them into the snug goose house with pans of food but to no avail.

The family that had built our house nearly a century before had first built a small house to live in while the big house was going up. The small house was near collapse and we had tied ropes around it to prevent it from wracking, tying it off to a nearby oak tree so the whole thing wouldn't cave in while we replaced studs and beams and eventually the floor. It will be a charming guesthouse someday we told ourselves. Our whimsical plans included a stained-glass window that I had already started, skylights over a sleeping loft, but the whimsy faded fast when the geese moved into the open basement, odors of authentic farming wafting through the floorboards. We soon relinquished our dream, renovations stopped and the hay bales were moved in for the squatters that winter. The guesthouse was now the goose house.

The driveway to our house was nearly a half mile long and we could hear approaching cars crunching the gravel long before we saw them. While Mr. Blue enjoyed the romp to welcome visiting cars the ritual had changed. In full attack formation the geese led the charge, wings stretched out amazingly wide, hissing heads held low running fearlessly head on toward any approaching car. It was always the car that relinquished but that didn't end the battle. The geese would slowly waddle to the side of the road and hiss from the flanks pecking at the tires as the alien machine crept on.

It was getting out of the car that presented the greatest challenge. The minute the car stopped they launched a pecking attack on the grill plate and front bumper. We surmised it was the squashed bug tidbits they loved but they always had their eyes on the driver and the click of the door handle alerted them to the fact that someone was about to escape. Charging around to the side they pecked like a pair of machine guns at the opening door.

I started commuting each day with my broom in the front seat beside me. I learned that if I clicked the driver's side door, leaving it slightly ajar, then quickly crawled over the stick shift and slipped out the opposite side I could often make it to the front porch before the geese reached my heels. Often, but not always. We advised guests to remain in their cars until we could reach them with an escort broom.

When the Wisconsin winter came in its full fury the water in the tub outside the goose house froze solid. Twice a day broom in hand I plodded through the snow with a sprinkling can of warm water to replenish the tub. The geese took great joy in waddling under the warm spray, preening their feathers, craning their necks. They were in ecstasy and I felt in some strange way that they truly appreciated my efforts. In fact there were times I almost detected a smile in the way they held their beaks under the warm drizzle. That is until the water ran out. There was barely a moment's pause before the smile turned to a hiss and they'd begin attacking the empty sprinkling can and then me. It was what we termed goose gratitude and the term has stuck within our family to this day.

We had by now reached a low point in country living. Mr. Blue seldom left the front porch and I was tired of living the pastoral dream broom in hand. David continued to vow it had never been like this for his sister Eleanor and her geese. They had chased the dogs, and the dogs had chased them and the family sat on the lime green hill. He was lost again in that childhood memory but not for long. That night he called Eleanor to see what it was she had done right with her geese. Perhaps there were training techniques, something in their food.

"Geese?" she said in surprise. "I don't know anything about geese, David."

He was evidently stunned.

"Don't you remember — when I'd visit you when I was little. The big house and the pond and the dogs would chase the geese and we'd all sit on the grass."

"Those weren't geese, David." Her voice was soft but matter-of-fact, not knowing what territory she was treading. "Those were ducks, David. Ducks. Good lord, geese are vicious."

There was a long silence as the pastoral childhood dream sank slowly to the bottom of the purple pond.

Throughout that winter the geese remained a part of our lives but fate had its own agenda for them when David's daughter Megan came to visit us from college bearing an unidentifiable creature in her arms. At first glance it looked like a limp monkey with its long dark brown legs curled inward, its body fixed in a fetal position. She had found it in a snow bank on the campus of Beloit College where she was a student. The poor creature had obviously been beaten and was now dying. She was fearful if she took it to the pound it would be put down. We named her Annie for little orphan Annie and Mr. Blue took to her immediately. We made a bed for her by the wood stove and Mr. Blue lay next to her wrapping his body around her. We had little hope for Annie as she couldn't hold her head up well but Blue began licking her and wouldn't stop. Nuzzling her head, licking her face, her legs, prodding her with his nose trying to move her. He was on a mission to rouse her. It was about the third day when she lifted her head and stood up on wobbly legs that we recognized what she was. A Doberman pinscher. Stretching out eventually to her full height she was stunning.

By the time spring came Annie had grown tall and regal, romping with grace across our three acres of hills with the geese not far behind testing out the areas where snow had melted. In retrospect it was inevitable. David came back with the news. Annie had killed a goose.

We called our neighbor with the wisdom of his farming years and asked how to train Annie. His words were chilling. Once a dog kills a farm animal and has tasted blood it's difficult to stop it. He had a lot of chickens and ducks nearby and we could hear the urgent concern in his voice. His guidance was clear. Tie the dead goose around her neck and leave it there for four days. The stench might do it. We gasped.

David found some wire and fastened the dead goose around Annie's neck. We could hardly watch as she dragged herself across the yard and up the porch steps, bumping the heavy goose on each step. Mr. Blue kept his distance speaking with his eyes that he wanted no part of this while Annie stared at us, the dead goose like an albatross draped across her neck, her doe-eyes pleading. We held fast for almost a day but the sight of her in such anguish got to us. She must have learned her lesson by now we rationalized as we cut the wires. The dead goose dropped with a thud and within seconds she sprang from the porch, raced toward the other goose and grabbed it by the neck with an audible snap.

We buried both geese just beyond the goose house and found a new home for Annie away from farm animals. With the geese gone we walked the hills fearlessly and sat on our lime green hill with Mr. Blue. It all felt peaceful and pastoral, but it was never quite the same.

Life at the farmhouse was evolving. I continued to meditate, the inspiration of the *Kalachakra* melding with my life as a whole, unsure of what lay ahead. I was eagerly anticipating something. David was unstoppable, adding a solar greenhouse, renovating the kitchen in between poverty program work while I prepared lectures and wrote. We'd sit together on the front porch swing at day's end as though we had spent a lifetime together, kindred spirits, something I had never experienced, never knew enough to long for. The geese were gone, Annie was with her new family, Mr. Blue flew off to Alaska to join my youngest son Christopher in his long-dreamed adventure. Our children were all on their own life path and even the chickens we tried raising were no longer with us. David saw the last one hanging by her neck in a fox's mouth as the culprit cleared the five-foot fence surrounding the coop we had built. David went out on a foxhunt and tracked her down in the woods behind the barn. Finding a scatter of feathers in a den, mother fox peering out surrounded by wide-eyed babies, he decided they needed the chickens more than we did.

As we continued to think of what our next chapter of life might bring, a nearly abandoned sailboat, a John Alden yawl named Genesis, took up residence next to the goose house. Aha, we could restore this antique beauty, sail off to faraway places, my father's story of sailing the South Pacific still haunting my dreams.

We set up a steel drum half filled with water with a downspout protruding, built a fire underneath it and steamed ten-foot oak pieces to sister the old cracked ribs. As though the old house wasn't a project in itself, we were now racing between steamer and yawl, up the ladder into the hull clamping the new piece down before it cooled. Each step forward revealed more rot and it didn't take that long before reality set in. We tenderly covered her cockpit in canvas and decided we needed time to reconsider Genesis.

Sadi, our old Mercedes with nearly 300,000 miles to her life, hid behind one lilac bush in hopes of one day restoring her, but for now we were preserving our tranquil rural views with lilacs. Old Jeep hid behind another lilac bush but what we really needed was a truck to haul wood so one day David got out his grinder. I got the job inside Old Jeep, squirting water at the ceiling lining to keep it from catching fire while David sawed off the rear top of the vehicle with the grinder, one of many life experiences David introduced me to. Voila, we had a pickup truck. It served us well in hauling lumber for renovations and firewood but its comical profile raised eyebrows even at the local dump.

I enjoyed my teaching. Graduate students in architecture are a unique breed of creative dreamers, fresh eyes searching for a better way to design spaces for life, a better way to live. My courses in design research and evaluation allowed me to accompany them into evaluating their ideas of what could be. Walking with them through their imagined spaces, what would people be doing here, where would the light be? It wasn't long before I tangibly caught their excitement, going out into the world, creating something new, making something happen. We had both reached a tipping point. We sent off a few letters of inquiry with our resumes attached. That was on a Monday. It was Thursday when we got the call. Would we be interested in working in Kenya?

The call was from Christian Church Disciples of Christ, the liberal denomination David had been ordained in but drifted away from after the civil rights movement faded. The council of churches in Kenya wanted to do an evaluation of the multiple programs they had been working on since the country's independence. They needed assistance with evaluating and documenting their work. Our resumes landed on the day the request came in and the match seemed uncanny. Africa itself was uncanny. Before he was born David's parents had been missionaries for ten years in what was then the Belgian Congo. Stories had permeated his childhood of his dad teaching people how to bake bricks so their mud houses wouldn't dissolve in the rain, smuggling milking goats on a barge up the Congo River past the Belgian governor's outpost so village children would have milk, earning him the title in Lonkundu that meant 'he who pulls arrow out of eye and still you see,' his two sisters raised in Africa taunting him, 'ha ha, you never got to ride a camel.'

David gave notice to the state energy office and I finished the semester at the university. We began learning a few phrases of Kiswahili, reading everything we could get our hands on about Kenya. We put Sadie and Old Jeep up for sale, but there sat unmovable Genesis in all her rotted glory until a man showed up who really wanted Sadie despite the nest of mice in her air filter. He agreed to salvage what he could from Genesis and haul her to the dump in exchange for Sadie. A deal. We sold the house and in the chaos of departure, our bags packed, a young man came to buy Old Jeep then drove off without paying us. It really was time to move on.

INTO AFRICA

I pressed my cheek against the window of the plane as the thunderous gray hills of Africa emerged from the clouds. Lush pregnant mounds of primal vegetation rolled flat into languid savannahs that reached for the sea spilling in from the east. On the other side of the plane hills rose abruptly to tropical snow, frozen crystal peaks that punctured the clouds. As the plane drifted downward the skyline of Nairobi gradually came into view. High-rise structures, elegant concrete pillars clustered together suddenly gave way to the surrounding wilderness embossed with mud huts and fingers of smoke.

I reached for David's hand. Everything about coming here had happened at warp speed and now the African landscape was rising up to catch us. The airport stretched into a game reserve at the edge of the city, its runways fringed by a grass and thorn bush landscape that brought into focus every preconceived image of Africa I ever had. Eland and zebra scattered in alarm as our silver beast approached the strip invading their land with pilgrims and blasting jets.

"We're here," David whispered, squeezing my hand.

"We're here," I repeated, hardly believing my own words.

Making our way down the steps to the tarmac we were instantly caught up in a chaotic crowd propelling itself towards an unmarked entrance to the airport. With shoulder bags sliding off we followed a fast stepping couple holding US passports looking like they knew where they were going. Inside the building there was a line leading to a booth so high we had to stretch to submit our passports to a broad faced man in uniform who stared at us unblinking, then loudly stamped them without comment.

A troop of boy scouts in short pants and knee socks swarmed around us, sagged under the weight of their bulging backpacks as they inched forward now in the customs line. Our luggage including several aluminum cases had arrived without mishap and lay open for inspection. Seeing the contents – cameras, laptop computer, video equipment – the agent hailed his supervisor then turned toward us studying our passports.

I unfolded our document pouch and spread a series of letters and official papers in a line down the counter. We had come prepared. The warnings from others who had been on assignment in developing countries may have been exaggerated, but we had determined to take no chances. Everything we had was meticulously recorded as development related equipment for the humanitarian work we would be doing with the churches in Kenya.

The supervisor leaned over his broad belly staring at the papers one after the other working his way to the end of the counter where his eyes fell on the open cases of cameras. He straightened up abruptly. A woman with a cartload of luggage squeezed past us and a cheer rang out from the crowd waiting in the arrivals lounge as she pushed through the door.

Staring at the equipment the supervisor shook his head. We began explaining about the projects we would be working on, the letters validating our assignment, but our words seemed to float through the air like the nonsense verse children recite to distract elders from their appointed task.

"This is all on the list," the supervisor declared as though it was self-evident. "You must pay the value of each item plus one hundred percent duty for each of these." His hands swept over the array of equipment, his face as flat as his voice.

"That's two hundred per cent on each! That's impossible! We —." David caught himself.

"Sorry. It's all on the list. Go to a bank. Get a bond guaranteeing the equipment won't be sold in Kenya. Come back with the bond tomorrow."

"A bond? Tomorrow?"

"Tomorrow. When the customs office is open."

My hands were clammy as I closed the cases and locked each in turn, then a cold sinking feeling settled into my stomach as the agent slid them off behind the counter. David patted my shoulder.

The scouts were singing some trekking song and pushed past us as our aluminum cases were stacked on a cart and wheeled away. We stared at the tissue thin receipt with a blurred purple stamp on the bottom. This was not happening. Our new video camera, our laptop computer, 35mm camera, a case filled with lenses all being rolled through a paint-splattered doorway out of sight.

"It'll be OK," David said under his breath. "Let's just move on."

I fixed my hands firmly on the cart handle that held our remaining luggage. A swarm of tourists converged behind us. A tour leader in a safari suit and slouch hat held up a sign at the head of the group corralling all of them behind luggage carts slowly easing them along like one massive body toward a convoy of zebra striped mini buses waiting at the curb. Bobbing signs with names printed on them floated above the mass of people.

We were circling the perimeter of the crowd when a woman with a halo of black curls pushed through waving at us.

"Havens? Havens?" she called out.

We waved back and within moments were swept into a swaying hug with Kadzo.

"*Karibuni, karibuni!*" she repeated, her glowing black face, wide eyes, flashing.

We couldn't have felt more welcome. Kadzo was in charge of urban programs at the council. She was the force behind getting us hired and had been anxiously awaiting our arrival. In a cascading collision of greetings, back and forth sighs of relief and questions she led us through the parking area. Steven, a council driver, would take us to a hotel where we could rest for a few days while other accommodations were being arranged. With apologies she explained an urgent situation had just come up, and she had to leave immediately. She would be away for a week or so, but Steven would be available for whatever needs we had. Dinner at her house as soon as she returned. A promise. A last hug and she was off.

My eyes fixed on the thorn bush hills. I took a deep breath. David was rapidly explaining to Steven about our equipment, everything we needed was still at the airport. Steven just smiled nodding as he pulled away. Did we have the forms? It seemed evident this was a familiar problem. "Forms? What forms?" "Forms you must have to get the bond. "No, we don't have any forms." "Then we must get the forms," he said still smiling. "No problem."

I was exhausted from the flight and so exhilarated in being here that the words were just floating. I rolled down the window. The air was sweet with the fragrance of strange blossoms. Shafts of sunlight split the passing scenery into frames. Palms and hibiscus in pinks and crimsons edged the road alternating their color with scrap wood shanty vegetable stands. Crowds of people clustered around the market stalls, walking the edges of the road, massing at corner bus stops. Beyond the highway lay the humped silhouette of Ngong Hills, fading from morning mauve to the deep green savannah of the Nairobi Game Park below.

A truck ahead of us wallowed under an off-sided load, straddling both lanes. An approaching battered white pickup, its back end loaded with people, thumped onto the washed-out shoulder of the road in a shower of dust. People and goats fled from its path. I stiffened and grabbed David's hand. We were bearing down at full speed on a large truck that was clearly stalled in the middle of the road. Steven suddenly swerved into the on-coming traffic, swung around the truck and back into his lane, slamming on the brakes for a red light.

David squeezed my hand. He chatted calmly with Steven who never stopped smiling, carrying on how thrilled everyone was that we were here, most of them were away at a conference just now; we would be staying in a hotel until our apartment was ready and how terrible Nairobi traffic was.

A sea of faces hurried past the window, peering in, women with babies on their backs tied close in colorful wraps rushing on. A man with withered legs hobbled toward us propelling himself with a solitary pole that was twice as tall as he was. He tapped on the glass, his hand cupped to receive a coin. Next to him several children crowded in, calling out "*shilingi moja, shilingi moja,*" hands extended.

When the light turned yellow Steven shot out into the roundabout, vying for a lane with a city bus then slowing down for a large Mercedes with Kenyan flags flying from the front fenders. "Government," he said. We swung around a corner through a rush of people hurrying across the street barely missing a woman bent low under the weight of a vegetable basket. I let the next streets pass without speaking as we swerved through two more roundabouts, and around a corner and in what seemed one continuous frantic motion we had arrived at the hotel.

Inside the hotel compound the garden wall blocked the view of everything that lay beyond its thick lawn and enameled tables. Steven lined up our luggage inside the lobby saying he would be back to pick us up and take us to the airport after lunch. "After lunch? To the airport?" "Yes, to get the forms for the bond. The office will be open after lunch. No problem. You see, the vehicle is very ready."

The drive back to the airport took on the fever of an ambulance run in a national emergency and the fact that we had just survived this journey, didn't lessen the terror. Steven swerved from lane to lane, tucking in between a pick-up and a large truck then darting out to pass.

When we arrived at the airport customs desk a solid looking woman with a tightly braided hairdo was locking the door. The customs agent had left, she said. Someone in his family had died and he had gone back to his village. Couldn't we just get the forms? Not without the approval of the customs agent. Come back tomorrow.

"Perhaps tomorrow," Steven said casually as he ushered us back to the car. "Someone dies and people must go back to the village. No problem."

Masses of fuchsia bougainvillea cascaded from the stone wall surrounding the hotel grounds and at the foot of the wall a pool of water stretched like a stream punctuated by fountains and exquisitely thin stalks of deep purple allium. An enormous bird coasted overhead, his wingspread casting a fleeting shadow across the glare and with a shattering squawk he settled in the branch of a jacaranda tree ripe with lavender blooms just overhead. Our equipment was gone. The air was filled with the fragrance of frangipani blossoms. The bird looked down at us over his stubby hooked bill.

LETTER HOME: ARRIVAL

Dearest All,

We are sitting here drinking cocoa, listening to a Mozart tape and the night sounds of Nairobi. It is the eve of our first week here and we're writing this not only to share our first experiences with you but as a log for ourselves, so bear with us if there are some repetitions of happenings we may have already related when we phoned.

The Fairview Hotel is a secluded small old hotel set in an exquisite garden with high walls draped with flowers and a splendid lawn with enameled tables for afternoon tea or beer in the evenings. It is pathetically British and jolted us into our first look at the vestiges of colonialism that are everywhere. Very little local food except for the luscious fruits. Chopped kidneys on toast, boiled leeks and beef is more the fare. The head of the council, stopped by and gave us a fatherly lecture on thievery warning not to leave our cameras and equipment in our room, then left. We slept out this phase of jet lag then had a tea tray delivered to our room, 70 cents including tip. Our full six-course dinner was $3.50. We walked to the city, took a quick look around and hurried back feeling uneasy leaving all of our gear in the room. After three days of tea in the garden and only hurried phone calls saying our house was still not ready and the bond wasn't processed, we finally got word that we could go to the airport to present the bond to customs and move in to our house. Alas, the day proved to be a trial in third world bureaucracy.

Out to the airport by early morning, the customs agent is having coffee so we are told. We wait 45 minutes before he returns, looks at the bond and sends us to the freight customs agent – at another airport. Oh, you don't have the right forms this one says, you must get the right forms – downtown at the Customs House. We barrel downtown, but alas the customs offices are moving from their old building to a new building next door. A procession of workers is carrying drawers, bookcases, armloads of files up and down stairways. The lifts are not yet working. Does anyone know where the forms are? Somewhere in the procession of worker ants of course. What's the hurry? After an hour the right stack is found and we are given five sets of forms that we begin to fill out perching on a windowsill since there is no furniture yet. "No," cries the clerk, "they must be typed." She is shouting through a pane of solid glass since there is no voice hole. "Can we borrow a typewriter here?" "No, and whatever you do, don't put a pin in the papers or they are not valid." We learned they use stick pins not paper clips. Back to the council, thankful for Steven as there seems to be no logic to the traffic. We capture a secretary who types out our four copies and almost puts a pin in them before we scream. Back to the Customs House thankfully before the lunch hour when the whole city stops everything and most civil workers don't show up afterwards, we are told. We shout through the glass that we have the forms holding them up so the clerk can see since there is also no pass-through for papers, which being the entire function of this office seems a bit awkward. She comes out the door and around to take our papers. Sorry, you put the wrong name first. You will have to do them over. This time a customs worker who has taken pity on us hops in the car with us to head back to the council since he must witness signatures anyway. Something we hadn't been told until now. He directs the secretary, we sign each set, then take off to the bank where he is supposed to witness the signature of the bank manager for the bond, except the manager is out to lunch. The saga continues and ultimately all is signed, stamps affixed and so far, no pins!

Out to the airport by three o'clock where after four different offices look it over and record things in fat musty books with two close calls with pins, we are given more forms to fill out. Patiently we do so and it is nearing five o'clock when the last official hauls out a catalog of equipment with prices and asks for the value of each item which he begins to counter check in his book. This video recorder thing, is this a TV? He apparently has prices on TVs but little else. No, it's not a TV, it just holds batteries, not worth more than $25. He begins writing down the values we give him, adds 16% tax, then 150% duty. I can hear David's brain gasping as he pulls out his calculator and tries to keep one item ahead so the whole thing bingos out at the amount of the bond that we hold in our dripping wet hands. Solar calculators had seemed like such a good idea for Africa but in the dim customs office they were useless. Our security alarm appears. A battery charger the agent announces, pleased because he has a price for one. We don't correct him. Then the video monitor, is this a TV? No, it won't show TV programs, it's just a viewer, and so on. Somehow the total miraculously comes out a few dollars under the bond and we calmly roll our luggage out to the parking lot where Steven has been praying the whole time.

The house originally arranged for us won't be ready until August, so we are taken to what is called a maisonette sort of a townhouse arrangement that reminds us of student housing, stone block construction, clay tile roofs, big private yards with high privacy shrubs, hibiscus everywhere, alley access to the rear. It's more modest than the house they're getting ready for us but it has some advantages – we're within a walled compound with an *askari* (guard) night and day. Neighbors seem to look out for one another and there is a gardener who cares for each private yard — all of which we'd have to hire separately in a house. We have a back enclosed porch, living room, dining room, shower-powder room, and kitchen with a pantry and off of that a greenhouse. There are three bedrooms upstairs, a toilet room and a tub room. The windows all have iron grillwork for security and jalousie openings. Every room has a lock and key including closets – even cupboards and drawers! The furniture is tacky modern, draperies in dreadful splatter prints, no evidence of African design, but there are compensations like triple mirrored vanities and huge desks.

We took one full day to scrub and shop and told Steven we'd try to find our own way to the market. The council has given us a VW beetle from their vehicle pool for our use. Beyond local use we'll get a driver with a different vehicle. Vegetables and fruits are beyond imagination, half of them I can't identify, but we stock up on avocado, mangoes, papaya, eggplants—David accidentally bought twenty pounds of potatoes when he really only wanted a few – and we don't yet have the heart to bargain which seems to amuse all the vendors. Plastic things are outrageously expensive. Vegetable mamas come by the house in the morning, their backs bent under the weight of immense wicker baskets of vegetables strapped to them by a leather strap around their foreheads.

Saturday we braved the maddening business of driving and went to Nairobi Game Park at the edge of town to practice driving on the left. Heading down the gravel road we saw a stream ahead with a bridge of sorts, two wide boards for your wheels. We stopped to check it out before driving onto it and saw a car in the creek that had apparently slipped off the boards. Several people were climbing out seemingly unscathed. When we stopped to help they waved us on calling out, "Just another day in Africa." That may become our new slogan.

We made it across the bridge. Not much further down the road we saw a pair of lions, two males, in the middle of the road heading straight toward us. Being in this small car does not give much feeling of protection. When they got to us, they split apart, one to the left, the other to the right, passing us, glancing in the windows at close range and meandering on. It was a glorious experience with giraffe close enough to reach out your window, which you don't do, gazelle, warthogs, ostriches are immense, zebras, antelopes. We rolled down our window to photograph two rhinoceros standing nose to nose, horns crossed, just standing there as though they were wondering what to do next. We named them the kissing rhinos.

At one point you're allowed out of your car to hike down to the hippo ponds. It was a bit disconcerting to turn around and find a large baboon on our trail, but we were told they're not usually aggressive. Monkeys were everywhere in the trees above us, squawking away. We couldn't help but listen to every crunch in the brush wondering what was there. After seeing the sleeping hippos, the bank was high enough for safety from crocodiles, we headed back to the car where a ranger was waiting offering to ride along with us as he had to do a game count. He didn't have a vehicle. We spent the entire day with him while we practiced driving on the left. What an experience.

Today is Sunday and we woke to the sound of a choir running past our house – a lively crowd in purple choir robes chugging slowly down the road. Every now and then people in purple robes came out of nearby houses and joined them as they passed. We have since learned that these are church groups, circling neighborhoods picking up their members like a human bus. They eventually reach their place of worship, typically a sprawling shade tree where they will spend the entire morning singing and praying together.

As we start work tomorrow we treated ourselves to a cultural tour of Nairobi – on our own. We went through the museum, a magnificent collection and perfect setting in a flowered park, then walked to the City Market, a glass roofed structure with hundreds of stalls selling flowers, vegetables, baskets, pottery, and carvings. Fishmongers, butchers, and bakers rim the building and we determine that this is where we'll shop, as it is the first place we've seen with African merchants. We walked down to the famous Norfolk Hotel, watering hole for Hemingway and the like and had lunch on the terrace, people watching.

The city is lovely though sections quickly change from posh hotels with top hatted doormen to shanty markets. Traffic is a menace with *matatus*, small buses or trucks privately owned, jammed with people hanging out of every window and door, perched on top, crazy drivers defying you at every point. There is no speed limit and with the crazy roundabouts at every intersection it will take a good deal of getting used to while learning to drive on the left. So far, I have mastered the city map and navigate every turn while Dave braves the wheel with me constantly repeating, keep left, look right, like a crew captain.

And so, we have reached the one-week mark. We find ourselves sleeping a lot, deeply, perhaps the subconscious is busy processing all of the new experiences. The weather couldn't be more perfect – cool mornings, days around 75, chilly evenings. There seem to be few bugs, no screens on windows, though we do have a house lizard who eats the gnats and such. He comes out at night and is considered good luck, so we are feeling comfortable with his presence and have named him *Chui* (leopard). We set our alarm clock, leave *Chui* to his evening meal and await our first day of work.

We love and miss all of you, hoping somehow our letter writing will help share all that we are experiencing.

Lani

THE CHOIR COMPETITION

The request came immediately on the heels of getting our equipment back. The council asked us to produce a video documentary marking its fortieth anniversary. We were to film as many of the council's projects as possible across Kenya in time for a huge celebration in the spring to be attended by African leaders from across the continent and donors from around the world. Some of the projects were decades old, such as the nation's polytechnic school system, numerous mother-child health clinics, and agricultural and water development. Others such as small business development were relatively new. With nearly four hundred council staff working with communities on virtually every sector of development it was a daunting assignment to say the least. They told us to plan to be on safari for months, but not to worry, they would provide a driver and vehicle

We argued that our humble equipment was not professional quality, also totally new to us, also we had no experience whatsoever, had never even done a video before, much less produced a documentary, edited it, added sound tracks, much less brought anything to a polished showable production. We also managed to remind them that we had been told we would have three months of Kiswahili language training before our duties were to commence. Our excuses were waved off with confident smiles and promises that there would be time for learning Kiswahili, reminding us we should be prepared to be on safari most of the time to film as much as we could. With this said they handed us our first assignment — to film a Maasai agricultural project as well as a choir competition that was being held there.

"Tell me about the Maasai."

Kadzo and I were having lunch at a small kiosk near the office.

She smiled. "Not easy to describe. Nomadic cultures have the most difficulty adapting to changing times. Traditionally they followed their herds from place to place, open savannah everywhere, but now of course, that same land is a game park or somebody's property with a fence around it. It's hard, especially for the youth. They go to school, learn about other places, other ways of doing things. Still, they are very proud to be Maasai. I tried to help one young woman from the agricultural project. She came to me asking questions. I had been working with a women's group there so she knew me. Mara. You might meet her. Where you're going, it's a small community. A very tall, pretty girl. A sensitive issue. She didn't want to be circumcised, hard to believe this horrid practice is still going on. The government finally made it illegal but of course they never enforce it. Her family was insisting. I offered to talk to her family but she said no. She was thinking of running away, with another girl, her family was also insisting on circumcision. The ceremony had already been arranged. Mara was so frightened. I would have taken her home with me but that would have been a legal mess. Nothing's simple. Then I found a scholarship opportunity, preparatory program at the university. I was so excited. I had the enrollment papers waiting for her but she never showed up. I learned later she was very fond of a young man in the tribe." She hesitated, "Tipis, I think that's his name, working with the cattle program there. Maasai life still revolves around cattle as you will soon see, but Mara wanted to study agriculture. Such a smart student. I've been wanting to catch up with her, but she's been elusive."

We talked into the afternoon. My mind was struggling to absorb everything, hoping to learn what we were heading into on this first trip. How can you film what you don't understand, how do you even put a frame around what you are seeing? A few days later we were heading out of the city to begin our filming with Steven asking endless questions about America and filmmaking.

"You criticize even your president. Right on television. We heard this, yes?"

"Yes, we criticize everyone, even the president. You see, we have freedom of speech."

"See, it is so," he declared slapping the wheel, obviously pleased at his insight. "And no one gets picked up?"

"Picked up?"

"By the secret service."

"No. But we do have other problems," David began just as a truck passed ahead of us barely missing our front fender.

Steven kept chattering about Hollywood and Kung Fu as though we were actual film producers. We were heading up a steep hill on the wrong side of the road. Just before the crest a truck appeared directly in front of us and Steven swung wildly. We swerved onto the washed-out mud shoulder of the road then bumped back onto the tarmac. I hugged my bag and closed my eyes. It was happening again. I couldn't keep shutting my eyes like this. I reached for the comfort of David's hand. The vehicle jerked to one side then back, I opened my eyes as a bus bore down, head-on toward us on our side of the road. Steven swung off at the last instant hitting the broken edge of the road to avoid what seemed like certain disaster.

A line of women filed by, each one carrying a five-gallon jerry can of water on her head, some with babies strapped across their chests. Their eyes were silent, deep, almost startling in their intensity.

Steven threw the vehicle in gear and bumped along the rutted road edge, pointing out potholes and the black spot signs posted along the roadside indicating this had been the scene of a fatal accident. He seemed disinterested in any questions about the Maasai, he himself was Luya he said as though that should explain it, but he did know some fine Maasai youth at the agricultural post. Then he leaped to the choir competition, what an exciting thing it was, the entire nation was riveted, which choir was expected to win the trophies, who would go to the national finals. It all sounded like a national sport, which we were soon to realize it was.

Toward the bottom of the steep hill we suddenly turned onto a dirt road swerving between two boulders jutting from the washed-out soil.

"Over there," Steven said, his puckered lips pointing. "See the green *shamba*, the field with all the brown grass around it? That is the irrigation scheme. The Maasai agricultural post."

The air felt cool and the clear outline of the green *shamba* of the training center stood out like an etching on a subtle background. Piece by piece Steven told the story of how the center had started more than eight years before. The land had become so overgrazed that it could no longer support the cattle of the nomadic Maasai. At an abandoned prison grounds, a former *Mau Mau* detention center, the council began to teach the people how to cultivate crops. There had been great reluctance to learn agriculture within the Maasai settlement at first, they were nomads with cattle to graze but gradually as land became scarce more young people were learning to grow. The rains however had been poor for the past few years and the experimental fields had been failing season after season, so the council assisted them in installing a well and an irrigation system, and now the *shambas* could be cultivated all year long. I scrawled in my notebook as fast as Steven was speaking which evidently pleased him since he continued to embellish the story staring at his words becoming ink.

"So this is now where most Maasai live?" I asked.

"Oh, no. So many Maasai still live in Tanzania since before it was Tanzania."

42

"Maasai in both countries?"

"Oh, yes. You see the Queen Victoria, she had all this land and her cousin, he was the German Kaiser and he thought it wasn't fair that she had two African mountains with snow on top. That is why she drew a line on her map and for his birthday she gave him Kilimanjaro with snow on top and with it came more land and she kept Mount Kenya with snow on top for herself. So, you see that is how Tanzania became Tanzania and Kenya became Kenya and how the Maasai they became split into two pieces.

I couldn't respond. A small herds boy waved at us as we passed. He held a tiny bow and a few arrows and wore only a red-brown *shuka* draped over his shoulder. The large herd of goats he was tending had wandered onto the road and he ran to shoo them from our path as we approached. I wondered how much of his people's history he knew, whether he had cousins he had never met just across the border.

Several women were at the gate of the training post, sitting in the grass, their brilliant red and blue *kangas* draped about their shoulders. They wore heavy collars of beads and enormous rings of beads and wire dangling from their ears. As our car approached, they ran toward us, their hands filled with necklaces to sell. I rolled down my window but Steven waved the women off and turned sharply down the long driveway.

The training post spread out across the dusty compound. The director, Simon, had been expecting us and led the way to a tool-making shop where young men were hammering out scrap metal. David had the video camera rolling as we made our way around the center. At a tree nursery, women were watering seedlings in black plastic bags, nearby there were fields of maize and beans with irrigation ditches running between the rows. Images shuffled together then merged as we roamed the compound. Simon's voice droned on, almost inaudibly, like the hum of a bee buried in the monotony of its task until a tall young man approached us.

"Ah, here is Tipis," Simon said.

I sucked in my surprise. We shook hands.

"He is a worker in the cattle-dipping project. So many ticks and things that make the cattle sick."

Since Tipis spoke English, Simon suggested he take us to his home to see how Maasai families live. Tipis seemed pleased at the suggestion. He went ahead of us to notify his mother while we scooped up our gear, loaded the car then drove down the dirt road toward the small settlement at the edge of the center. In the distance we could see a ring of thorn brush built up around a few low mud huts.

"My mother is most honored," Tipis said as we approached his *manyatta*. "She has never had *wazungu*," he smiled broadly. "White visitors."

The compound was sparse. In front of a low mounded, oblong hut stood a woman, her shaved head gleaming in the sun. Her eyes were part of a broad smile growing wider as we approached.

Tipis spoke to her in Kimaasai. She stood tall and shook our hands with both of hers. Tipis translated as we asked our unending questions. Her name was Joyce and she had built this house herself of mud and dung. She patted the humped roof with her hands in great sweeps to demonstrate. Most of the older women preferred their traditional food of coddled milk mixed with cattle blood, she explained, they were not accustomed to eating vegetables. But they were learning. Before the irrigation scheme women had walked four kilometers each day for water, now many of them had less than a kilometer to walk. Tipis had gone to school and for this she was very proud.

Simple questions, simple answers but it was growing late and smoke rose from cooking fires around the settlement. The drone of chanting dancers enveloped us as we said our farewells and headed back to our vehicle. Tipis darted off toward the dancers like a fawn before the wind.

The next morning choirs began gathering in clusters around the compound and the sounds of African songs carried across the treetops. The music pulled us toward it into the full light of day. Before first light buses were arriving from all over the area, men, women, children in flowing robes, brilliant blues, purples, and crimson, clustering under trees, greeting each other, rehearsing their songs, the morning gathering of birds at the stream, each warbling over the sounds of the others.

People were crowding into the small church where rows of narrow benches were jammed together with barely enough space to slide between. Four judges arrived, wearing thin three-piece suits. Each carried an immense silver trophy that they placed on a table in front of the high wooden stage.

Our shiny camera cases looked garish stacked against the rough benches. We set up our tripod and tape recorder trying not to be any more conspicuous than we already were. The choirs would each sing their own arrangement of the assigned competition hymn plus a hymn they had composed in their tribal language.

People were pouring in the door, vying for a patch of standing room to witness what was about to unfold. Outside, a dozen different choirs were each warming up with different songs that tumbled together in the hot air. Someone sent a hush through the audience as a solitary drum swept like a heartbeat through the packed room. The drum was joined by the sound of steel clangers and in a ribbon of color, children in billowy white robes edged in crimson, danced in, thumping out the beat of the drum with their stomping feet, voices singing out in full volume as they rhythmically edged their way forward, then back, then forward, onto the stage. Adults in matching robes followed the children, blending their voices in a harmony that at once seemed haphazard yet intricate beyond comprehension.

Slim girls, lean young men, heavy and thin women all carrying the same grace swayed as they pounded the rhythm into the floor along their path. Faces gleamed with perspiration, eyes fairly danced out of their heads as they held chins high so their voices would soar upward, the soft folds of choir robes draped around them like royal gowns. I fixed my zoom lens on the line and snapped away. Voices were bursting all around like an explosion of human energy translated into a primordial harmony.

Two young men with tall traditional drums squatted before the assembled group and several women with circular steel bands and clanging rods stood behind them, beating out the rhythm. The glowing smiles and swaying bodies were as much a part of the song as the music itself.

I noticed Tipis looking in from outside through an open window. He apparently had chosen not to come in. His *shuka* and bare brown shoulders stood out against the sea of brilliant blue choir robes that surrounded him, waiting their turn to sing. His eyes were fixed on one tall young woman, stomping and swaying as the line crept forward. I wondered if that were Mara. When the group was at last on stage the music shifted without pause into another plane carrying the church filled with people with it. Everyone rose from their benches, joining with clapping hands, stomping out the song in their confined spots. Our bodies pressed together, welded one to another, the choir voices pushing the spirit from the deepest recesses of our souls.

It was impossible to escape. The music rushed up from the earth itself, through our bodies and suddenly David and I were standing, cameras abandoned, stomping in rhythm with the growing thunder. We felt as though our feet weren't quite touching the ground, the hot moisture of crowding bodies was holding us up so we couldn't fall even if we tried, supported shoulder to shoulder inside a mass of singing humanity. The video camera on tripod rolled on its own. The room was alive with people, drums, and music. A toothless grandmother was standing at the side of the stage, her old eyes with their sagging rims suddenly alive as the choir burst into a higher plane and warbling squeals from several of the singers pierced the air.

Everything was rushing together. Something tingling, alive, rushed over my skin. I looked through my lens, my hands shaking on the shutter. The toothless grandmother was singing, hands raised to the heavens. With a burst of warbling squeals the music ended into an explosion of clapping hands that rolled across the church. I glanced toward the window. Tipis had gone.

Steven knew Tipis. I asked as we drove back.

"So smart, that boy. His cousin you know is now an airplane pilot. Went to university. He can drive one of these big jets you see flying over. But Tipis, he loves his cattle."

Steven's chatter was welcomed on the drive back as I prodded him with questions, every detail of being Maasai. The documentary was one thing, trying to capture on film what it meant to be Maasai caught in changing times. Separately, a story was forming in my head.

MAASAI

With head held high in an ancient elegance his spine glided effortlessly back and forth in a serpentine rhythm. He breathed heavily in cadence with the chant as though his chest were the drum that beat out the pace of life. Then with an unconscious ease he suddenly thrust his body upward in a leap like an arrow leaving the bow. It seemed as though he hung motionless in the air for a moment, his lean body erect above the earth, then in a soft pounce he landed and pushed off again. Higher, straighter, leap after leap, his eyes pitched high at the distant hills, he sprang as if his life depended upon the height he could reach in this dance. In a way it did.

Beside him Sarone was leaping till his heart nearly burst. But Sarone was not as tall as Tipis and though they were age mates and had been circumcised together they each knew Tipis would draw the glances of the prettiest girls in the village for his leaps were startlingly high and graceful.

Sarone stumbled forward, recovered his balance and danced back to the chanting circle of young *morani* leaving Tipis alone in the center. With one last heaving breath and undulating thrust of the head, Tipis threw his body upward. Sweat glistened on his smooth black forehead and rivulets of ocher mud and fat meandered down his temples in another rhythm far removed from the dance yet dependent on it. His arms and thighs glistened giving him the sheen of ebony, like a statue polished and elongated to make some statement about the human spirit. Caked ocher mud covered his long hair and his intense dark eyes held the far horizon. The leather head straps, the scarlet beads that bounded from his flapping ear slits, they were all as much a part of him as his long, bony feet and supple back. All this had evolved over the generations as surely as had his people's beliefs, until now he, and what he wore, and how he danced, and what he thought, were completely one. He was Maasai.

He wore only his *shuka*, a brief shoulder drape that flew loosely as he reached the apex of his ascent, chin high, spear held parallel to his lean body together casting pencil thin shadows on the red earth. The soil beneath the pounding feet had powdered into fine red silt and each man's jolting body returned to it as surely as the birds returned to the river sending out puff clouds of red talc that clung to their sweaty legs in mottled patches.

He had seen Mara arrive and he felt relieved as she laughed with her sisters now, all teasing one another as they admired the *morani*. He felt a surge of pride watching her. She was taller than any of her age mates and her quick sense of humor had attracted him when they were very young. She was always the first to understand, the first to laugh, and the first to console when even the tiniest bird had fallen wounded in their path. She was also beautiful, lean and strong and held herself with that unconscious grace born of hereditary innocence. Tipis' pulse quickened now just thinking of her clear black eyes and smooth skin. He had watched her from afar when he had gone hunting with the other boys as she sat by the riverbank whispering soft words to a monitor lizard that was meditating in the mud. He knew she was fearless.

Tipis landed as though it were his decision to come down to earth rather than a gravitational force. Without losing the rhythm of the chant he eased with small leaps back into the circle.

The pounding chant of breathing filled the air in a low humming drone. Black bodies drawn tall, arching in supple ripples upward, they formed a half circle. Mesmerized by the grunting cadence of their own breath, they stood tall as acacia against the equatorial sun. Now the women joined the chant. Clustered in a tight group they inched their way forward, spines swaying in the same snake-like waves. With shaved heads glowing black against the strands of leather and beadwork that draped across their brows, they carried the dance with them as if it were coming from the earth itself, winding its willowy way through their bodies to somewhere far above them. Like brilliant stalks of blossoms shaken from the soil below, they undulated, their huge beaded necklaces bobbing over their breasts. The cloud of red dust rose around them until their feet vanished and they sank into the earth and floated above it within the same graceful, timeless motion.

Several women eased from the group, inching their way toward the line of *morani*. Others joined them. Tipis watched anxiously. His heart leaped when he saw Mara approaching with two of her sisters. Each of the young women danced slowly toward the line of warriors, closer and closer, swaying, changing directions and weaving until each directly faced the warrior she had chosen. Mara danced toward Sarone in a tease, then swung around, bobbed and glided toward Tipis until they were face to face. Like a lion swinging his mane, he swished his long hair across her face, accepting the compliment of her selection and she slowly danced back. They would be together tonight.

As each maiden selected her *morani*, other women joined the approach, some giggling, others deliberately averting their eyes and changing direction to confuse the awaiting warriors as to whom they would choose.

The circle of dancers stretched broadly across the bare red earth of the *manyatta*, the *morani* wearing their decorated bodies like the ancient ceremonial robes of a royal clan. The field of women swayed in the breeze, their flowing capes of crimson and white blossoming about them, and standing like a protective hedgerow, elders in darker wraps, and *morani* proudly indifferent pulsated to the chant that had begun before memory. Though even now the men hunted naked lest their clothing catch in the thorn bush and restrict their running, some came today in blue jeans and tee shirts bearing the names of faraway places — the University of Chicago, the Pepsi Generation, Baha Surfers' Club. Next to painted bare feet were striped tennis shoes, leaping side by side in chaotic exuberance.

From each of the seven huts wisps of smoke curled upward, for even in the heat of the day the fires were kept burning inside. Three stones in the small fire pit held up the open pot of boiled milk tea. Smoke was part of life here, spiraling around the people and cattle, the mud walls and skin mats just as surely as the spirits of their ancestors would hover over and around them until there was no one left to remember them. Fingers of the milky, smoky spirits eased their way through the maze of cracks along each wall permeating the air and the life of the *manyatta*. Everything smelled and tasted of smoke as though the past could never leave the present even in the tea. Perhaps especially in the tea since the milk was stored in long beaded gourds that had been cured with smoke forever imparting the pungent flavor of yesterday to the nourishment of this day.

The low huts crouched softly over their families. Cocoons of dung, they pushed their backs from the earth just high enough for people to sit around the fire awaiting the cycles of life as they had since time began. Laid out like the curls of a snail their squatting low doorways and winding entrances gave the inhabitants the opportunity to waylay any intruders.

This *manyatta* belonged to Mara's uncle. He was wealthy, having many head of cattle and four wives. There was one hut for her uncle, the *mzee*, each wife had a hut for herself and her children, and as their sons had grown older, they too had each built their own huts in their designated places within the family compound. Long ago four wives would hardly have been the sign of a wealthy man, but today things were changing. The land was growing dry. Neither the long rains nor the short rains had come as before. As far as the eye could see across the vast open lands there lay only scrub brush, *pori*, bush country. The scattered persistence of elegant acacia trees here and there sent their lacy lime green branches skyward, swept into long horizontal reaches by the winds, offering what little shade they could to the parched earth. Yellow brown grass bent over in exhaustion and bleeding wounds of red earth scarred the once rich plains speaking of a death that was not far away.

The richest grasslands had long ago gone to the white settlers and to the *Kikuyus* for farms and cattle ranches. Now the great herds that once freely roamed the plains had dwindled to a struggling mass, wrenching from the land what little it had to offer, trampling its attempts to send forth new life buds as each creature fought to survive. What little growth cattle left behind the goats destroyed and today the elders could only look with faded eyes across the landscape and tell stories of what once had been. Now broad tarmac highways rolled across the plains, splitting the vast land into remnants, carrying busloads of tourists to the game parks, and sleek white motorcars to their unknown destinations.

The *boma*, a thick ring of fierce thorn bush bramble that ringed the *manyatta,* had successfully kept out the lions and hyenas as long as anyone here could remember. It was a ring of protection from the outer world so that life within the *manyatta* could go on, built of the scrub brush of the savannah itself as though the land were offering what it could to its people. Seemingly delicate in its form, the *boma* held millions of thorns each four to five inches long and as fat as a pencil, deadly sharp to anyone fool enough to plunge through. Each evening the young herder boys drove the cattle within its protective circle pulling the last of the bramble closed after them, sealing off the lions and other terrors of the night.

Nine girls had been circumcised this time accounting for the huge celebration. Mara stared at the hut where they lay. Her cheeks suddenly felt hot as she walked slowly away from the gathering to the edge of the *boma*. It had been only a year since her own circumcision, only a year since she had lain on that mat listening to the chanting outside while her body convulsed in burning pain. The women had led her into the river that dawn before it all happened in the belief that the cold water would help numb her loins, but even Sarone's grandmother knew that the waters were no longer deep enough to chill.

This grandmother was revered in the village. Since she herself became a woman she had been trained in the ancient ritual of female circumcision and now she was the only one in the village permitted to amputate the clitoris of girls reaching puberty and thus sanction their passage into womanhood. Her hands were strong and sure, her eyes sharp as her blade, and now with the ceremony completed she watched over the girls binding their wounds with leaves, taking care lest infection or heavy bleeding begin. It would take more than a month for them to heal and during that time the old woman would keep the watch of the hawk over her brood.

Mara's parents had hesitated when questions began to be raised about her circumcision. The old ways were passing and they had heard many people speaking against this custom even saying the government had prohibited it. Mara had pleaded against it desperately trying to hold back tears that pushed from the deepest part of her being. One night, fearing they would never listen to the arguments of a girl no matter how reasonable they might be, she made a plan to run away with her best friend Sarah whose parents had already made the decision that she would be circumcised. But at dawn Sarah was not at the river where they had agreed to meet. Confined to bed, Sarah's older sister said later when she found Mara sitting alone under a tree. There was a stiff scowl carved into her lean face as though she knew everything they had plotted and dared Mara to pursue the matter.

Sarah looked groggy when Mara caught a glimpse of her that evening, her eyes dull, her movements slow and deliberate, which was the same evening Mara's grandmother, toothless and unmovable, spoke with her parents and the decision had been made. If she were not circumcised how would she know that she was now a woman? Besides, uncircumcised girls ran off to the city to become prostitutes. Running away to Nairobi alone without Sarah, Mara thought, took more courage than she had, to push aside all of the people she loved telling her of how things had been, of how things must be if the world is to stay balanced. She felt sucked down a slippery riverbed with nothing to grab onto. Fast and sure was the current and she had flowed with it.

The dancing had not stopped since early morning and now the festivities took on a more intense fervor by the light of the fires. Many of the men had been drinking beer all day and at the edge of the *boma* several lay in a stupor, their huge beer gourds beside them smelling of the now putrid brew. Reinforced by their delirium, several elders, the *wazee*, had joined the dancing *morani* staggering among the elegant youth in the pathetic contrast of life.

One old man with folded flesh over his scrawny arms stumbled forward in the remembrance of a leap he had executed as a young *morani*. His great cracked feet and ankles had been leathered by the soil and bristly stubble into painless thick boots which he wore each day without thought. His slit ear lobes had stretched over the seasons of the plains until one hung down to his shoulder like a limp intestine and the other held a bright blue Vicks bottle with his tobacco stuffed inside. A long white feather protruded from his bushy hair giving him the head of a secretary bird studying the earth through cataract eyes before he left its surface in his attempted flight. And though his soul levitated indefinitely into his forgetfulness, his body fell into a soft heap of dusty brown skin and the matted gray blanket it had worn before it took to flight. Some young boys scurried to help the old man up and carry him to the long grass where he could sleep in peace.

Tipis and Sarone squatted comfortably on their haunches, their long legs damp with sweat. Unconsciously their heads lurched forward with the distant chant, chins thrusting rhythmically into the night as though it were impossible to cease the dance that had begun before the lions were born.

"Do you remember when we went on our hunt?"

Sarone nodded. His thoughts stretched to the far hills inside his eyes and Tipis could see that he was thinking. It had been three years since Sarone and Tipis had been circumcised. They had not killed a lion as their fathers and brothers had. The government had made strict rules. But they had hunted together, living in the bush, eating meat for a

54

month until it was time. But each one of them knew in his heart he could kill a lion alone with his spear if he had to. He knew it as surely as he knew he was Maasai.

Since the earth had been created, God had given all of the animals into the care of the Maasai, and that was why to this day they could walk fearlessly in the bush. The animals knew it too and they could tell a Maasai from other men even from a great distance. Animals know Maasai are the bravest men on earth and respect their presence among them for they can smell bravery as it is carried by the wind and left in the grass they walk on. Some of the boys had actually killed lions, one had gotten caught by the police, but the chief had argued for him, pleading it was their tradition, and the elders had given them two goats and there had been no trouble. Now the lion killers would be allowed to wear the lion's tail and mane at dances. Tipis envied them. He and his age mates were caught in a time between lions and police. Still he knew if a lion would stalk his cattle, he could kill it alone as surely and swiftly as his father had done.

Tipis had always been grateful he had not been born Kikuyu. God had given the Kikuyus the care of the crops and the fields which must be a very boring and tiresome task. And if Kikuyus wanted to hunt, they must first learn how to be brave. For the Maasai, bravery was not something you learned. You were born brave when you were born Maasai.

"Mama has the food spread out," his sister called running toward him. "Will you eat with us?"

Her young face was bright and glowing with oil she had spread on for the occasion, and her new red *kanga* made her look suddenly older and more graceful as Tipis looked at her with pride. She had a bright, quick mind like a gazelle that leaped over and between ideas with an unlearned grace, and he watched over her with more care than he gave his other sisters. But today he wanted to stay with Sarone. He shook his head and the young girl darted away shyly.

He remembered how she had looked the last day he was a boy. She had teased him for the last time and his mother had said goodbye to his childhood with a look that was both sad and proud. The next day he would be a man and his mother would never again address him or treat him as a child. She had been well prepared in her heart for she had had other sons become men. But it had been hardest for his little sister. She had still seen him as Tipis the boy, not Tipis the man, and yet she too had learned to respect him in time. For him it was a swift transition, but one he had been prepared for over the years by the elders. From the day he was circumcised he received the full rights and respect of an adult man in his society. He had felt more than ready when that day had come and he had never doubted who he was since then.

Now his eyes searched the crowd for Mara. He remembered the times they had run off together in the long grass and the secret place they laid together near the river when the earth had swallowed him into the blackness of her ancient night, the night he determined he would one day marry Mara.

The last slanted orange rays of the sun mixed with the blaze of the fire to cast mysterious long shadows all about. He had heard the men talking. The cattle had dwindled. Food was scarce. The garden of the agricultural center nearby looked green and rich. He tried not to think of Mara going away to school in Nairobi, to study agriculture, like a Kikuyu. Still he was proud of her for wanting to help her people. But for Maasai to go away is different than for other tribes, he thought. Maasai do not just leave home, they leave their identity. In the city, how would one know one is Maasai? No, he would never leave. That would be to walk away from the entire history of his people, the history of the world as he knew it.

Tipis hadn't seen Mara slip away from the dancing for he was watching a giant jet slice through the clouds overhead, its drone joining the chanting as it grew louder. He had heard from Sarone, whose grandmother was the village circumciser of girls, that Mara had not cried out, at least not so others beyond the hut could hear. He felt a surge of pride thinking of her. Now that she was circumcised he would be able to pursue her as his wife, though most of his age mates had known for some time of his feelings.

"Maybe that is Boniface," Tipis said, elbowing Sarone as he looked up at the jet. "He is learning to fly a plane just like that."

"Maybe, it's him," Sarone agreed.

Boniface was their cousin, older by almost ten years. He had gone away to the university and then the air force, and though they had not seen him for a long time, they knew he was studying to be a pilot. His brothers still tended the family cattle in the fading yellow grass, and when Boniface came back to visit he went to the hills with them. One of them had gone to the city to visit Boniface last Christmas and had sat inside one of the planes with him. He had said it was round inside, like a steel hut, and they had all been silent together as he spoke of every detail he could remember of that day.

"He will come back," Sarone said, pulling each word from his thoughts. "And probably buy more cattle than anyone else."

They stared at the jet silently as it descended slowly, keeping their thoughts unspoken lest they take form.

LETTER: INTRODUCTIONS

Hujambo,

We have now been here one month and if today is any indicator the experiences that are in store for us here are beyond imagination. Our friend Kadzo had us over for dinner, a memorable occasion for many reasons. We arrived to find a chicken tied by its leg to a chair near the entry, Kadzo with a *kanga* wrapped around her, far different than the business look when we first met her at the airport. Hardly missing a beat in an enthusiastic hug and pulling us inside, she untied the chicken, carried it to the kitchen, snapped its neck and began plucking it. We had a wonderful spicy chicken dinner, filling us not only with good food but a treasure of advice on the inner workings of the council and all the travels that lay ahead in documenting more projects than we could imagine.

Last week we headed for Isinya, an area about an hour due south of Nairobi, into Maasai land where we had previously filmed a choir competition. We wanted to share some of our video footage with people we had filmed, so today we set out prepared for just that. When we arrived a huge celebration was in process. The people had been forewarned of our arrival – fortunate, as the Maasai have been notably abused by tourists taking pictures. It was a circumcision celebration and we were allowed to shoot as much video and photos as we wanted though a mania sort of set in with everyone wanting to pose, asking for pictures. One of the young warriors, hair packed with ochre mud and wearing only the traditional shoulder drape, carrying a spear, invited us into his family hut for tea.

The hut is squatting height and despite the eighty-five-degree day a huge fire was burning inside. David didn't quite fit inside the door with our video gear as there were already several warriors inside, but I braved the heat and shared the boiled milk tea, the air so hot and smoke so thick I could barely breathe.

Outside the dancing and leaping carried on most of the afternoon. Several young *morani* escorted us to a sacred wooded spot beyond the celebration where several cattle carcasses were hanging from low branches of a tree. Hoofs and hides lay all around us as they skewered a stick with the best tasting beef we ever tasted. It was considered a sacred place where the young men about to be circumcised fed on their kill prior to their circumcision. They assured us if a lion appeared it would only take one of them to slay it and the rest of us could go on eating. It was obvious they had all wished they had killed lions instead of cattle. With their sideways glances we wondered if some of these morani had actually killed lions but given restrictions didn't want to reveal this. With amazing comfort, we sat on stumps near the fire eating fresh beef, stumbling through a conversation part Kiswahili, part English, part waving hands, part laughter. We could have lounged there the entire afternoon, but we had come to share the videos we had taken with Joyce and others and somehow made this known in gratitude as we excused ourselves.

Once again bush-telegram was working and Joyce and Tipis were waiting for us, smiles and hugs all around as friends and neighbors rushed over to greet us. David hooked up our tiny monitor to our car battery since there was no electricity. At first there were shouts then laughter as people pointed to themselves on the tiny screen. With squeals and exuberant chatter, they hailed others over for repeated showings. It was thrilling to watch, but also embarrassing, as though we were dazzling them with our technology which wasn't our intent. They had dazzled us and we felt it a simple courtesy to share with them the images they had so freely allowed us to capture. There is a fine art in knowing when we have overstepped cultural sharing. Undoubtedly we felt we had friends for life with that family as they hugged us goodbye, inviting us back. We will be sending them prints of the photos we took as they dearly wanted some pictures of themselves in their festive attire.

The week prior to our Maasai visit we were at Meru on the slopes of Mt. Kenya, a rural area in the highlands with another council center there. A marriage counselor training session was going on when we arrived. Everyone got so carried away by the video camera that they decided to stage a play for us on how they counsel marriage problems. In the gardens of the center they rigged up costumes and props and went into a full production of current methods of counseling. Over dinner afterwards we asked about traditional methods of resolving family problems. They seemed pleased at our interest and decided it would be good for others to see how many villages still resolve family disputes.

Early the next morning we all piled into cars and drove along the mountainside until the road stopped. Then we all walked a good distance to a traditional family compound tucked away into a setting Cecil B. DeMille would have envied. Banana trees, mountains in the background, flowers everywhere and an old *mzee*, an elder, sitting in front of a round thatched hut wrapped in a blanket. Our entourage of about thirty-five explained to him that they wanted to stage a play for us to photograph. He agreed and asked if he could be in it. While we set up the cameras, others led in the cattle, sheep, goats, an old woman with beer gourds and then lit a fire in front of the hut. Fire symbolizes wisdom and the length of time needed to work out the problem, a large fire for a large problem, a small fire for problems that will be resolved quickly. We were amazed at what natural actors they all were for when we turned around they had shed their Western clothes and wrapped themselves in traditional *kangas*. It all looked like some scene out of another time. Without any prompting from us they came up with a storyline and started in full force, the old *mzee* hamming it up with the beer drinking gourd, stomping his spear when he heard the husband

60

who now stood before him had abused his wife. He would have to give her parents three goats for his misdeeds and apologize to his wife. The family members seated around the fire agreed this was a fair settlement and the errant husband left to fetch his goats. We felt a rush of excitement just witnessing it. We're not sure how much of this raw footage will ultimately be used in the documentary, but for us it's a treasure nonetheless.

That evening the training group gathered after supper together to watch an American film that had been provided to the council by some outside group as a family training tool. We were mortified watching it, a "father knows best" production depicting a family in a glamorous house, a pouting teenager slamming her bedroom door and tearfully flopping on her canopied bed with its organdy ruffles, then the kindly father coming in to comfort her. The African trainees, eyes wide at the Hollywood setting, watched on the edge of their seats in total fascination, not understanding a word of the dialogue. We felt a need to separate ourselves from such images, to say how much we value what they were sharing with us, but we still don't know enough Kiswahili to express ourselves.

Each time we're picking up better filming techniques, learning more about our equipment and improvement in the tapes is beginning to show when we review them. We're now hunting for access to an editing setup so we can clean up the bloopers.

After our Maasai celebration today we stopped in at the Norfolk Hotel to have a cold beer on their terrace – a *wazungu* (westerner's) hangout. We could hardly believe everything we've experienced since last we wrote. So now, after hot baths in our incredibly deep tub we're limp. We have two more days scheduled in Maasai land this week, then we're heading to Lake Victoria and Kisumu on Friday. It's really hard to believe this is work yet the fleeting moments in between trips we're hassling with confusing committee meetings as an immense workload on other projects grows daily. We're learning how to say no, but it's hard as they are so short staffed at every level. Still our schedule right now permits little else.

Hope this finds everyone well and happy. Mail seems to take from 8 to 10 days and is appreciated more than you can guess. Much love to all. Lani

ZACHARINA'S STORY

"You ask to hear our story. That is not a small thing." Zacharina stared straight into my eyes. "Are you a storyteller?"

I looked into the strong black face in front of me. "I want to be," I whispered.

"Ah, that is good. For it is in the story that you touch the heart of what it means to be people together. But as women we have always known this, haven't we? We have been the keepers of the story since the story began, passing the lessons of the soul from one generation to the next, from our hearts to the children we bear. It is our spiritual bloodline, a quiet task for quiet moments, but it is because the moment is so quiet that the story sinks deep."

I held my breath. Zacharina leaned back.

"This boat was fishing alone because a young girl grew very ill very suddenly and no one could know why. We burned a candle all night in the doorway and folded a blanket around her, but still she trembled and even her younger brother Uma could hear it through the blackness of that night, though his hut was across the compound. He poked his head through the window, for I saw him. He was listening, sucking in air as if he might change the wild beat of her breath by making his own so powerful.

"It was just before dawn that she began to scream out strange names, sitting up as though she were struggling with some creature. Her face folded into stone so that she looked like an ancient woman who had slipped into the village from the past, escaping from some unknown terror. Streams of sweat poured from her face and her tongue grew swollen and blue, her eyes wild like a night animal that had fallen into the hunter's pit. Her mother tried to bathe her with damp cloths, but it was of little use.

"Just as the sun broke over the low rise of trees to the east, she went limp and made no further sound. The silence was heard across the compound. Uma stood in his doorway when the shadow drifted through the skies from the lake and hovered about us all. I could see he was waiting for the wail of the women to begin.

"That is when he went to the hill above the bay to be alone, to sit looking at the slippery green water with the hot orange sun on his back. The lake was still that day and no wind shook the papyrus by the shore. I sat down with him for you never know how things are when the shadow passes over and someone is so young.

"He talked about Uganda across the lake where his cousins lived. He had never met them, but an uncle had come to visit once and told of his village on the other side of the lake. They were fishermen too and Uma spoke of one day visiting them though just now the great waters of the lake seemed endless, as though there were no other side. Perhaps someone would come again, to honor his sister's death. Yes, they would surely come once word reached them. It would be unthinkable that they wouldn't come, being of the same tribe.

"While we sat there a few small boats set off down the canal that led through the swamp to the open lake. Their hulls were spattered with bright colors, their long noses hung with animal tails for protection from the evils that lurked in the water. Perhaps today, he said, they would catch a giant Nile perch and it would be a day to celebrate for them. His uncle had once caught a perch that was bigger than Uma.

That was the day Uma made a promise to himself — he would be a fisherman and one day catch such a giant fish.

"His tongue fluttered on with his thoughts as though I weren't there." Zacharina took a deep breath, "He wiggled close to me, the way young children do when they do not quite want to be alone. His grandmother had been the first to teach him about the lake – *ziwa*, that is our Swahili word for lake. It also means breast, for the lake is flowing with food and life to nurture us. He remembered the older boys who had been to school talking of the Nile that flowed from the lake north through Uganda, winding its way through the Sudan and Egypt until at last it flowed into a great sea that even touched the shores of Europe.

"He wondered how the water could continue to flow so far away from where it was born and whether the fishes went with it and the lake would one day be empty because all of it had flowed away. You see, he wondered about all of these things on that black bright morning because he didn't want to wonder about other things. I knew of course that his sister, who was right that minute being wrapped in cloth, had been his companion every day he could remember. She was the one who taught him how to paddle a log in the lake and how to lie still in the grass and watch the hippos as they grazed the shallows of the swampy shores. She was the one who told him the stories at night about the magic of falling stars and other such things.

"We watched the fishermen spreading their nets out in the morning sun to dry. Uma could hear their voices and wondered if his father's voice had sounded like that. He had died when Uma was only a baby and with no older brothers, Uma's uncles and older cousins were teaching him to fish. They brought part of their catch each day to Uma's mother and if Uma were ever caught in mischief, it was his father's brothers who took him to task. His grandmother had told him that he must respect all elders as though they were his own parents, for of course being of the same tribe they were, and therefore, she assured him, he had many fathers.

"Now you see, all of the members of Uma's tribe lived near each other on the hill toward the lake side of the village. His grandmother had told him that those who cultivated the same fields for their food would share the same burial ground for their dead. That is the way of our people, the graves clustered together as the people had been in life with the trees and rock outcroppings built up like an underground village that spread its way across the hills through time. He remembered this as we sat there.

"You see, most of the people in this village are of the same few families and Uma knew this land had belonged to our tribe since the lake had been born. That is why he knew the men would continue to dry their nets and the women would come for water like birds returning from the sky. He knew that life would go on in this village, even though his sister had died.

"When the lake grew blurry, Uma wiped his eyes and headed back toward his home. I did not see him again until the witch burning was about to begin. But that was later."

Zacharina untied her *kanga*, shook out the droplets of water, wrapping it around her shoulders again. Then she continued.

"When the boats returned from their night fishing, the men were told the girl had died, so the elders gathered together that very night. Oh, many people had accused Oki, the herbalist, before this. During the last rains one elder had accused him of witchcraft when the elder's wife grew suddenly ill after taking his herbs, but the accusations faded when the woman recovered. And when he had healed one whole family that was near death with the fever during the harvest, no more words were heard. Still, bad thoughts stick like tree gum in the hearts of some who said he took money to cast hexes or to give poison, and now this girl had died after drinking his *dawa*.

"And so that is why the herbalist Oki was brought before the council of elders and accused of witchcraft in the death of Uma's sister. They sat in a hut around a small fire and called for Oki. He was so frightened, his head hanging low. I shall never forget. He sat with the elders but what questions they asked and what Oki said no one knew, for no one's ears are allowed except the elders. At noontime, several of us brought food for the elders, but we were silent and kept our eyes down so that no thought in those old gray heads would be lost.

66

"You see how far back our village sits from the lake?" Zacharina waved her arm in a sweep toward the hill. "That is because in days long ago there had been floodings and the stories sit in our hearts to this day of water that crept over the land and cattle and huts floated away like fish in a stream and children and even old men and women washed away, perhaps as far away as Egypt, while their families clung to the tops of the boulders until they too were covered with water and only the frogs and a few strong people survived to warn the future people that houses must always be built back from the lake.

"What I didn't know then, but came to know later, was that some of the older boys of the village had gathered near the council hut, whispering together, watching for any movement from the small doorway of the hut. They remembered the night the elders had judged a man for stealing another man's cow. It had not been his first offense and we all knew the elders would have to make a difficult decision.

"Well, that man was found guilty. They nailed him inside a hollowed-out beehive log and rolled him down the hill into the lake to his death. The boys described his screams and the way, the crazed bees swarming the log as it rolled, menacing the last moments of the man until he sank beneath the waters.

"Uma had heard this story before, though they say he folded his ears over so he would not hear the boys tell it again. He loved his sister more than he would ever let anyone know. Though he must have wanted to blame someone, the story of the man rolling to his death in a beehive was making him sick to his stomach. He told me this later.

"Then an older boy, Odeng, began to talk wild talk among those waiting boys. 'We shall be elders one day, sitting in there. So why do they keep us out? One day we will be responsible for the village. We should at least be allowed to listen.'

"But Elijah was cautious and warned them the *mzee* by the door might chase them away if they were not quiet. But Odeng was determined. He puffed words out like smoke and they sounded strong and true, about burning a witch to destroy the evil. And so they all shared in remembering that witch power passes from father to son, mother to daughter, for that is the way it is with witches and that is why a village must protect itself from such forces. The boys were swallowed up by their own talk, and suddenly rose up.

"Okiki — he was the only son of the herbalist — he struggled but he did not cry out when they pounced on him and dragged him off down the hill toward the lake. They used fishing rope from the nearby boats to tie Okiki to a tree, and because none of them were sure about tying knots, they kept winding the rope round and round the boy until an immense mass of rope bound him stiff to the tree like an insect caught in a web. That is when word spread across the village and more boys arrived filled with the boredom of a day of waiting and the flame of feeling young and full of power.

"Uma sat away from the group when they stacked kindling in a great pile around Okiki, Odeng yelling hot words to keep their spirits flamed. But then, you see, no one had a match to start the fire so Odeng offered to fetch one while the others stood guard.

"There were no families living near this beach because of the great flooding many years ago, so he had to walk a great distance before finding a family compound. The mother had just put a pot of water on the fire and was squatting beside it when Odeng came by. He tried to act politely, as though there was nothing going on, but she looked at him with a knowing mother's eyes when he asked for a match — she told me this later. She had only a few matches left for her cooking fire and she wasn't about to part with one for the needs of a young boy. Then he pleaded for a piece of burning stick from the fire, and so she agreed though her eyes followed him suspiciously as he headed back down the path.

"Now it was a long walk back to the shore and the burning stick became short and too hot to handle. He stopped to light a longer one from it, but then when he walked fast it flickered and began to go out. Several times he had to stop and gather a clump of dry grass to get a flame going from the almost dead stick and begin again.

"While he was crouched in the shelter of a boulder at the edge of the tall grass, fanning the stick, that is when I saw him with these two eyes."

She stuck her fingers on her lids and looked at me. "A storyteller must have very clear eyes. But you know this to be true."

I nodded, too spell-struck to say a word.

"That is why I stood on the hill just above, watching, but of course he did not see me. Odeng blew on the stick then added a few bits of dry grass that burned brightly for an instant and soon the stick was glowing red. He stood up slowly and started off once again, his hand cupping the stick from the moving air, walking very slowly.

"I followed him for his arms jumped and his legs were stumbling and something was not right with his deed. Then I could see in the distance the crowd of boys circling Okiki and the tree and I knew in my heart what they had done. Now these old legs are stiff but I glided down the hill like the swiftest young antelope searching in my heart for what I could do, one old woman, for there were more than eighty boys boiling in the fever of this witch burning.

"I could see the sun was growing low over the lake and that is when the idea came to me. There were only a few fishing boats going out that evening, cutting like knives through the waters of the bay, disappearing around the point. The murmur of the boys' voices rose and fell as they awaited Odeng and his flame.

"I had no breath left and I did not want to seem excited so I stopped behind some brush and swallowed deep air. Then with my walking stick in hand, for such things are noticed by the young, I came upon them.

"'And what have we here? I asked them in my wise woman's voice, and that is when I saw the eyes of Okiki hidden in that bale of rope and twigs. 'His father is a witch, so we are going to burn him because he will be a witch one day.' That is what they told me. So I sat down slowly on a nearby stone to give myself time to think and laid my walking stick across my legs with my arms wide so it would seem an important act. That is what you must do with so many children. The sun was hanging low over the lake and it was then I could see Odeng approaching out of the corner of my eyes, holding the glowing stick.

"But I am afraid you are too late today, I said slowly and quietly so that each of my words would echo against the wind and they would gather closer to listen. If you burn a witch after the sun goes down, his evil will pass to each one of you. I made the words stand out one from the other looking in one pair of those young eyes, then the next. That is the way we must talk if we want the young to listen. You must wait until tomorrow. Unless you all want to be cursed and wake to the next sunrise as witches. Of course, they looked toward the lake and could see the sun had already touched the green water turning it into a blazing pot.

"Odeng had not seen me of course so he marched proudly to the tree, calling for the others to join him to light the fire. Elijah grabbed his hand, throwing the glowing stick to the ground and stomped it out. The others shouted their warnings and then watched, not breathing, as the sun slipped into the lake.

"Elijah took Uma by the hand. The others followed, at first slowly, then feeling the darkness near some started to run like gazelle before the storm. When they had all gone, I pulled the piles of twigs away from the tree. Like a spider I walked round and round the tree, pulling away the ropes from Okiki.

"It was late for the moon was high when Uma came back to the tree, running alone over the hill, thinking now that he would free Okiki since the elders had decided that his father, was innocent. Oki had willingly taken the same *dawa* he had given the girl and his heart had spoken the truth. He was not a witch — they had declared it so.

"When Uma saw the empty tree, he sank to the ground and his sobs rang out until his sorrow for his sister floated across the lake to Uganda. I sat with him for a long time that night so that my prayer would enter his heart. He asked if I knew, even before the elders decided, that Oki was innocent. I told him there are some things you know in your head and other things you know in your heart, like what it is like to be young in a crowd all excited about something, and what it is like to be old, sitting around a fire trying to decide the fate of someone you have lived with all your life. Neither is an easy task."

Zacharina folded her arms across her heavy chest. She had not paused in telling her tale, only casting her eyes now and again toward the rainy shore, then back to me with the intense concentration of a practiced storyteller. "But you must know some stories continue on through many years and they are not all sweet. You see our people heard the elders say he was not a witch, but they never took Oki's innocence into their hearts. The men would go out on the lake together, but Oki and Okiki were left to pole their way alone on the waters. This was not as it should be."

She knelt down and leaned closer, taking hold of the *ziwa kanga* I had wrapped around my shoulders and pulled me close.

"The heart of a storyteller breaks over and over for the stories are not always sweet. They are sometimes salted like desert wells when there is no rain, salted like tears, and the most frightening thing of all," she paused her face so close it blurred my vision. "Often you meet yourself on the path."

I could feel her breath on my cheeks. "Remember this *ziwa*," she said pointing to the lake. "We are meant to be mother's milk to one another."

When she stopped talking the silence became overwhelming. Hesitating, I finally asked, "And Oki and Okiki?"

She looked out over the lake as though she were searching for something. "One day on this lake, they were there alone when it happened."

She pointed to a stretch of shallow shoreline. "A hippopotamus rammed them, tipped over their boat. Then it attacked Oki while he thrashed in the water, bit him nearly in two pieces. Okiki was not strong enough to save him. Their people were not with them, you see. We do not survive the lake or life if we are separated from our people.

71

That is a lesson our ancestors knew well, but today, how sad that our memories grow dim."

JOURNEY TO VICTORIA

They were sending us a driver who would take us as far as Nakuru where he had family. From there we would go on our own to Western Province and Lake Victoria. They had said two o'clock at the latest. It was now well past five. We shifted camera gear around and looked at the clock realizing this was all part of what we would have to adjust to. Time was not a critical element in life here and those who let it rule their lives would find no solace in Africa.

Bougainvillea bushes exploding with color beside our door. School children in maroon and gray uniforms returning from school swarmed across the street in a gay cackle. Then in one frenzied blur the car arrived, the driver jumped out. He was Joshua, a short, slight man smiling ear to ear as he hustled our luggage into the rear and with no explanation of his tardiness, we were off careening through the traffic of Nairobi toward the hills of Limuru.

We were racing to pass a huge overloaded lorry struggling to climb a hill when Joshua swung back into our lane just as a bus came barreling head-on toward us. Chatter continued without pause as we swerved half onto the dirt shoulder to avoid the collision and eventually bumped back onto the tarmac.

Ahead a donkey cart loaded with water barrels paraded down the edge of the road driven by a lone child cracking a long switch on the animal's rump in a constant staccato seemingly unaware of any pain being inflicted. Kiosks along the road bore piles of brushed sheepskins with bundles of rhubarb hanging from swooping string across the front.

We stopped behind a bus loaded with bananas while a lorry in the opposite lane lumbered across a cavernous pothole. More women passed, bent over from the waist under enormous loads of firewood that spread more than a body length across their backs. Barefoot women following each other from the hills, back to the hills. I took a deep breath and blew out through puckered lips in a steady stream to slow my thoughts as we pulled ahead.

Gradually the roadside market areas evaporated into scattered fields of clumped maize. The air became suddenly cooler and clearer as we climbed higher into the hills of Limuru. Donkeys pulling carts loaded with firewood crept slowly up the road. David was chatting with Joshua, reminding him we weren't in a hurry. I felt myself breathing easier trying to take in the richness of the hills, thatched roofed huts, grazing cattle. I pressed my forehead against the window. It was beginning to feel real. All of it. The traffic, the startling beauty of the land, the strong handshakes of the people, the intensity of life alongside the acceptance of it.

Leaning against the window staring into the landscape I was suddenly aware someone was staring back at me. A woman bent over with a massive load of firewood strapped to her back was walking slowly at the edge of the road. We had slowed down behind some donkey carts so now we were looking at each other, two women, our faces only inches apart creeping up the same hill. I felt a flush rise in my cheeks. Bent under her burden, her gleaming black face cocked at an angle to the rest of the world, her eyes set far apart and just above them the leather straps that balanced her load cut into her forehead puckering it into deep furrows. Her face filled the entire space of my vision and though my instinct was to pull away since even through the glass our faces felt uncomfortably close, I returned the steady gaze with a hesitant smile. Slowly the woman smiled back, the furrows in her forehead buckling beneath the straps. Each pore, the gleaming sheen of sweat across her cheeks, the pink veins in the corners of her creamy eyes, the mass of hair tucked behind her ears all came into sharp focus magnified by the glass that separated us. Her eyes looked older than her face. I wondered what she thought of mine. Inch by inch we crept on at the same pace, moving up the road together. Neither of us wavered in our gaze making it strangely intimate, as though each of us knew we were intruding on sacred space and knowing it refused to leave. Then with a jolt our vehicle shot ahead but the reflection of the woman's eyes lingered in the spotted glass.

Climbing through the thick green countryside I could glimpse here and there the lime green mounds of tea bushes, their perfect rows reflecting the once grand colonial plantation, now contrasting sharply with the carefree clumps of banana trees and maize edged by ruffles of *skumawiki*.

We swung around a curve far into the opposite lane. My fingernails dug into my knapsack. Joshua seemed content with his path and continued on it until a *matatu* heading toward us blinked its lights, the local signal for you're in my way and I'm coming through. We drifted back to our side of the road onto loose gravel skidding to a halt, David and I clutching our bags as we lurched forward.

"Look," Joshua excitedly said pointing out his window.

Struggling not to shout something I'd regret I looked out and gasped. It lay below us like some primeval landscape. We got out and walked to the edge of the road where the earth changed before our eyes dropping down three thousand feet into the sprawling basin of the Rift Valley. Undulating hills, greens fading to dry browns then to a beige purple haze before the limits of eyesight drew the horizon. Looking straight down we were staring into the belly of an ancient crater, just beyond it a narrow lake, slate blue with soft shrimp colored shores, ethereal in the low rays of the sun. We hung onto each other not daring to move as a coral pink cloud lifted up from the shores splitting off into streaks.

Flamingoes, we whispered. Breaking away each pink streak, hundreds strong, broke gracefully from the cloud gliding low across the lake then settling down in a new part of the salty shallows. Each flock moved as if it were one life form changing its shape and direction from some shared spirit. Whatever power it was that had shaken this earth in prehistoric times to split an entire continent and form this great rift had compensated life by leaving behind this valley with its salty lake thick with shrimp and now these thousands of exquisite birds of the same shrimp color thrived in their own world.

The sound of the car engine starting pulled us back from the edge.

"The night it is coming," Joshua called.

We climbed back in and before we could settle between our bags we were swerving back onto the highway, speeding off. Ahead a mother giraffe with a gawky yearling by her side lumbered along the roadside staring at us as we shot by. Through the spattered rear window, I watched her as the last rays of sun created a mirage dissolving her silhouette.

Evening is only a moment on the equator, the sun drops with a flash leaving little time between the brightness of day and the darkness of night. Dark shadowed grasslands swept by with sudden rises of orange trees, then in a moment the landscape was black. It was disquieting to lose sight of the land for now the road took on a menacing presence without the relief of distraction. Headlights shot at us dead ahead then swayed to the opposite lane just as we met. Heavy rains and soft soil had eroded the edges of the road leaving dramatic drop offs and potholes so deep and broad that drivers hugged the middle until forced over by oncoming traffic. Giant lorries held their middle road position forcing oncoming traffic to the crumbling edge. Even when both lanes observed their side of the road there was barely passing room. Each approaching car appeared to be heading straight for us then would somehow streak by within what seemed a fingers reach.

I felt the tension in David's body, his eyes pinned to the road ahead in the pale headlights. He was an experienced driver, rebuilding engines from teen years on, racing his patched together car with buddies on the country roads of Indiana, earning money during college as a taxi driver. It was evident he had difficulty relinquishing the wheel to anyone else. Though he was silent his hazel eyes were growing wilder with the energy it took to restrain himself.

Suddenly a black wall appeared directly ahead. Joshua swung wildly into the blackness of the opposite shoulder and without slowing down recovered control, easing us back onto the road. The black wall was a lorry, stopped dead in the road, no lights or warning. We tried breathing deeply as we shot on without comment.

Within minutes the tarmac ended, and we were on a dirt road that seemed one lane wide. None of us had been speaking but now the quiet was distinctly different. It was evident Joshua was uncertain of this route but also evident he didn't want us to know. Without warning we hit a rock careening off it with a shattering screech. Headlights rose in the distance as we lurched around a scattering of boulders spread across the road. An immense bus appeared swerving from side to side before it brushed past us shooting a spray of gravel and dust across our windshield. Before we could see clearly, we hit a pothole with a sudden thud that threw us against the front seat. My heart was racing and my face was growing cold. I felt an anger welling up inside me that couldn't scream out. This was total madness. We would all die in this lunacy and without cause. One close call my nerves might tolerate but we were now hours into a continuous barrage of road terror that had no reason. I was too enraged to cry but a child-like fear had settled inside me beyond tears. The night was without stars and in the purple blackness each flash of light ahead was a new threat. I closed my eyes in silent resignation but they blinked open refusing to resign their watch. David's jaw was set tightly as he cautioned Joshua in increasing volume to slow down. Now! Every swerve he repeated what sounded more like a command. We had promised ourselves we wouldn't criticize African ways of doing things but this suicidal frenzy was our limit.

"Driving is crazy here," Joshua said glancing back at us with a smile. "Nobody cares if they live or die, but you'll get used to it."

I slumped back and leaned against David trying to relax my muscles. Meditate, I told myself. Float within. I took in deep breaths, blowing out, eyes closed, the oncoming headlights crossing my lids with fleeting iridescence I tried to push into coral veils swirling around my head, the sway of the elephants, the droning of monks. David's shoulder felt warm and strong. I tried focusing on just being close to him with each breath. Again and again lights passed and I was able to keep my eyes closed as the glowing flashes shone through my lids. There was a strange feeling that the glowing light through my eyelids was growing inside of me. Then without prelude she was there. As clearly as if she were lit from within by a noon sun, she stood there on the running board of the car glowing an iridescent white. Even her hair was a startling white, pale caramel hands protruding from her flowing robes. She held her arms open wide like a child in a keep-away game, head flung back in silent laughter facing a pickup truck as it sped by, shielding us. I opened my eyes and she was gone. Quickly I closed them and she was there tossing her head in a carefree laugh without a sound. Her skin golden, her eyes intense black and somehow it felt like she was me, more beautiful than I had ever thought myself, more gracefully at ease with herself yet I knew she was some form of my own being shifting into a dream-like survival mode. She faded in and out of view, back arched, head tossed back, then on the hood springing up like an ancient ship's bowsprit sending a faint light into the blackness around us. A mellowness was flooding my system. I laid my head back on David's shoulder and studied her as now the half-seen traffic careened by. She was neither frightening nor strange. There was a happy wildness in her eyes that was familiar, perhaps something I recognized in myself but could not fully be. And yet she was.

SUDDENLY THERE

She was no ordinary angel,

Appearing as she did in the African night,

Wispy robes fluttering free as we flew through the chaos,

Cars careening past, some with headlights bursting halos around us,

(Had we already died?)

Matatus shrieking past, dark in the darkness,

Lorries swaying, the road disappearing,

She with her glowing bronze Buddha belly,

Suddenly there,

Dancing eyes, silk white hair,

Hardly the guardian angel of my childhood prayer,

"Angel of God my guardian dear

To whom God's love entrusts thee here,

Ever this day be at my side –"

And so she was, arms flung wide,

Holding back the madness, hovering there

Holding off my despair,

You shall live to tell the tale, she smiled,

And so I have.

WOMEN AND FISH

It was late when we arrived at the small hotel in Nakuru. Joshua shook our hands vigorously and walked off into the night still smiling. His home was a few miles through the hills he said. This was his leave from work, and he was happy to have had the lift home this far.

The hotel kitchen had chapatis and curried beef left. We sat at a small table staring at our tepid beer. We were numb. I wanted to share the glowing woman still so vivid in the recesses of my brain, but I had no desire to form words. We were both too exhausted to do more than clutch each other's hand over the stained tablecloth with half smiles of disbelief. I had drifted asleep in the car and she had faded, like the mother giraffe fading with the limits of my eyesight but in that moment, I knew she would always be there.

The harrowing drive of the night faded when we woke to the fresh smell of morning air and headed out on our own. We would be staying that night with Julia and Edward at their ranch in the Rift Valley. We first met catching snippets of their conversation at a dinner party, raising camels and zebroids, part of their past running wildlife expeditions. Of course, we had to ask questions and their eagerness to share led to an invitation to their ranch. Now we were following their sketched map, winding our way downward, broad switchbacks descending into the richness of the deep valley.

The main house of the ranch sat on a rise, its wide porches under deep protective roofs, surrounded by long grass grazing lands with a scattering of sheds and barns. We were suddenly swept into a part of Africa's history we never expected to see. Gracious arms pulled us in, hot tea waiting.

"*Dawa ya moto ni moto*," the cure for heat is heat, Julia beamed filling mugs of sweet tea. "The hot dust of the road is best cleared with hot tea."

The front rooms of the house were filled with mounted animal heads staring down at us, relics of past days when this had been a hunting lodge. Photographs were propped up on mantles and bookshelves, hunting poses. I recognized a photograph of Hemingway holding up the head of a just killed leopard but decided to hold my tongue. Here was this kindly older couple with clearly a passionate love of the land, having lived here in the Rift for decades, through times when norms were different, through the Mau-Mau uprisings and the new independence, the archeological discoveries, the ever changing awareness. Now what they had left were their tales of how it once had been. After tea they took us out to meet the camels they still bred.

"No more ha-ha's from your sisters," Edward said as he saddled them up.

David had told them the story of his sisters' taunts. We were both soon mounting camels, lurching forward then back as they rose under us, swaying us slowly across the fields. The zebroids were kept in separate pastures, a cross between a zebra and a horse, their beautiful tan bodies with black zebra stripes wrapping halfway across their backs. Zebras being immune to the tsetse fly, their hooves not needing to be shod, and horses being trainable, their backs able to carry a load, resulted in a perfect pack animal for expeditions. Tales of past safaris emerged over sherry in the evening on the porch, long lines of camels and zebroids heading out over the Rift.

I asked about the photograph of Hemingway.

"I was his guide." Edward said quietly. There was a long pause. "The great white hunter. He was not a nice man."

He spoke of long hunting expeditions with the famous author over the years, his heavy drinking, telling African bearers to sit up in the tree branches at night, telling them they were spotters when he really wanted them to attract the large cats. Edward's voice trailed off. I wondered how bittersweet those memories were or just bitter. I couldn't find the words to ask. Our conversation shifted to the latest archeological digs, the clarity of the stars. Then we all just sat listening to the night sounds of the ancient valley. I kept wondering if buried bones could talk what stories would they tell.

With hugs and a warm invitation to return soon we set off early the next morning, the lunch Julia had packed for us on the seat between us. The lingering images of animal heads against the warm hospitality of this couple, their complex history, their enthusiasm for what we were doing, everything was weaving in and out of all we were learning about Africa past and present. Given the road conditions it would be a long drive but we felt more at ease being in charge of driving. We would take our time.

Clouds hung dark around the mountains as we threaded our way up the highway winding through the forested slopes. It was late afternoon when a sudden chill wind swept down from the high plains. Within seconds the sky opened up and the rain fell with such force that the narrow mountain road was instantly awash. Thin red mud filled the ruts and potholes spilling swiftly down what had moments before been a discernible way out of the hills. Now there was nothing to see but a rushing wall of water on all sides.

David held his speed. We needed to make time before the caked red earth softened into a quagmire though with the force of the rain it was inevitable. We headed downhill into the wall of water lurching from side to side. It was nearly impossible to see anything ahead. Suddenly the road turned sharply to the left. We swerved wide onto the shoulder, glanced off a fallen tree branch and recovered in time to round the bend. Almost as soon as we had regained the middle of the road the rain abruptly lightened. The road ahead was barely wet and the sky seemed distinctly brighter. A misty drizzle continued for another kilometer or so and then low in the west the sun returned. Below us a clear road swept out of the mountains.

Thick trees gave way to tea plantations on each side, the brilliant yellow-green tea bushes glowing in the soft light. A few pickers remained, their yellow rubber aprons stiff about them as they stooped under the weight of the wicker baskets strapped to their backs. Soon the dirt road turned to tarmac and our mud-crusted wheels whistled on the smooth surface. From the hills we could see the road slope steadily downwards to the Lake Victoria basin and Kisumu.

We would be staying at the hotel there tonight. We could see it on the rise just above the bay, solid and non-distinctive except for the flashing pinks and purples of the bougainvillea that cascaded over the half-rotted fence as though nature were trying to compensate for what humans had done to the landscape. She had almost succeeded for there was an undeserved air of elegance about the old hotel that had nothing to do with itself. It was more the fronds that rimmed the terrace, gracefully erect, the flowering arch poised between the cracked plaster pillars and the slope of the land that gave it charm as it rose from the edge of Lake Victoria. Depending on the disposition of one's eye, it was entirely possible to ignore the stained cracked stucco, the soiled red carpet that lay crooked on the front steps and still see simple elegance.

The lobby smelled of dampness and stale beer. Heavy chairs clumped awkwardly around squat round tables while guests hunched over their knees to reach their drinks. We picked our way through a raucous group near the door and headed for the desk. Everything in the room seemed unduly dark — dark green walls, the furniture, even people's clothing, except for the startlingly white starched coats of the waiters. These stood out in a ghostly glow against the sullen brown shadows of the room.

We registered for our room. Two servants passed by, lighted candles in hand. They stopped at each table, secured a candle in an empty bottle, took another candle from their pockets, lit it and went on. Slowly the room took on a new tone. Faces glowed in the flickering bits of light and the shadows grew darker as the last faint glow of dusk over the lake blackened into night.

"There is no electricity in town this evening. So sorry. There is no hot food. Only sandwiches. The storm, you know," the clerk explained.

He was Asian and spoke in an Indian-British rhythm that was both melodic and mechanical. "You wish something from the bar?" he sang out in his up and down tones.

We sat down near the window on a lumpy sofa that smelled of mildew. The waiter brought thin sandwiches and beer, then fixed a lighted candle in a saucer on the table. We touched glasses in a toast. The lake was barely discernible as the reflection of the candlelight gleamed back from the glass, blocking the view of everything that lay beyond.

Through the dimness of the room a young couple approached. Did we mind sharing our table, the place was totally packed. We gladly made room for them and shared introductions. They looked travel weary. They had just driven in from Uganda, working on a Quaker project demilitarizing children who had been snatched by various militias and were now finding their way back home. The children had spent years with their captors raiding villages, setting fire to homes, watching their young friends get blown up by mines when they were all made to walk ahead of the soldiers, first carrying weapons, then learning to use them with deadly accuracy and abandon — all to survive. But now, returning home, the habits of war were hard to lose and their families soon realized these weren't the children they had known and lost. A danger to their families, rejected by the schools, there was an entire generation of children, mainly boys, now social outcasts. Homes were set up for them to provide basic shelter and education and most importantly to help them relearn social norms, to deal with their nightmares, the demons reminding them of what they had done, to make still the habits of violence. For most there was no hope of rejoining their families. They spoke lovingly of the boy who still slept under his bed for fear of being snatched back by soldiers, another who screamed so much in his dreams he feared sleeping and far too many who struck out at others with uncontrollable force at the slightest upset. They spoke softly, no anger, no frustration. They made this trip to Kenya once a month to replenish medicines, school supplies, powdered milk, things that weren't available in Uganda. Getting it all back across the border was the challenge. Their voices were so soft it made their story seem like a secret to be kept. Our stories felt so pale. We were all tired and said our good nights. The lake was barely discernible as the reflection of the candlelight gleamed back from the glass blocking the view of everything that lay beyond.

"*Wazungus! Wazungus!*" the women shouted the next morning when they saw us approaching in our mud-spattered vehicle. Massed together holding papyrus reeds high, waving them over their heads they seemed like one exuberant creature winding its way down the road. Their voices rang out in shrill warbling hoots and then into song as they danced toward us.

David swung the video camera out the window to capture the images and sounds as they approached. The music rang through the swamp, interrupted by their shrill cries like birds calling to one another, women weaving from one side of the road to the other, waving their reeds. When they got to our vehicle they went into higher pitch of squeals, reaching for me, gently pulling me out into their midst.

One woman, stouter than the rest, dressed in a dandelion gold *kanga*, danced forward, her voice leaving the song to laugh, the laughter growing into a hooting warble. The group turned around, heading back toward their shelter, never breaking their rhythm, arms around me from every direction, enveloping me as they danced me to the squat shelter that was their project center.

After sipping a welcoming tea, struggling with our few words of thanks we were swept off to their *shambas*, green gardens that stretched in every direction. They guided us through the swampy edges of rice fields, rows of cabbages and *skumawiki*.

They told us the story of their project and how several years ago Lake Victoria had flooded terribly pushing the shore back several kilometers leaving a swamp where there once had been a field with a cleared path leading to the lake. The swamp had blocked all access to the lake and the men were no longer able to reach the lake to fish. Their boats had been destroyed in the floods. After sharing all their thoughts, the women had devised a plan. They would dig a canal through the swamp so fishing boats could reach the lake. They had heard that a council of churches had been helping women's groups and they wanted to tell their story in hopes of getting help. Though none of them had ever been to Nairobi before they each gave a few shillings so that two of them could take a bus to the city. When they arrived they asked directions to find the council. Hearing their story and their compelling plan the council assigned a social worker to guide them and gave them a loan.

A channel was dug through the swamp out to the lake and with the funds they also bought three fishing boats and nets. The women decided to lease the boats to the men so they could fish. Their strategy went way beyond simply reaching the waters of Lake Victoria. Prior to the flooding the men had fished the lake, sold their fish and gotten drunk with the money. If there was anything left the women might be able to buy food for their families and pay school fees for their children, but most often there was little left. With the flooding the women saw an opportunity to change the situation not only by having a canal dug. By owning the boats themselves, leasing them to the men ensured there would be income to support their families. Now while they waited for the men to return from fishing each day the women worked on their gardens near the small shelter they had built at the head of the canal, each taking vegetables to sell in the market or bringing them home to feed their families. With pride, their eyes bright, hands flying as fast as their words they carved out their story in the air, evidently thrilled that we would be filming their work.

With gear loaded we all climbed into long narrow canal boats. A young man with a pole twice his height stood in the rear and pushing against the mucky bottom eased the heavy boat through the narrow slip of water. The other women followed in two other boats. All around us papyrus reeds stood tall, iridescent in the brilliant sun, some bending gracefully like lacy umbrellas over our heads. The women giggled and poked each other as they chattered, smiling broadly anytime they'd catch our eye.

We asked about crocodiles and were told there were a few. It was hippos they feared. Since the men only had poles to propel their boats they had to stay in shallow water. It was in the shallows that hippos grazed and slept unseen beneath the surface, easily charging and toppling over a boat if they were disturbed. But if they drifted into deeper water beyond the length of their poles they lost control of their boats. The explanation was shared without drama, a simple reality of the lake and what it meant to catch her fish. Perched in the bow I was scribbling notes, pausing to take photos as we were propelled through the papyrus swamp.

Before we had gone more than a half-kilometer, I felt a prickly chill. The papyrus surrounding us was so thick it was impossible to see either end of the canal, and for long stretches even the sky was hidden from view as great fronds bent in sweeping arches above us, cocooning us. Papyrus brushed us on either side as we slid through the narrow canal barely room for planting the pole for each push. It was as though we were floating through a mysterious tunnel to an unknown world. The words of the women drifted all around, unfamiliar sounds in the swamp echoing in the grass, and now and then the scream of a bird rang through the hot air with a bristling clarity like the warbling hoot of the women's song.

David put his hand on my shoulder and pointed ahead. The reeds were beginning to thin and patches of dark water lay like miniature lakes around us as the swamp gave way to the lake. The light weight of his hand felt comforting. Ahead of us Lake Victoria spread out its mauve mantle fading into the glare of the sun like a mirage without edges. With swift ease the pole man swung the craft to the right, heaving his body into the thrust of the pole with new energy in the open water. Birds swooped overhead, diving now and then into the mirage, shattering the stillness of the waters.

Far in the distance I focused the video camera on the silhouette of three fishing boats. As they drew nearer the hunched figures of fishermen became more distinct, emerging from the glare like figures in a dream. They were motionless except for a lone pole man in the stern of each craft bending with the weight of his task.

They don't look alive, was all I could think as I zoomed in on the huddled men feeling intrusive as I filmed. The stillness of their bodies was frightening. As we grew near enough to see their faces there were no greetings, no waving hands. Slowly the boats of the men and our boats carrying the women converged on a sandy strip of shore beyond the swamp.

We had no idea what was unfolding but wanting to capture every image we kept filming and taking pictures. It was why they sent us here, but it seemed to be so insensitive, even rude. One by one the men's fishing boats landed and one by one the fish they had caught were laid out on the damp sand. Women walked down the long line of fish and the deciding began — which fish they would take for their lease payment, which they would buy outright. No scales, no calculators, few words spoken, just nods. The agreements to the process had been made long ago and now each played out their role with an efficiency of motion without words. The men would sleep in the grass hut on the beach this night, heading back out each morning to fish, and each day the women would come with their pots of hot *ugali* to feed the men and collect their fish. Every week or so the men returned to their homes and families. It was now the pattern of their lives.

I noticed one thin man bent protectively over his catch studying each fish with great care. His hands were long and bony, his hollow chest bent in as though his body had not straightened up in many years. As the women approached to look over his catch his hand fell on one small, fat fish that he slid from the pile. This one he would not sell. It had been a hard decision, but he had decided in favor of his hungry belly.

The women hauled out great cooking pots, hot with *ugali*, the stiff cornmeal mush that is the staple of every meal. A large kettle of tea was set securely on rocks. As if in slow motion the men pulled their heavy nets from their boats, spreading them out on the hot sand to dry. Women came by each boat with gourds heaped high with *ugali* and passed them out to the men. Small fires were built and the men propped up the smaller fish they had saved for themselves on sticks over the flames.

Though the sun was still brilliant overhead the edges of the sky were growing dark. Despite the clouds the women served fish stew over rice for our lunch, far more elegant than what the men were eating, and while we ate a circle of women danced around us, hooting out with shrill cries as they stomped and swayed to the rhythm of a small drum, some with a huge fish draped over their heads. We were told this was not just for us. They danced and sang every day celebrating the catch to keep the spirits of the men and their own spirits high. One of the leaders wore a crown of warthog teeth on her head and several of the women carried swishing sticks fastened with animal tails swinging them in great arcs over their heads.

The leader of the group came to me, pulling me into the midst of the dance. She held a folded cloth, a *kanga*, as deep blue as the lake, a gift, she said, because the pictures we were taking would be shared and seeing them would give other women hope so that they too might be able to feed their families. For this they were thanking us. Their own *kangas* were worn and thin. I felt tears well up. I tear easily, a problem I've had since childhood, and now tears were streaking down my cheeks. How could I accept something that cost more than any of these women could afford? How could I refuse? As the leader wrapped the *kanga* around me, the dancers clapped and spun around us warbling like a rookery of colorful birds. David huddled over the camera, framing us, the dance, the fishing boats, the faces of the women, the exhausted men.

Our dance went on amidst laughter and my embarrassing tears until a sudden gust of wind swept across the beach and the sky lost its light. The water that had been still as glass now rippled with the wind and stinging bits of sand whipped against our legs. Men rushed to the shore to haul their boats higher onto the beach. One man went out in a canal boat, poling in circles to test the wind. He returned saying we must leave now.

As we headed back through the papyrus reed canal, I found it hard to form thoughts much less the words that would be needed for the narrative for the film. Once again, we had been invited into another world that could only be described with every one of our senses in play. It wasn't just a matter of capturing images of the great lake, it was the tactile grit of sand, the taste of just caught fish, the smell of the mud, the singing, the palpable joy of dancing women with warthog crowns and fish on their heads and the exhaustion of men who fish all night. How do you ever share the whole picture? With each lunge of the pole man propelling us back through the arch of papyrus reeds I felt a silent sadness in leaving. There was so much more to learn from these women, more stories to hear, so many more images and dances to capture, and a strange longing to be part of a simpler life.

LETTER: OUR NEW HOUSE

Dearest Family all,

Our new house is great! We have five huge African mango trees, five avocado trees the size of huge maples back home all loaded with fruit, guava trees by our front door bending nearly to the ground with fruit, passion fruit vines, loquat and custard apple trees, a new treat. Flowers are everywhere. The compound is huge, surrounded by a high concrete wall and a double gate across the driveway. A car enters the first gate from the road, then that is closed behind before the inner gate is opened. All of which was declared necessary by the council. They suggested we get dogs. David suggested we get geese. In the end we decided against both. We will be planting a small vegetable garden this weekend when we hope to complete our moving in.

The house itself is lovely — white stucco, red tile roof, two bathrooms, a huge fireplace, three bedrooms so there's room for anyone who wants to visit. We have a garage with a studio type garden room attached, plus servants' quarters behind the house with two small one-room apartments and a courtyard. Alice has moved in, which has been a strange experience, as we never intended to have a housekeeper. It seems she was hired several years ago by an expat working with the council and it was presumed we would hire her as soon as we moved into our permanent home. Given her desperate need for income we agreed and now are realizing more every day how important she will be in our crazy lives. Laundry is all done in the bathtub and dried on a clothesline in the service yard. Alice can wring a sheet, even a blanket nearly dry with one mighty twist of her strong arms. She tucks the bed sheets in so tightly we can barely undo them enough to crawl in at night. She speaks not a word of English and with our struggling Kiswahili it's often an amusing interchange.

After a few trials, we decided Alice will only make tea for us but will not cook which has apparently disappointed her. It's for the best. Our first week here we had an open house for about twenty new friends from the council and NGO community. I made a large pot of lamb curry and some wonderful mango chutney from our own trees and asked Alice to prepare the rice so it would be ready just before we were to eat. She apparently put the rice and cold water in the pot hours in advance then turned on the heat when the guests arrived. My own fault as I presumed she knew how to cook rice. The giant glob of gelatinous paste that she turned out into the serving bowl bore no resemblance whatsoever to rice and of course it was too late to start anew. Everyone was very sporting about it and we had learned a valuable lesson.

Philip has also joined us. He works at the council serving tea and delivering messages earning next to nothing there. He needed a place to live and we were approached since everyone knew we had an extra servant's quarters. It all seemed to have been decided before we got here. We also learned he will take care of our yard and lawn on weekends in exchange for rent and be here as a night guard when we are away which makes Alice less anxious. So here we all are.

The past few weeks we've stayed put in Nairobi trying to wade through the politics and complications of doing development work in Kenya. There are supposedly nearly 400 different non-governmental organizations (NGOs) based here, major foundations plus the UN's development programs, mainly due to the relative stability of Kenya. We've been meeting so many amazing people working in humanitarian assistance and development, staff of Ford Foundation with ears to the ground for new projects dealing with women in development, Quakers and Mennonites working with peace and reconciliation groups on the borders, and University of Nairobi faculty searching for solutions to tribalism and justice in a developing democracy. Everywhere we go it is evident that it is the women who are developing Kenya. Men seem unable to work together in groups. They have a high rate of alcoholism and little ambition. The women are dynamite, forming groups to become literate, to earn some income, to support one another, yet they have no land ownership rights and are typically excluded from community or tribal decisions. Women grow most of the food in Africa, and most often raise the children with little financial support from their male partners. That is why, though it is Saturday, we are in the office writing more funding proposals under the umbrella of women in development.

The madness of driving in Kenya has been our greatest adjustment, both the traffic and trusting to vagaries of the vehicle pool. We decided the only sane thing to do was search for our own vehicle and do our own driving whenever possible. The good news is we just bought a used Range Rover. All of the "Rs" on the nameplate fell off so we've named her Ange Ove. It just felt too precarious depending on overworked drivers for these long journeys. Thankfully Alice keeps us in clean clothes between trips, scrubs the red silt out of our socks and keeps the house immaculate.

Last week we had houseguests from the States, they had been to one of the swank tourist safari lodges and saw next to nothing. As a final send off, we drove through Nairobi Game Park on the way to the airport and what a bonanza. We saw five cheetahs, six lions, a freshly killed zebra covered with vultures right next to the road. Back on the highway heading to the airport we had to stop abruptly, all traffic, both directions, four lanes at a standstill while a stampeding herd of wildebeests charged past us on both sides. We sat breathlessly frozen listening to their thundering hooves on the tarmac of the highway, their curled horns flying past within inches of Ange Ove's windows.

We're honestly thriving on this hectic schedule, feeling absurdly healthy and sleeping like a pair of babes no matter where we are. Every Friday the US Embassy across the street from our office shows a week's worth of CBS news so we're able to catch up. It was

95

disturbing learning of the South Korean plane that was shot down. When big things happen it feels even harder being this far away from all of you. Give each other hugs for us and please stay safe. All of our love,

Lani

WAMBUI

Wambui picked up the piles of potatoes and the last withered cabbage that remained on her plastic sheet and put them into her basket. The money she had earned from the day's selling was already tucked safely inside her clothing, and though there were still people rushing out of office buildings who might stop to buy something, she was too tired to delay the walk back home any longer. Heaving the basket onto her back she adjusted its straps across her forehead and headed for home.

It had rained heavily the night before in Nairobi and puddles still blocked the crosswalks. A bus careened around the corner, sending a wall of water across the crowd of pedestrians waiting to cross the street. Unable to move from the weight of her load she bowed her head to the inevitable deluge and felt the cold muddy water splatter through her *kanga*. She picked her way through the crowd slowly and steadily and seeing a break in the traffic hurried as best she could with the heavy basket on her back. A *matatu* bearing down on the flow of people in the street blared its horn and skimmed past just missing her. She pushed past the people waiting to cross on the other side of the street and continued on, head thrust down under the load.

Secretaries in high heels and flowered nylon hose clicked past, their plaited hairdos in new African chic swinging as they ran. A group of men in suits stood outside a French pastry shop laughing loudly and beyond them a group of tourists was disembarking from a zebra striped bus in front of the Hilton. The doorman in top hat and red tailed coat stood straight and tall beside a carved pillar of African masks, each with an expression of amazement and horror. The top hat rushed to help a group of tourists climbing out of a zebra striped tour van.

The rubber thongs Wambui wore had grown thin and her feet had been strangely swollen for over a month. It had not seemed possible to take a day off and wait at the clinic for someone to look at her feet, though each day she reminded herself that soon she must.

She stopped briefly at the corner and looked up as a *matatu* swerved by. It would cost two shillings to take a *matatu* home but two shillings would also buy the pencil Jeremiah needed if he were to go to school tomorrow. The teacher had sent him home yesterday because he had not worn his uniform shirt and had no pencil. The shirt had fallen off the stool onto the floor while they slept the night before and in the morning it was soaked with mud. She had washed it immediately but it was wet and Jeremiah was unable to wear it to school. That morning she had spent the last of her shillings buying the vegetables she would sell and a bit of maize meal for their dinner so Jeremiah had gone without his pencil. But today she had a few extra shillings and tomorrow Jeremiah would have his pencil and a clean shirt.

Though her other children had tried going to school they were too slow to learn and one by one they had dropped out. Jeremiah seemed different, and though he was not bright he was very determined and for this Wambui thanked God every day. She was grateful she had six children. At least some of them might take care of her when she grew old. Other women with only a few children were doomed. Children can die and some will marry and go away. You need many children if you hope to survive through old age.

Another *matatu* shot past as she adjusted her head straps and went on. Shops selling music cassettes blared the latest African hits and shop windows filled with watches and calculators were crowded with young people gazing at the glitter. The last few hawkers still had their wares spread out across the sidewalks and office workers paused to buy a few mangoes or cassava. It had been a good day for Wambui for the police had not chased any of the hawkers from her street and she had sold all but one of her cabbages. This last one they would have for dinner and there was enough maize meal left from yesterday even for porridge in the morning.

Beyond the city center the streets wound in slow curves past Asian shops selling foam mattresses and hardware and small African kiosks with beans and maize bubbling in giant pots. The landmarks on the way to Mathare Valley had become engraved on Wambui's senses over the years and now she was able to walk the four kilometers to her home without having to look up.

Wambui had been born in Mathare and though she had once visited the village from which her mother had come, the land had been divided so many times with each generation there was no land for them now, no relatives who could help a young girl, so she had returned to the valley and had borne her six children here.

It was almost evening when Wambui turned down Juja Road. The clanging of hammers against steel bars could still be heard from the small shops of the metal workers, and goats scurried over the heaps of garbage that stood at the edge of the road. Two young men were beating a mound of blanket cuttings discarded by the factory, their wire whips turning the waste edges into fluffy stuffing. Beside them an older man was sewing plastic sacks for mattress covers. As far as the eye could see mudded huts and shacks stood crowded together, clumped on top of each other down the narrow streets that led to the river. Sheets of polythene were stretched across caved-in roofs and cardboard sheets were woven in and out of poles where mud walls had washed away in the last rainy season.

Near the river the huts were nothing but lean-tos for the waters rose predictably during the heavy rains carrying everything along the bank

99

with them. But for the newest squatters this was the only land they could afford. As the houses climbed up the hill, they took on a more solid character and some here and there even had metal roofing sheets and smooth mud walls. But for these the landlords charged more than one hundred shillings a month, more than a vegetable mama could afford.

On Mathare's main road each house was also a business with a broad window and fat windowsills to display small stacks of charcoal or neat rows of onions piled in tiny pyramids for two shillings each. For those who could not afford to buy a sack of maize meal there were vendors selling small newspaper cones of meal for a few shillings and the profit made from those who had less paid for their own supper.

Wambui hurried down a side alley past the butchers with tables spread with stacks of meat. Slaughtered goats hung from the eaves of their shops, blood dripping into great pots and kettles of innards standing ready for selling. With darkness coming, the valley was soon to take on a different character.

Plastic cups and basins, batteries and tin cans that had been pounded into small lanterns were spread out on boards in front of one kiosk. Wambui stopped and bought the pencil for Jeremiah and tucked it securely inside her *kanga* before going on.

The hot sun had dried out the morning's mud and now the road past the clinic was once more thick dust littered with garbage and droppings from goats and people. Wambui nodded to a heavy woman in a long blue jacket standing in front of the clapboard building. It was Theresa but hurried on. No time for visiting now. If she stopped her tired legs might not feel like starting again though she must ask Theresa about her swollen feet soon.

Theresa was the nurse in charge of the clinic. Her head was covered in a blue scarf and she wore large white plastic earrings with gold speckles that bobbed and swirled as she called out with expressive nods to Wambui as she hurried on. There was something in Wambui's walk that didn't seem right and Theresa called out but Wambui didn't turn. Then Theresa noticed her colleague Charles approaching.

"*Habari*, Charles." She had been expecting him since morning and here it was the end of the day.

"*Mzuri, mzuri.* I found more children for you, Theresa," he said without pausing. Charles was a Catholic priest, teaching children to read at his sidewalk school. Chalk and charcoal letters drawn on fairly intact stretches of concrete constituted his classroom where children clustered around him each day, absorbing his caring energy.

"I don't need more children to feed —."

"At the dump," Charles said, his smile fading. "Children, I couldn't believe it, they've built their own village there."

"A village?"

"There must be fifty or more igloos — sticks and polythene sacks. Only children. No adults. I kept asking. Just kids."

"Living off the dump?"

"Quite well, considering," Charles said. "You know the spot, where the garbage trucks from the airport dump the leftover food from the planes. It seems the drivers have gotten to know the kids and they take great care to dump the food in one area the older ones have cleared off with a tarp. It was amazing to watch — a whole small society, older kids line up the younger ones, sort through the food, really quite just in the way they hand it out. They even keep track of kids who are missing that day. It was amazing. I spent the whole morning there. They're a bit cautious about talking to me, but perhaps in time they will."

Theresa thrust her hands on her hips.

"And while you find more children, I must figure out how to feed the ones we already have. I spent the entire morning at the import office and I still do not have clearance on the powdered milk! I know they are looking for *chai* and I simply refused to slip them something. 'You come with me and see our children' I said to them 'and you will sign these papers *sasa hivi*,' but they just laugh. I looked for you all day.

101

There were so many tiny babies, Charles, you wouldn't have believed. We didn't even get them all weighed before more began arriving and we had to send so many away hungry. And with a shipment of powdered milk waiting for us in Mombasa. Now you're telling me a whole village of children?"

Charles sat down on a bench outside the clinic and folded his arms across his chest, his long legs stretched out in front of him making him look even taller than his two meters. His deep eyes were lively, yet serious, which prompted people to confide in him easily since it seemed so evident he was listening.

Theresa sat down next to him and continued. Her voice was hushed as she peered around.

"And as if that wasn't enough, the landlords have been making threats again to the squatters of *Kwajuma* village. Some think it could be serious this time. They want them off the land now! Word is that big money is coming for new housing. The squatters know they will not be the ones to get it so they're not budging."

She did not pause for a breath but continued to stare straight ahead swinging her head as she talked. "Then wouldn't you know that women's church group from America was here today, of all days, a whole busload wanting to see for themselves, so I sent Mary with them into the valley so the chiefs wouldn't be upset, and Charles, you know that latrine that has been over-flowing behind the school? Well that road has been flooded with sewage for weeks and the bus driver had really never driven in the valley before and wouldn't you know they got stuck in all that filth. The tires were half buried and some of the visitors got out in that muck and tried to push but it was useless. The bus is still there. Everyone had to walk back here. Poor souls. Mary said they were a mess and of course there wasn't much water left in the tanks here at the clinic by that time of day so they cleaned up as best they could and took a city bus back to their hotel. Won't they have some story to tell back home?" She heaved a deep breath. "All I want to know is what am I supposed to do next?"

Charles looked at her.

"Tomorrow I will meet you here first thing in the morning and we can go together to the import office. Let's give it one more try." He smiled and cocked his head. "Then —."

"Then?"

"Then you could come with me — to the children's village."

Theresa closed her eyes and shook her head.

"I'm going home. Look, it's almost dark and there will be no buses. I may just wake up tomorrow morning and decide not to come back here."

"You'll be back, Theresa. I know you will," he said softly. "And so will I."

Darkness crept over the valley. Kerosene lanterns were lighted and hung from the ceilings and set in the doorways of kiosks. Beyond the school in Kwajuma village stretched an area of cardboard and paper houses. Heavy rains last season had washed away the mud walls and the people had salvaged what they could of their poles and plastic sheets and built the rest with cardboard scraps.

Wambui had rebuilt her house here with what she could find and moved her treasured sacks of charcoal inside. Her oldest girl Lucy sold charcoal from their only window while she was in the city and though she tried her best Wambui was sure people were cheating the girl.

She blew on the coals of her fire until they glowed red and when a few flames shot out she set the pot filled with the chopped cabbage and water on to boil. Jeremiah had folded his uniform shirt and lay next to it on his cot fingering his new pencil, watching her. The older boys would probably not be coming home again tonight. They spent the day in Nairobi trying to earn a few shillings pointing out and saving parking spots to passing cars and though Wambui feared they would soon begin stealing she wanted to believe them that it was just too far to walk back, especially if they had not eaten all day. But something in her knew they didn't want to look her in the eye and face a mother's questioning look.

The baby was fussing so Wambui spread a thin, worn blanket across the top of two sacks of charcoal and set the child there. Lucy took care of the baby each day while Wambui went to the city and though the girl was almost ten, Wambui was fearful she was no longer trustworthy. Today the baby was crying too hard, as though she hadn't been fed. She had left some porridge from breakfast, but Lucy admitted she had eaten it herself. If she could no longer trust Lucy she might have to stay in Mathare to sell her vegetables, which would mean less profit. The girl sat outside the door staring at her mother, hoping for a glance of forgiveness, but Wambui refused to look up from the steaming pot. Lucy would get no supper tonight and Wambui was too tired and hungry herself to be pestered about it. She had taken no lunch today and now the aroma of the soup was making her dizzy with hunger.

Across the valley wisps of smoke curled into the black night air and the yellow flicker of lanterns dotted the shadows of the narrow streets. Thumping music thundered from the bars and loud voices called to each other across the confusion of the outdoor beer kiosks. Women who had brewed beer or *changaa* were bringing it now in the darkness to be sold and others with nothing to sell but themselves wandered toward the bars in search of men with shillings to spare.

Wambui sent Jeremiah with a penny to fetch a jug of water from the tap down the alley and pried open the tin where she kept their maize meal. She stared inside the tin. Her heart felt suddenly heavy and very old. She knew the tin had been nearly half full, she knew it as surely as she knew her name, and yet now it was almost empty. Only a few handfuls remained.

She turned around to look for Lucy but the girl had anticipated her anger and was nowhere to be seen. It was then she smelled the smoke. At first she thought it was her own cooking fire, then she saw it sifting in between the cracks in her cardboard walls from outside. She grabbed the baby and ran to the door. A black billowy cloud of smoke caught her in the face and all around flames shot like a storm bursting over the valley. People were screaming and running and before she could think she heard the blaze burst as it hit a tin of kerosene in the house next door.

She called out for Jeremiah and Lucy as a thick wall of smoke blanketed her voice. Suddenly the flames from the neighbor's house shot through their roof, the cardboard burst into flames. Clutching the baby to her breast, she ran through the smoke out to the street.

Spears of fire shot skyward in the black night engulfing the shanties in an inferno that crept steadily towards the river. Screams echoed through the darkness as women vainly searched for their children, men scooping handfuls of dirt to throw on the blaze. Goats fled before the smoke, stampeding through the crowded streets. People clutching cooking pots, babies, and blankets ran toward the river, and all-around shouts and cries broke through the smoke, more people emerging frantically seeking safety from the blaze.

Men banged on the door of the chief's house. He had the only phone in the Kwajuma area to call for help but his door was locked. The public tap was running too slowly to provide enough buckets of water so people dug frantically in the dirt throwing tins of dust on the flames to hold back the edge of the fire from the school. For more than three hours the flames burned undisturbed by the human frenzy about them until out of the darkness a soft rain began to fall, at first gently, then pouring down in a blessed deluge.

The flames hissed and bowed to the rains and eventually great clouds of smoke and steam rose from the quieting fire bed. A government lorry rolled slowly down the flooding street to the burning mass and a half dozen men in uniforms got out, surveyed the scene, then slowly climbed back in the lorry and left. Here and there a few fresh flames sprouted up as the blaze caught a kerosene patch from a spilled lamp, but the force of the fire had spent itself on the already devastated rubble. Some people hovered in the downpour at the edge of the road hoping once it was cool enough to venture in to salvage what they could from the disaster while rivers of ash and mud ran through the smoldering debris.

Wambui searched for Jeremiah and Lucy in the streets surrounding their house and in desperation made her way to the clinic when the downpour began. Soaking wet and cold she huddled in the doorway with a crowd of other villagers seeking shelter on the small veranda. The baby was crying weakly and she could feel her own strength leaving her body with the bitter chill of the night air.

It was more than an hour before Theresa got back to the clinic to open the doors. Jeremiah had run with some older boys to fetch her then without words came to his mother, leaning against her. Charles came minutes later.

When the doors to the clinic opened Wambui pushed her way inside and sank to the floor propping herself against the wall with Jeremiah and the baby. She stared through the smoky darkness most of the night hoping to see Lucy as stragglers wandered in like ashen figures in a dream but she did not have the energy to move much less go out and search for her.

It was just before dawn when a neighbor came in, her face smeared with soot and tears. Lucy's body had been found. She had run back into the house calling to the baby, thinking she was still there and it was then that the roof had collapsed on top of her. The words came like a distant echo. Wambui had no more tears. She was too hungry and weak to cry. Jeremiah sat by his mother on the cement floor holding his baby sister in his lap staring out into the wet morning as the first rays of sun burst over the valley.

MATHARE AND BEYOND

Upcountry the Mathare River winds through deep green hills, fields of maize and mud hutted villages. Near Nairobi it flows past elegant two-story houses with red tile roofs, horses on the green, past the sprawling estates that edge the Muthaiga Country Club before dipping into the gully called Mathare Valley.

It was during the battles for independence that the rural poor began to pour into Nairobi in search of food and jobs and finding neither built their shacks on the shores of the Mathare River at the edge of the city. As their numbers swelled beyond count humble shelters stretched across the valley until Mathare became a world unto itself. Mudded shacks crowded together, clumped on top of each other down the narrow streets that led to the river. Sheets of polythene stretched across caved-in roofs, and cardboard sheets fingered in and out of poles where mud had washed away in the last rainy season.

There were nine villages in Mathare Valley at the time we were there, each with its own chief, its own identity, but for visitors we brought wanting to see first-hand what poverty looked like, they all ran together in a squalid, indistinctive mass with hammers ringing against steel singing out from small stalls, men pounding metal scraps into bowls next to young men with wire whips beating mounds of blanket cuttings into mattress filling for polyethene sacks they sewed together.

Our first visit to Mathare left me in emotional distress, angry at the history that had created this place, personal feelings of guilt for being unaware, so privileged, angry that the world had not responded, and knowing that now, being here, seeing this, I would never be able to let it go. The visions, the smells, the sounds, the faces, especially the faces, were mine for life — a mother with a toddler strapped to her back, a newborn wrapped to her breast, arriving at the nutrition center, staff with illustrated charts speaking about food, hygiene, family planning, demonstrating cooking. Those mamas who had stayed to listen received plastic bags of weaning food prepared in great grinders in the back room — powdered milk, cornmeal, peanuts – small enough bags that women would have to come back regularly meaning babies could be weighed, those who were not thriving spotted in time and mothers hearing another lesson in family planning and nutrition.

At the clinic we saw a two-year-old girl the size of a four-month-old infant, her huge eyes half closed, spindly legs, swollen belly, strapped to the back of her eight-year-old sister who had come to get a ration of powdered milk. The nurses suspected her sisters and brothers might be drinking her ration as they were usually hungry when they came to the center for their morning porridge.

At the weaving project women were learning to knit, crochet, sew simple pieces of clothing, using scraps of donated fabric to create patchwork panels and coverlets they could sell. Bulky wool was being spun, woven into thick rugs on simple looms, literacy groups were learning to read in Kiswahili. At the clinic mothers lined up with children to get vaccinations, medicines for colds, rehydration salts for ever-present diarrhea, advice on birth control, pregnancy, abusive husbands. Nearby was the school for physically and mentally handicapped children, nearly twelve percent of the population. Boys were learning to pound a nail into wood, girls learning to care for dolls as they would for a baby, teachers knowing, given the vulnerability of these girls, many would be pregnant before long.

We came back often over the next months. Sadness and anger gave way to admiration for the ingenuity, the perseverance of people who had nothing, and the commitment of those trying to help. Mathare became a constantly moving collage of humanity with increasingly familiar faces I could call by name.

They called us before dawn that day. There had been a major fire at Mathare and staff were overwhelmed. Could we assess the situation for what would be needed. The sky was a clear azure blue when we stopped at the head of the drive that led to the clinic. There were no words. As far as we could see an ashen blanket spread across the valley. A soft warm breeze was sweeping between the remaining shanties sending up a low cloud of ash, thin dark figures poking through the cloud. I could hardly focus my lens but I had to.

A stony quiet had settled over those still sheltering in the clinic. Families had been prodding with sticks in the charred heaps since early morning dragging out whatever looked familiar. Most had marked out where they thought their homes had been so that others would not steal what little was left and across the blackened field families sat on makeshift stools declaring which heap was theirs. Metal cups and bowls, dented pots, here and there a steel cot frame or lantern was pulled out of the hot ashes and claimed. They sat like stunned heirs to the ruins, each staking out the pitiful hill of blackened trash with which they would begin again.

A young girl had died. The police had taken her body to the city morgue and her mother was sitting in the clinic. She didn't have money for a wooden box to bury her daughter or to buy the cabbages she would need to sell today. Her son had pulled a kettle and some spoons from the rubble. That was all they had.

"What do you need most, Wambui," Theresa was asking her.

Her eyes were swollen from crying but there were no tears left. Her words were slow and deliberate. "A school uniform for my son. And a pencil. They will not let him back in school without a uniform, without a pencil."

I stared at my notebook trying to write down what was unfolding, I couldn't move my pen.

The newspaper's reporting had obviously been controlled but we later learned that latches had been thrown from the outside on a number of the dwellings, the morgues overflowing but no count of the dead. Negative images could impact the lucrative tourism economy but not knowing who might be listening, few at the council dared speak of the lack of information.

While the devastated area seemed to spread endlessly across the landscape, most of Mathare had been spared. Council staff were scrambling to deal with the overwhelming immediate needs, food, medicines, shelter materials and still carry on with their usual programs. Our job now was to find the resources needed. Telephone service was sporadic at best, so while David stuck to the phones, I drafted requests for urgent funding trying to put into a few succinct words that could be wired to donors in the U.S. and Europe what had happened, what was needed. Responses were almost immediate. Meanwhile squatters were pulling the scraps of their lives together with what they could find. Over the next weeks shanties rose like mushrooms from the ashes, alleyways were getting cleared and small kiosks claimed ground where they could. Rumors circulated that the new housing would soon be going in. Tensions were high. The clinic became a distribution point for food, blankets, clothing, as aid came in.

Mathare's needs were vivid in our heads when we got the invitation from an American businessman, head of an export firm in Kenya hosting a party for expats, mainly donor agencies, NGOs. Given the overwhelming needs of Mathare a gathering of donors and agencies was something we needed to explore. I began mentally framing a description of the needs our staff had outlined. I needed something brief but clearly stating the devastation we had just seen.

"It's a small place," he had laughed on the phone when he called with the invitation. "Only six acres. You can't miss it. Just look for all the lights. I have more lights than any house in Nairobi. If you get lost, just ask anyone where I live. Everyone knows my house. Just watch for the lights. You can't miss it."

As we set out beyond the Mathare river the forests of eucalyptus blocked out the last glow of the city and only the faint outlines of estates could be seen, stone pillars embracing black iron gates with only a hint of what lay beyond them. Punctuating the sprawling estates, low round coffee trees, Kenya gold as it was called, stood in groomed rows emerging from the blackness of the hills. Mile after mile of coffee estates rolled by before small star bursts of distant lights began to puncture the veil of rain. Now the gates we were passing took on more grandeur. Elaborate iron lions stared with dead eyes from their stone perches. Lampposts lined graceful winding driveways with formal garden edges. Lights blazed everywhere around stone mansions and after several inquiries at well-lit entrances we at last spotted a spreading blaze of lights that outshone the rest.

Lights ringed the circle drive, marked the perimeter of the tennis courts and lavish flowerbeds, and flooded the sprawling house from every angle. The edges of the drive were crowded with cars. Two night watchmen, clubs in hand, closed the tall iron gates behind us.

The front door stood wide open and the sound of voices grew louder as we entered the foyer. Embraced by a huge bay of windows and mirrors, the entry was lit by a massive chandelier reflecting itself over and over above our heads. Beyond the foyer lay a long receiving hall lined with heavy polished mahogany tables, each set with an oversized Chinese vase, each vase backed by an elaborately framed mirror multiplying the display of wealth, the emptiness of the room. A trio of musicians was playing soft jazz somewhere. People had congregated in the great room toward the back of the house. Some were dancing on the veranda that overlooked the gardens, others hovered over the long buffet table spread with food.

A colleague was hailing us. He was with a man who was evidently the host surrounded by a small cluster of eager faces. We joined what appeared to be a captive audience listening intently to an animated monologue from our host.

"Transfer of technology — that's what development's all about," he said, his eyes swinging mechanically from side to side, seemingly talking to no one in particular. "Technical skills, technical transfer. Plain-and-simple," he punched the words out like bullets. "Just drop all this other development crap. Doesn't take long to figure that out now, does it? Just give these people some technical know-how, the right equipment, this place is going to take off. Hell, with these natural resources, business will be booming – which is the whole reason I'm here." He chuckled out each word.

I felt the chill from the faces. Most of the people gathered around him were field-experienced, caring NGO staff desperate to get some project funded, each awaiting an opportune moment to provide a counterpoint or insert a creative segue to our host's remarks, something that might catch his interest for potential funding or at least inform his perspective. The images in my heart about Mathare were vivid, the urgent needs, the words I had hoped to speak hovering in my mouth but he had made it quite clear that he was only interested in funding projects that would economically lead somewhere. Everyone was hanging on his words trying to figure out where that somewhere was and whether the critical needs they knew all too well and the groups they served might get needed resources.

A waiter came by with a tray of wine glasses so we took the opportunity of distraction to move slowly toward the veranda away from the tight circle of hopeful faces. I was suddenly swept over by a wave of sadness, an overwhelming need to leave this place of mirrors and convictions. We slipped from the back veranda following the path around the house flooded with lights. With no words exchanged the guard opened the gate for us and we drove home.

Responses were coming into the office from our grant proposals. In hopeful anticipation of funding the council had already mobilized extra staff, supplies were going out to Mathare families, new funds would replenish the stockpile. It became evident they had done all this before.

Before we could take a breath, we were notified. Arrangements had finally been made for our trip to review and film projects in the Far

North. We were reminded producing the video documentary was our primary task. I gave Kadzo the stack of pending requests for Mathare and started packing. The trip would be rough, crossing a desert that stretched to the Somali and Ethiopian borders, many had warned us about it, but we would be given a strong truck, so not to worry.

RAPSU

We set out in our strong truck, a Toyota pickup that drove like it had already been around the world on non-existent roads at least once. Dust belched from holes in the floor, it was consuming gas at an alarming rate. We were skirting Mount Kenya when David slammed on the brakes for a baboon in the road and we spun around a full 180 degrees before stopping. We hobbled into a mechanic's shop and confirmed our worst suspicions, three of the four brakes were gone, brake pads had to be replaced, carburetor rebuilt, replace the master cylinder and fix a few other critical items like leaking fuel lines which apparently accounted for our outrageous fuel consumption — all before we could even visit the resettlement project on our way much less cross the desert. It would take at least a full day's work and we guessed it was going to cost more, cash only, than we had with us.

Is there a hotel in town? A bank? We were already worrying about our camera cases. No, sorry, no hotel, no bank. There was however an American family, missionaries, who might accommodate us. We drove out at a crawl in search of a rescue promising to be back as soon as possible for the repairs.

What unfolded remains a bizarre dream — a pleasant couple took us in, cashed our check so we could pay for the repairs and fed us a gracious supper of potato soup and cornbread. He was a building contractor and they were building a school here, an impressive sprawling structure, on behalf of an independent church that had never done mission work before and provided little backing for them other than funding. That evening they shared a video they had made and sent back to their church. They had dressed their African staff in animal skins staging them behind a makeshift cardboard boiling pot while the missionary family danced around them with spears. They said the congregation had thoroughly enjoyed it and funding was flowing in for their project.

Words wouldn't come. We couldn't even glance at each other for fear of what we might reveal so we claimed exhaustion and went to bed early.

Thankfully, miraculously, the truck was ready the next day, we said our thanks to our hosts and followed our well-worn map toward Rapsu. We were to film a resettlement project the council had started more than ten years prior. I read my notes from the briefing aloud as we drove. Nomads dying in desert, extended drought. More than two hundred families at one point, a school was built, *shambas* planted, maize, cotton, beans, an irrigation system dug from the nearby river. There was a paragraph I had circled – drought had driven elephants from the adjacent game park in search of the lush vegetation of the *shambas*. Men were killed protecting their crops, villagers were taking shifts, making noise to scare elephants away, two men just recently killed, five elephants charged, trampled them. That was where my notes ended. We were to assess the situation and make recommendations. Recommendations, I had underlined the word. I barely had space in my head for the images of the Mathare fire and now we were heading towards a village ravaged by drought-starved elephants.

When we arrived at Rapsu an older man led us to a dilapidated cottage, an abandoned missionary house by the edge of the river. An awkward structure, its window openings were roughly boarded up with a few sticks where glass had once been. Inside there was a single large room, empty except for a few chairs and a bed frame strung with sisal rope leaning against the wall. A small bathroom protruded out the back an obvious after-thought with buckets of water sitting next to the standard British enameled tub and toilet. Evidently it once had running water. In defiance of the crumbling remains of half plastered walls and layers of dust a pleasant light was streaming in, but there was no time to linger.

Aman, the project leader would not be back until evening so we walked through the settlement. These were Boran, distinct in their tribal culture, rounded thatched huts standing like upright shaggy brown eggs planted next to glossy green gardens, lean graceful people greeted us, women with scarves loosely draped over their hair, long *kangas* slung across their shoulders, men wearing turbans of white or striped cotton, long robes, *kanzus,* flowing around their legs. They moved silently between the huts, a small curl of black smoke wisping through the air from each.

Greeting people as we filmed, we stepped over the narrow irrigation ditches that spread fingers of water from the river. Several men eagerly demonstrated the small floodgates controlling the flow through the rows of maize, bananas, cotton and beans. Here and there a few cattle were penned up in tight thorn bush *bomas* while goats and chickens ran free. Beyond these first *shambas* stretched heartbreaking destruction of the land. Banana plants were shredded, irrigation gates lay in shambles, row after row of maize lay crushed in the dirt.

"*Tembo*," they said. Elephants.

After our tour we hiked up to a rock ledge that rose high at the bend in the river at the edge of the settlement. The savannah spread low and green across the horizon half veiled in the haze of the late afternoon. We stretched out on a ledge like a pair of lizards sunning ourselves. A few trees were scattered here and there amongst the tall grasses, their scrubby branches twisted into shapes, mythical creatures rising up from some strange world.

In the distance we could see a herd of elephants, several dozen huge gray humps blotched with the red clay of the riverbank, beautiful in their graceful sway through the yellow grass. One huge elephant with a broken tusk lowered its head and walked slowly into a tree. With a thunderous crack, the tree toppled over, not all of a sudden as under the ax of the woodsman, but gracefully as if in slow motion, the roots pulling up from the soft soil reaching high into the sky as the huge tree eased buoyantly down on its outstretched branches, arms trying to break its death fall. Some had young ones with them who moved toward the stricken tree and began feeding, now able to reach the tender leaves that had once been too high. It was like a lioness taking down a gazelle for her cubs. Most of the elders seemed content to mangle a few branches, ripping them apart with their trunks for the young, then moving on.

I focused my lens at the spectacle. In the space of less than an hour more than fifteen full grown trees fell gracefully, gaping holes of raw, wounded soil in the grass bed marking where they had once grown tall. The herd had toppled an acre of trees for supper. The peacefulness of the scene was mesmerizing. Watching the destruction of the trees, the young elephants feeding, there was an inevitability about it all that was strangely non-alarming. This was the life of the savannah, life as it had been for uncountable years.

The herd eased its way toward the river. One by one the lead elephants waded in, cautiously at first, feeling their way as the water quickly grew deeper and swifter. More followed, some younger ones, one old bull covered with scars, then several mothers with calves. The center of the river was evidently deep, for the lead elephants with heads high and trunks pointing skyward were swimming. The swift current carried them down river a ways before they could recover footing and wade ashore on the opposite bank. The smaller elephants were struggling with the current in the middle of the river. The rushing water caught one small calf turning him around as he struggled to hold his trunk erect. His mother nudged him from one side toward the opposite shore, another female was nudging him from the other side but the current caught him, water washing over his head. In a flailing explosion of water he cried out, trumpeting his terror to the world and at last regained his footing in the shallows and waded back to the bank where they had first entered the river.

He stood looking across the river at the rest of the herd. They had all reached the opposite bank but him. The young calf trumpeted across the river. The others responded to the call. They all stood watch, waiting. The young calf answered again with a wailing squeal. The others repeated their calls several times, swinging their heads as they bellowed to him. Then there was silence, they all waited, watching. Then slowly, the elephants on the far side of the river waded back into the water. The entire herd swam back across the river to rejoin the small calf that couldn't make it. When they reached the bank where he stood, some nuzzled him, others started walking down the river's edge in a single file toward the hills. The small calf trotted beside his mother at the end of the line. A very faint breeze stirred the tall grass around them as they faded from view.

Back at the cottage Aman was waiting, greeting us with a pot of tea.

AMAN

"So you ask about us and how this settlement came to be. Of course, it is not really my story to tell. It is the story of the old woman who really led these people out of the desert and it is her feet we embrace, *shikamoo*."

He sat on the steps with us and poured tiny cups of mint tea. His pale blue eyes looked like clear crystal against his sun-leathered face, still there was a youthful energy I could immediately feel from him.

"You must forgive an old man to tell but the desert is not always kindly to people. For many years it had been growing more dry, the rains did not come on time, aahee, then one year they did not come at all. The land beyond the river had always been green, but it too became dry, as though the desert had swallowed it alive while we all slept. It stayed like a mirage though, fooling our eyes. Aahee, how easily we are deceived to think that water flows and life is possible because a few thorn bush grow. Yet before our very eyes, grain by grain the sand was baked by the sun and the dry lands spread into the

119

green, creeping slowly, sucking what moisture and life they found near their edges.

"Aahee, how we hoped. We prayed that Allah would spare us this, but each season the hot dry air swirled up from our feet to the highest heaven where blue begins, taking whatever water the coming winds held, driving rain away as surely as an evil spirit with a death wish. That is how the desert grew, before our very eyes, as far as even the youngest eye could see — like a sprawling monster that only the vultures that fly overhead, circling with hunger, can see how quickly the monster grows.

"You see these Boran knew they were a dying people. Their cattle were dry — they could give no milk. People could not draw blood for their food from sick herds — aahee — now to slaughter even one head of cattle is to admit one's doom, you see. Cattle are wealth. Not because a man sells them for great money. Some men live a whole lifetime and never sell one cow. But when you have great herds you know you are wealthy and if you have few animals you know you are poor. So in this knowing, the rich and the poor they wander side by side eating the same clotted milk and blood, walking the same sands. Aahee, but deep inside, the rich and poor — they know they are different.

"But the desert doesn't care, it dries-up everyone equally, and equally they die. Even the goats grew thin and weak — still, these Boran crept on behind their bony herds leaving their dead under the hot sands.

"That is when I came upon them, and praise Allah for that day — I was so thin when I called out 'Salama' to them, yet they took me as strong, this Somali man with three dying camels and two young sons, having just buried my wife. Of course, I could see in their eyes the fear that I was shifta, a bandit who would steal whatever they had, for that is what they think of Somali — but I prayed to Allah with them and I carried no weapons. It was Fatma who accepted me and for this I shall give thanks to my dying day. She was old, living longer than three husbands and all but two of her ten children and she had a cautious eye. Elders and young, they all listened when Fatma told of the old days when their people had herds that spread across the

120

horizon beyond the hills, and when the rains came the grasses grew tall enough to hide a man and yellow blossoms covered each stalk and floated through the air in fragrant clouds so that is was hard to see the setting sun, and cattle were so plentiful it would take a man a week to count his herd. Aahee, yes they listened. Who would not?

I studied Aman's face as he spoke, his compelling expressions changing with each part of his story as though it was all happening for the first time right before his eyes. He leaned closer to us.

"Without words I could read the questions in the old woman's eyes and greeted her with respect whenever we passed, a tribute she saw, silently, but I knew. There were so few strong men, only Sa-id, and he was with a weak mind and I could see that Fatma and I hoped for the same things. I also knew if we were to survive it was our spirits that must be rekindled for the desperation of these people would kill them before the desert would.

"I invited them to sit by the fire each night, to meet as elders, as though life were continuing, and it was there I learned their language. By the next moon, they asked me for each decision, though I still spoke with Fatma before I gave the words on where we should go and when we should rest.

"Then one week I walked far ahead of the group and returned bearing sacks of maize and beans. Sa-id saw me coming.

"'And now what has this Aman brought with him?' he called out. "I have been to a village — just beyond the hills," I told them. "With no money," Sa-id said, for you see I am sure he still thought me a *shifta* who was trained by my father to steal, but I said, "The officials were handing these sacks out freely. They said it is relief food. There have been no rains for so long that many people are hungry. Someone from overseas has sent food to be given away. But that is not the most important news," I told them.

"Fatma looked at me with her silent eyes, then she pulled a stone close and sat down." "Tell us the most important news," she said. The others gathered around, so I told them what I had learned. "The government has some land. They know the people of the desert are dying and they say they cannot forever bring sacks of food. The desert will not give back the lands it has swallowed and the rains that once fell are still not seen on the horizon beyond the hills. Aahee, you see they agreed with me then, except for one old man who said, 'It is our fate. We must accept it.' But I went on quickly so this bit of hope would not blow across the sands and told them what I had been told by the officials, that if we register in the book, we would be given land, by a river that always flows."

He stood up pointing to the river just beyond the old house. "See for yourselves."

We walked a bit from the porch to get a better view of the river catching the light of the late afternoon sun.

"See how it flows so swiftly? Not even drying up when the rains have gone."

As we walked back to the house he continued. "'But Fatma asked the hardest question of all. 'Is it land enough for our herds?' I had to tell them that in truth it was land for growing things, for staying with the land, not wandering. Aahee, that news was bitter at first, but as they huddled around the fire to watch the boiling pot of maize the idea grew slowly soft among them, like the kernels in the pot. Perhaps it was something in the fire itself, or perhaps they saw the fire in my eyes, for I was very keen for the idea. After we had eaten, it was then Fatma looked at me and nodded, and so it was we came to this river that always flows."

"From the reeds that grew near the river we wove our huts and the women made new mats and we built our *bomas* to keep out the lions."

He must have noticed the change in my face. "Lions?"

"Oh, yes. Lions. They can smell us from so far, our cattle, our chickens."

I couldn't help but scan the horizon thinking of the fragile house we would be sleeping in, the windows barely covered with sticks. Still I was mesmerized by his story.

He filled our cups then continued. "You see, that is when it began — first just a moist shadow in the morning sky, then each day the shadow grew more gray until one day the rains began to fall. We stood there, not believing, letting the waters flow over us, washing great streams down our backs to our toes until ponds of rich red mud blossomed at our feet. The river had been blessing enough but now the fragrant smell of damp earth filled the air. Fatma seemed so calm at first with the rains. That is when I spoke with her of the project. Some churches wanted to build an irrigation system for the people. Ditches would bring the river's water right into the *shambas*. We could plant all year even between the rains and grow enough food to feed the whole community. Once the *shambas* were growing we would not need the food in sacks from outsiders."

"Fatma looked out at the rain as it poured from her hut. I shall never forget how beautiful it was, great swirls of red mud — flowing like perfume across the land. She said it was good news but she was not sure about these Christians, why would they help a band of Muslims. Something didn't taste right in her mouth, this irrigation project. There was something in her voice and I knew she could not rejoice. Her eyes drifted beyond the river, across the great plains that spread far to the North. She said, 'Perhaps it is raining over there too.' Even though a misty veil had come over her eyes she could see farther than ever before, she said, and she told of a faint greenness spreading slowly across the north plains and tiny birds darting among the new buds in the distance. 'See, the tall grasses are growing once more,' she said. 'And the wells that were too salty — they are already becoming sweet again with new rain,' and she believed it to be so, so I listened as I always had."

"When the digging began for the irrigation canals, she would not move from her hut. My heart heard her fear. The more the people worked on this land, the more they would forget the North. You see, she knew this land would never hold great herds. These plots were for vegetables, the land of farmers, not herders. Boran could eat vegetables when they were hungry but in their hearts, they would always hunger for the meat of the plains. Some days she stood in the doorway of her hut for hours looking to the North at the spreading green that only she could see. She had not left her compound since the irrigation system began. Her eyes seemed further away every day. There were no relatives. She had never heard from her last two sons since they left for the city when the drought began."

"Then these foreigners like you came with seed. For that we will thank you beyond this day."

He placed his hand over his heart and nodded to each of us in turn. Not knowing how to respond, we did the same in return.

"So these foreigners, they gave each family maize, beans, cottonseed, peanuts, even banana plants. They worked alongside us, showing us how to plant the seed, how to let inlets of water flow between the rows, how to keep the canals clear. Then these Boran, they wanted to appoint me the leader of the project, but of course I knew I was still a stranger to them and it would take more than a river to change that, so I said if Fatma would share this honor with me, I would agree. She gave her consent, but she did not plant one seed. Aahee, her heart was heavy, but eventually she shared in the work of another widow and together they harvested more maize than two old women could eat. Still she walked through the village always looking across the river to the open plains that spread to the North. These small fields with edges, ditches of water marking off where one family's land ends and the next begins, she said it gave her a tight feeling in her chest seeing all of these edges, this nomad woman, and her breathing became heavy at night in the darkness."

"The village had grown — aahee, now there were more than a hundred huts and the *shambas* were green with cotton. Even the young children hoeing the canals talked of the harvest but Fatma's eyes grew more hazy. Each day she went to the fields beyond the *shambas* where the few cattle grazed and stood next to the small herd boys with their spears, and when they warned her of the lions she refused to move."

"This woman," he paused. He had tears in his eyes and cleared his throat. "She could see infinitely far now, even beyond the hills that marked the horizon. 'Do you see now, Aman?' she said to me. They had summoned me to persuade her home. 'The tall grasses have returned to the North at last. Praise Allah, all his children. Clouds of yellow flowers are drifting across the river, do you see them, covering the water, even blanketing the goats? We can return home at last.' Her face was alive like a new bride and she turned with the grace of a young girl. Just then some elephants began coming near, hungry for our green *shambas*. It was dangerous, but she said her husband was near, he was very brave and would protect her. So we took her back to her hut. All night we sat together by the fire as she talked softly, telling the people that I would lead them North to the green grass. When she died that night, I put out the fire."

He paused and stared into his teacup, then took a long last swallow.

"That is when these Boran made this Somali man the project leader, protector of the *shambas,* and the very next day the elephants attacked. It had grown so dry in the forest but our *shambas* were so green and sweet with water flowing through the little rivers. They came as a herd. They tore up the banana trees. You cannot see, but there was once a field of bananas that stretched to the river. We all came running, making a great noise to frighten them away. But the elephants did not run. Two men were killed, picked up by those great trunks and thrown like sticks against the trees. In my heart I was glad Fatma had not lived to see that night. And the nights that followed."

He stopped as though he saw something in the distance then brought his gaze back to us. I feared he had finished, but he slowly began again.

"So you see our *shambas* grow greener while the fields beyond wither in the drought. That is why the elephants keep coming. More than ten people have now been killed trying to protect their *shambas*."

He cradled his head in his hands. The sun was just setting over the huts. We were all silent feeling his pain of remembering. He looked up, his eyes scanning the settlement. "You see these nomads, I fear some may start leaving, returning to the desert. It is there they would choose to die."

We talked into the evening. There had to be a way. Park rangers could patrol, but this wasn't park land and there were already too few rangers available. Fences had been considered, but nothing they had was strong enough to keep elephants out. When David mentioned electric fences that might frighten but not kill the elephants, ideas started bubbling and the scratch pad came out. There was no electricity here. Solar panels could be used. Would an electric fence keep out an elephant? We didn't know. We would have to find out. Someone at the university might know.

Already David was scratching out figures. He'd need to calculate the weight of an elephant to determine how many amps were needed to provide a small spark but not injure the animal or people. Given how dry the ground was he was concerned about grounding. A second wire might have to be strung so both wires would make contact at the same time. Though David had dealt with solar before he wanted help on thinking this through. Aman wondered if the fence would enclose just the *shambas* or the whole settlement? He thought for a long time then decided it would have to be the whole settlement or the elephants might destroy the huts outside the fence trying to get to the *shambas*. How would people come and go beyond the fence? Baffle gateways might work, staggered overlapping sections wide enough for people to pass between but not elephants. David sketched it out. What would it cost? We'd have to estimate costs, find funding. Would the people accept a fence? We all worried, talking with these wandering nomads of a fence surrounding them on all sides would be like asking everyone to die inside. We all fell silent.

Aman got up to leave. He would call a meeting of the community tomorrow; they would decide together. Too many had already died. The elephants would always be here. If people left for the desert now, they would not survive. Something had to be done.

In the morning the entire community gathered under a cluster of sprawling shade trees, men seated in an inner circle, women and children stood crowding behind them. We found a perch on a log nearby not understanding a word of Kiboran, wondering what was evolving, what we were getting into. I shot a few pictures, children's faces, teachers we had filmed at the school. Some faces looked familiar but too hard to read. Speeches went on for nearly an hour, we were introduced, more speeches, a great deal of mumbling head to head. Then Aman came over to us carrying a huge squawking red and black hen. He handed it to me. I could barely contain its flapping discontent in my arms as I accepted it.

"We believe that once you have eaten a chicken that has been scratching its food from our soil, you will return to us." He was smiling. "*Mshala*, Allah be willing, we will build the fence – with your help."

CROSSING THE DESERT

We joined the line of vehicles waiting to cross the desert. Isiolo looked like a frontier town in the old west with a long row of buildings lining each side of the single road. People sat in front of shops and under sparse thorn bush trees. We watched a few donkeys waiting patiently with bulging sacks strapped to their backs while Somali women in shoulder drapes and long dresses waved their hands in animated conversation.

We were heading to the Far North as it was called to see a refugee resettlement and agricultural project. Rapsu was still heavy with us, every scene we had filmed there, the sound of Aman's voice, the image of the baby elephant caught in the river, the squawking red and black hen. Graciously, someone had prepared it for our dinner, a lovely mixture of coriander and rice and like everything that was happening it was still churning inside of me.

Obviously, we had a commitment to a solar electric fence to keep out elephants, but how that would all happen was beyond us. We woke up that morning with the same thought and now talked in an endless stream of all that was unfolding, words drifting even to childhood's small memories, wondering why our entire lives seemed to be so vividly present. In retrospect it might have been the first time we felt fear of what could happen to us on this safari. We always felt everything would turn out, we would be safe, but now that certainty was fading. Perhaps it was the air around us, still with heat, the sun beating down with no mercy. There was no shade except for the small strips of shadow found under doorways and beneath the lacy branches of the desert trees. Then there had been the repeated cautions from friends. Elections were very soon. There could be problems this time. It was best we be as far away from Nairobi as possible, which apparently was where we were heading.

Two soldiers came by as we sat waiting in the truck. They gave us instructions. Stay close behind the vehicle in front of you. Don't leave any gaps. If you have a puncture or mechanical difficulty, sound your horn. The convoy will stop and soldiers will surround you so you can make the repairs. The convoy will proceed with no stops except for emergencies.

I studied David's face wondering how he looked so calm. The lead vehicle was a large army truck with six soldiers armed with AK 47s and Uzis in the rear. Seven vehicles had registered to cross that day. A few were trucks carrying supplies, most seemed to be tough vehicles with various titles painted on their doors. We had six jerry cans of fuel in the rear, one of water, our truck was basically running, but hardly tough and certainly not strong.

"You have room for a passenger?" A lean young man with reddish brown skin poked his head through the window.

We looked at each other, then nodded hesitantly.

The man squeezed into the front seat and introduced himself in English. He was Ali, a schoolteacher returning home. He made this trip often and was grateful for the ride. Though we couldn't say so at the time, there was a bit of shared relief in having onboard someone who knew the road ahead, yet some awkwardness in how wise this was, beyond the fact that I was now straddling the shift stick while holding the aluminum case with our camera equipment in my lap and at least a six-hour desert crossing ahead.

129

A Land Rover loaded with soldiers with rifles poking out the windows took its position at the rear of the line. Small children pressed against the vehicles selling little paper cones of roasted peanuts. Four older women approached, pleading for a ride. They waved their arms indicating they could ride on top or in back. They carried huge baskets tied up in faded cloth, clusters of small children half hiding behind them. Their *kangas* were worn, their feet bare.

It was too dangerous Ali explained waving the women off with mumbled words. They could be thrown off too easily with the rough roads, they could even die, and then the driver would be held responsible for them, road justice, even by by-standers. We both started to say something at the same time when the barrier gate suddenly swung up and the lead army truck rolled out. We jolted forward. I felt my mouth go dry. Just thirty meters beyond the gate the tarmac ended and we dropped with a thud onto a rutted ribbon that threaded through the sandy desert. Within minutes the lead truck was lost in a cloud of dust so far ahead we could barely see it.

David clutched the wheel with sweaty hands. Several larger trucks passed us sending a dump of dirt and dust over our hood and around the edges of the closed windows. There was no way to see the Land Rover that was immediately in front of us. Far ahead, almost on the horizon now, there was a cloud, the lead army truck.

The road was a mass of corrugations sending shock waves through our bodies as we slammed over each one in turn. David's arms were a blur, shaking so hard from the vibrations it was evident he was struggling to maintain his grip on the wheel.

"We'll go into a spin if I push it any harder, unless this old truck shakes itself into pieces first." David was obviously trying not to sound alarmed but the wild shaking in his arms spoke otherwise.

With a silky layer of sand covering the road we were shimmying from side to side. Only the largest trucks were able to keep up with the speed of the convoy.

I clutched the camera case. Dust was seeping in around the windows and pouring in through the holes in the floor like belching dry volcanoes.

"I thought the army was supposed to stay with us. To keep us together," I said trying to sound calm.

Ali pulled a packet of green leaves out of his pocket. "*Mirrah.* You like it?"

He offered some to us. "It will help you stay alert."

We both declined the offer. He slid one of the limp green leaves through his teeth stripping the stem, shoving a bit of candy into the wad, chewing with wide swings of his jaw.

"You can be awake the whole day and night with *mirrah*, and you will still be smiling."

The Land Rover filled with soldiers was passing, guns poking through the cloud of dust as they passed.

"That was the tail guard that just flew by," I said no longer feeling alarm.

"I think perhaps you should have given the soldiers some *chai*. Maybe they would have stayed. But then, maybe not." Ali stared at the dust cloud dissolving in the brilliant haze ahead seemingly undisturbed.

"See those rocks over there? That's where the *shiftas* hid when they shot the MP. Just last month. Shot out his tires, then shot him and his driver." He slid another *mirrah* leaf through his teeth studying the rocks as we passed.

David gave me what looked to be a reassuring glance but it was taking all of his concentration to keep the vehicle from spinning out. We were both encrusted with a thick layer of desert dust running with sweat. Everything inside the truck was the same red-brown. Our teeth were red with grit. I was literally tasting the desert. Two vehicles were still in view, one ahead and one behind.

131

"No one trusts these Somali." Ali was looking across the empty landscape as though he saw something beyond the dust. "They are all *shiftas* you know. The son learns from the father and his father before him. Now they buy these American weapons, or the Russian weapons — very cheap — from the border villages. You can buy them anywhere, like tomatoes in the market. Ethiopia, Somalia, they are straight up this highway, you know. Many weapons on the border. Less than ten of your American dollars for an automatic with ten rounds. It makes a poor camel thief very powerful."

His smile revealed a row of green teeth.

With the army beyond sight David slowed down a bit trying to keep at least one other vehicle in view. The noise of the truck made it impossible to talk. Every fender and imaginable part was shaking like a tambourine on wheels. It was as if we each were reading the other's thoughts, hoping the pieces would hold together, fearful of speaking our fears aloud. Ali dozed on and off for the next few hours then woke up as if on cue.

"We can stop for a drink just up there," he said.

"Where up there?" I was staring into the dust shroud over the blank desert ahead. I had been clearing the inside of the windscreen, pointing out the ruts, hoping it meant someone must have gone this way before.

"Just over there," Ali said thrusting his puckered lips toward the blank sand haze. I had been told pointing with your finger was avoided because that was how tribal chiefs in the past designated someone for elimination.

The dust thinned to reveal the hazy silhouettes of a few huts in the distance. As we grew closer, we could see two palm thatched shelters and women selling a few limp vegetables and warm cokes, dessert wine, bottles smudged dull in the dust. Clean water was scarce but cokes were everywhere.

In the half shadow of the kiosk the acrid smell of animals and the white brilliance of the sun hung like a pall. A dozen goats and the small boys who herded them sat nearby, shivering off the flies. We added fuel to our tank emptying half of our cans. Splashing water from a bottle into a bandana we sponged off our faces and guzzled several cokes sticking extras in our bags. Daylight has no margin near the equator. Night replaces the brilliance of day with alarming suddenness. We knew we could not linger in the shade and headed on.

Bumping down the road as far as we could see there were no vehicles from the convoy in sight, none had passed us when we stopped, no more huts to indicate people lived here. We truly were alone. Now and then a solitary figure walked the edge of the ruts. Distant misty ribbons of glare and dust took on the appearance of camels and donkeys parading the horizon until the desert closed in around them dissolving them into her mirage.

Ali slept through most of the afternoon as we struggled to identify where the road was. The deafening rattle of the old truck threatening any confidence we had in her. The sun was starting its fast descent toward the low hills when we saw a barrier gate ahead. Neither of us gave words to our relief. Three petro stations stood in a row just beyond the barrier and beyond that a row of shops backed up against an old wall. The project office we were seeking was in town, Ali said. He thanked us for the ride and headed down a path behind the long row of shops pulling the last of his *mirrah* leaves between his teeth.

There was a small light in the window of the office. We knocked several times. No response. We called out in English, then "*hodi*" in Kiswahili to announce our presence. The door opened a crack. A man peered out then opened the door wide. He was Kimathi, the agricultural project coordinator. He spoke in soft clipped words. He was expecting us. He shook our hands with a hearty shake, welcomed us in then quickly locked the door behind us with a key and threw the bolt.

The tiny office had a desk, a filing cabinet, a few chairs and the two-way radio that kept him in touch with Nairobi. Behind the desk a blanket was strung on a long clothesline and behind that a mattress lay on the floor, a small kerosene stove with a steaming kettle on a table, a small sink. The solitary lantern cast a faded yellow glow on Kimathi's face as he spoke. It would be a full day's drive to the refugee resettlement and farm project we were to film the next day. He had arranged accommodations tonight for us with Pastor Joseph and his family. They lived just across the road he explained quickly as we sat down.

"My cousin is trying to find a job for me in Nairobi."

His hands were shaking as he poured us tea.

"This is a dangerous place. These people — you never know what they're going to do next. You will see, when we visit the projects. Some of these people are still naked. It is most difficult to work here. And now, these elections, very soon. No more secret ballot this time, the *Mzee* has decreed. People must queue behind a picture of their candidate with the army standing by. To ensure order, they say. Who knows what is going to happen tonight when they all get drunk. They are not fond of Kikuyus here you know, so I am staying inside. You must be very, very watchful too."

He cupped his hands around the warm mug of tea and looked down.

"I have been sick ever since they sent me up here. My stomach. Something's the matter. It just isn't right."

He led us across the road to a low brick house with a corrugated iron roof that extended over a wide porch. After quick introductions, Kimathi left.

Pastor Joseph was straight and lean with a warm but questioning look about him.

"You are most welcome," he said with a broad smile holding a lantern up studying our faces more closely.

Though it was dark we could make out the shadows of a square living room lined with huge stuffed furniture set flat against all four walls. Glaringly bright, varnished tables covered with elaborately crocheted doilies sat in front of the sofa and each chair. Near the ceiling, tiny photographs of family members were hung in large picture frames, ringing the entire room like generations of ancestors peering down.

134

We looked at the photos in the dim light until Joseph motioned for David to sit in the largest chair indicating the chair next to it for me. He lit two small kerosene lamps mounted on the wall, then disappeared into the next room and in a few minutes returned seating himself next to David.

I looked down at my clothes caked with red-gray dust, thin streaks of clean skin on my arms where water had drizzled from our brief wash-up at Kimathi's. David's teeth were still pink with dust and his face looked like a clay flower pot with two clean spots where his sunglasses had somewhat shielded him from the red desert dust. Mine must have looked the same.

Four children came in, each extending a limp hand to shake. They were followed by a tall quiet woman, Grace, Joseph's wife, and behind her a young girl carrying a heavy tray of tea which Joseph blessed with a long prayer, first in Kiswahili, then in English. The children sat tightly next to each other on the stiff couch, legs out straight in front of them, hands folded in their laps. Their bright eyes flashed between us with hesitant smiles locked behind closed lips. The young girl with the tea tray walked backwards into the kitchen never casting her eyes up.

Joseph noted that I was watching her.

"A poor child we have taken in," he explained. "Her parents couldn't afford to feed another mouth so we have taken her in."

I had the distinct feeling he was expecting a stream of praise for such kindness but I couldn't find words, only a weak nod.

The room was suddenly silent except for the clink of the teacups against the saucers. I shifted in my chair and felt the ache in my legs and back from the long ride. When I pulled my arm off the crocheted doily draped over the arm of the chair there was an oval brown smudge. I put my arm back covering the smudge.

The conversation turned awkward, Joseph focusing on the need for corporal punishment in the school he oversaw. Evidently, he had been told we were reviewing projects and as *wazungus* he presumed we would have funding. He went on about the need for the strictest discipline in the home, seemingly to impress us. Unless children and wives too at times were disciplined there could not be respect in the family. We made a few comments on children's need for encouragement, of positive reinforcement at which he simply smiled, his children and wife listening silently, fixed expressions, watching our faces intently.

Our room was just large enough for a bed and a small table. We bathed in a shared basin of tepid water grateful for the dimness of the yellow lantern light that let us ignore the red mud accumulating in the bottom of the bowl. We crawled in bed and held each other aware that even whispers would be heard given the tight cluster of small rooms. The small window revealed a blanket of stars with such startling clarity that it made the shadows of the house dissolve even further. What had really happened today besides dust and tea?

In the middle of the night I woke to a strange scraping sound. It was coming from right outside our bedroom door. Peering through a gap in the door I saw a candle in a small tin on the floor. In the blinking light the young girl who had brought us tea was on her knees scrubbing the hallway floor with a stiff brush, her thin arms bearing down with more vigor than such a tiny child seemed capable of. I was frozen in place, fearful she might hear my outrage, my silence.

In the morning when Kimathi came for us, we were glad to say our goodbyes.

"It was most difficult but the arrangements with the army have been made," he announced with a trace of a smile as we climbed into his truck. "The pumpkin farm is beyond the forest so it was necessary to find soldiers to go with us."

We suggested that from our experience having just crossed the desert, the army probably wasn't worth the bother. Kimathi persisted in a determined tone, shaking his head as we drove toward the army post. When we pulled up, two young soldiers with rifles climbed in the back of the truck.

The dense forest edging the solitary green hill sat in stark contrast to the vast empty landscape that surrounded it. It was evident that the hill captured what rain there was turning its slopes and skirts into a rich green island in a sea of sand. Women bent under loads of firewood walked in a long procession through the forest as we passed. The forest had many lions and elephants, Kimathi explained. People here did not walk through it alone. In groups it was always safer.

Kimathi's spirits seemed to rise the further we drove. Since he first came here, he had wanted to help these young boys and with a priest who lived nearby they started a pumpkin farm that became an example to the villages around. No one had believed squashes and pumpkins could grow in this soil but the sweet produce was appearing in the marketplace and heads were nodding with interest.

The road became suddenly narrower and rougher. Kimathi's face became brighter and his voice took on a new life as he pointed to some lost place up the mountain where there was a spring he needed to look at. Perhaps it could be another source of water for a nomadic community that was also trying to resettle here he said. The desert was killing these people. There was not enough grass left for their cattle, even for goats, and they did not know how to plant.

Suddenly his voice dropped away and he hit the brakes. Ahead in the road stood a band of warriors. Hair packed with red mud, elaborate headdresses, animal skins wrapped around their waists, long spears poised on their shoulders. They began leaping in place, spears raised high, aimed forward. They chugged in deep gulps of air, each heaving breath carrying them closer to our truck.

The tallest of the group wore a lion's mane wrapped around his head. He held his left arm straight up in the air, in his right arm his spear was poised, lightly balanced, rocking back and forth ready to thrust. He edged ahead of the others, his gaze fixed on us.

From the rear of the truck came a click. I had totally forgotten they were there. The soldiers were standing up, rifles cocked. The click was clear, loud, our hearts thumping. The warriors froze, spears poised in ready aim. From under the lion's mane the leader's eyes riveted on the rifles for one unending moment, then he lowered his raised hand and rested his spear on the ground. The others lowered their spears. They all walked slowly backwards into the brush. The tall brush closed over them as though they had never appeared.

Kimathi put the truck in gear and crept on. "They are just *morani*," he said with little expression. "They thought we might be cattle rustlers, after their herds, that is all. No problem." He smiled at David. "You see, the young men leave home after they are circumcised and live in the forest together for many years. They hunt and live like wild men. They are very dangerous when they are *morani*, coming to terrorize the villages. Even their mothers and sisters fear them. Then, after a few years, they return home, to find a wife, settle down as elders." His voice was matter of fact.

In the rear of the truck the two soldiers were once again chatting and laughing. The beads of sweat on my forehead were creeping into my eyes making them sting. I took several deep breaths scanning the brush as we rolled on. When would Africa cease to amaze me?

The farm sat like a green oasis between the dark forest and the gray desert beyond. There was an exquisite grace in the sturdy pumpkin vines as well as in the young boys who were cultivating the rows, tending each sucker like gold discovered in a new land. What had once been a barren Ethiopian refugee settlement now had a clinic, a granary, a school for the children, an adult literacy center, all surrounded by vegetable gardens and pumpkin patches.

Kimathi, the fearful thin figure that had bolted the door so securely against the night looked strangely robust as he strode along the garden rows, stopping to praise each worker, expressing amazement at the ripening squash. We fingered the rich leaves, the smooth ripening fruit springing from the edge of the caked desert. Kimathi kept repeating what a miracle it was, a simple miracle.

We filmed all day, interviewing young students in the school, every one eager to practice their English which by Kenya law was taught starting in the fourth grade along with British history and little else.

For them Nairobi was the other end of the earth and America only a place they had heard mentioned in fantastic stories.

The days passed too quickly, listening to their stories of wandering into Kenya from Ethiopia or Somalia, of days and nights in the desert, of what a blessing this isolated place was to them and now they were even able to go to school and learn of places like America and Nairobi which seemed equally far away. Their wonder at our humble video equipment, our clothes, everything seemed magical to them, yet it was we who were mesmerized by their stories and stamina given what life had dealt them.

After nearly a week of capturing images and stories we packed up. There were more than a dozen vehicles lined up waiting to return across the desert, one a simple station wagon with a sagging rear end. Just ahead of us was an old jeep with several expats leaning against it, everyone waiting for the army escort to assemble, waiting in the intense but familiar heat for the signal.

Some people left their vehicles and found shade where they could. One man paced back and forth in front of our truck trying to catch our eye.

"High noon on the desert," he called out to us with a British accent. "Great time to set out for the crossing!" His face was blistered red with sunburn and anger. "I was ready to cross before daybreak, but would they give me permission to leave? Wait for the convoy. Can you beat that! As though this old jeep can keep up with them. Fat chance. They leave you in the dust every time."

We sat on the running board acknowledging the man's frustration with half smiles, a nod.

"High noon on the desert." The man's face was growing redder by the minute. "But then if they were doing everything right, none of us would be here, would we?"

We both stood up and got back in the truck. I felt a vacant rush inside me, as though everything that was happening was happening somewhere else. The red-faced man kept pacing back and forth outside my window, behind him the contradictions of Africa as women walked their camels in a lumbering pace past us. They were just returning from an all-night walk from a watering hole, their leather water pouches bulging full on the camels' backs. It was a journey they made twice a week, babies strapped to their backs or tied on their camel amongst the water bags.

My eyes were stinging in the dryness of the air. A tiny baby lay on a leather water sack on the ground near our truck, stunning black eyes, women and camels, their only source of water miles away, women spending their days and nights carrying water and wood, things that would go up in smoke or drizzle away, barely noticed, so that if we turned around there would be no evidence that they had ever been here except that life had persisted. And we had come to take our pictures of how awful or how wonderful it all was and then run to our familiar comfort and safety to tell our tale to show how brave we had been to be there.

With no announcement, an army truck flashed by, the gates went up and everyone scrambled back to their vehicles. The huge lead truck charged ahead hitting the end of the tarmac with a loud thump sending up a cloud of sand and dust. Our convoy moved out, large trucks passing the smaller vehicles rapidly followed by the tail guard that swept past the trailing line in total defiance. It already seemed familiar except this time we were alone. David wiped the sweat from his eyes and hugged the wheel. In a few minutes we passed the old jeep with the red-faced man and then the small station wagon, trying to follow the disappearing cloud of the convoy ahead.

Through the dust an army barracks appeared, then vanished, and beyond that the landscape was vacant. A thin wisp of dust on the horizon became a faint line of goats that mysteriously disappeared just as it seemed to draw closer. All around the glassy reflection of vast desert lakes took form then evaporated.

I tried jotting down our departure time, the few letters scrawled and flew across the page with every jolt — the dust, the thudding vibrations, it was all beginning to have its own rhythm until a blistering crash pierced the air and shattered glass dropped around me.

David speeded up. "Was that a gunshot?"

The window on my side was gone, a mass of broken glass on the floor. Luckily I hadn't been cut. I looked back at the trail of dust. We both scanned each side of the road and behind, expecting another explosion. The vast expanse of dust stretched out on all sides with only an occasional boulder and blade of grass to break the bleakness. The air was still, no trace of a breeze, no movement in the landscape.

"Could have been the vibrations finally catching up," David said in a tone that was too deliberately reassuring.

I used my notebook to sweep the bits of glass down a hole in the floor. Within a half hour we heard a screeching thump as the rear end of the vehicle jumped abruptly to one side.

"Blast. Right rear shock. Feels like we lost it," David said.

There was a new feel, a new rhythm to the vibrations, a rattly clump-clank that punctuated the thudding. We had to stop. David jumped out, crawled under the rear bumper and tied up the shock. Our trip was now delayed more than an hour. We would have all we could do to make the crossing before dark. Within an hour another bang and a reciprocal clang set up from the left rear.

"Guess what," David said.

"Another shock?"

"Another shock."

His face was smeared with caked mud, two rings of white behind his sunglasses. His body jolted up from the seat with every rut, but there was something unflappable in his face that I truly treasured just then.

After he had tied up the second shock the clatter from the rear of the vehicle sounded more balanced. We continued on at a measured speed, the noise from the wheels and dust billowing in from my now shattered window made it impossible to hear each other's words. No other vehicles were in sight. The reality of our situation was setting in. No landmarks, no settlements, or road signs. The ruts barely distinguishable from the surrounding caked desert. Thoughts were colliding in my head, fears of totally breaking down, the stories of *shifta* bandits, the real possibility of not spotting the rutted road, getting lost. Eventually the small cluster of huts where we had stopped for cokes on the way out appeared just ahead, small comfort in knowing we were halfway there.

I bought an armload of sodas while David poured a jerry can of fuel into the tank, only one spare can left. No vehicles in sight so we set off once again in a syncopated rhythm of thuds and clangs. We had gone no more than a few kilometers when the vehicle jumped gears and we were thrown into a crawling pace. David tried to shift but the gear handle swung freely under his grasp without engaging.

"We now have a choice between second gear or second gear." He drew the words out, creasing the crust of dust on his cheeks with a smile.

We had to stop for repairs.

"If you need to stop, sound your horn, the army will stand guard," I said.

David, hardly amused, crawled under the vehicle and in a minute announced we had lost our gear link. It had apparently fallen out somewhere down the road. There was nothing in sight but the ruts ahead. I grabbed two soda bottles like clubs, one in each hand, declared myself to be the promised guard and paced back and forth, scanning the horizon, stepping over David's feet protruding from under the truck as I circled our wagon.

"Guess what? I need a wire!" he called out.

I searched under the seats, the glove compartment. Nothing. The ancient radio in the dash didn't work and I remembered seeing a wire hanging down when I swept up the glass. I felt around under the dash found it, a few firm yanks and I had it. David wired up the gear while I circled, coke bottles in hand, and soon we were back on the road once again, two gears working and not much speed.

"So much for our strong truck," David quipped.

I smiled. "Just another day in Africa."

It was evident we were both attempting to maintain confidence but the rutted road was without end. The sun grew hotter and it seemed as though the desert was watching, awaiting some chance carelessness, some false turn. The scenery no longer held even an abstract fascination much less beauty. It was easy to forget everything here, the monotony, the heat, the exhaustion of surviving the journey made its purpose disappear in the cloud of desert dust around us. The rest of the world didn't exist. Minutes drifted into the hours as we crawled slowly into the glare of late afternoon remembering the warning that the gate at Isiolo was locked by the army at sunset. Vehicles would not be permitted through once it was locked. Our eyes stayed fixated on the ruts ahead as the sun grew lower in the sky.

Somehow out of the heat haze the Isiolo barrier gate emerged. Before we could let out a recognizable word of celebration there was a deafening explosion. The left rear tire had blown. We did not even question the decision to keep driving rather than stop again. We had to roll on, this time the thudding vibrations and clanging rear end slowed to a new rhythm accompanied by the whacking of a punctured tire being dragged down the last strip of desert road.

Dust swirled around us as we bumped onto the tarmac. Soon there was only a cloud floating up from the desert in the fading light. Just beyond the barrier gate was a petro station. We rolled in as the army truck rolled past us, most likely there to lock the gate. Workers hurried over to help. I opened the door sending a new rush of glass bits onto the driveway. Without a word they took off the ruptured tire and dangling shocks. Someone was sweeping up the glass as though this was something they did every day. A mechanic with a pushcart of tools had his head under the hood with David, jabbering away.

We were lucky he said. "*Shiftas*. They just raided a village out there last night."

He nodded toward the desert. "Killed two people. Probably busy hiding now. That made you very lucky."

I must have looked astonished.

"They too busy to bother you."

Before I could process the news a small boy approached holding up an exquisite string of Somali amber.

"You want buy amber necklace?"

My eyes were stinging and filled with dust. My mouth was so dry I could hardly form words, but slowly the necklace came into focus, shiny, honey colored eggs. I nodded and bought it. For the first time I really understood the Kiswahili greeting we had learned whenever you arrive after travel. *Pole kwa safari*, my sympathies for the journey.

While David and the mechanics worked on the engine, putting on the spare, I sat on a rock, the amber necklace around my neck, staring at the desert road beyond the gate as the sun sank low and red. We had returned to tarmac roads, to running water. Still, there was this growing feeling in the pit of my stomach.

"Lani!" David's voice was urgent. He motioned to me.

Down the road a crowd of people had gathered in front of the school and loud voices punched through the hot air. Slowly the mass of people started to break up, streaming onto the road, shoving each other, arms waving. Two men, each carrying a photo mounted on a slab of cardboard, were leading the crowd, walking directly toward us.

I ran for the truck. Some of the men were obviously drunk. They pointed to the signs with photos shouting something. David smiled, slipped his arm around me as we slid into the front seat and locked the doors. I tried to roll up my window then heard the sound of gritty glass. Of course. There was nothing left to roll up.

We held our breath trying to smile as the crowd split up and walked past on either side of us. Their numbers had grown and soon the slow-moving mob was tightly surrounding us. Faces inches away staring through the shattered window slowly passing by. A seemingly endless procession of people squeezed past us, past the petro station compound, bound for somewhere else. A flurry of children scampered behind, teasing each other, faces filled with smiles that defied the mood of the crowd. As suddenly as they had appeared, they were gone.

It took David another hour to clear the filters and vents enough to get us going. The only lodging in the area was a game park resort. I squeezed close to David as we wound around the foothills of Mount Kenya.

It was pitch dark as we turned down the well-lit road toward the lodge. Zebra-striped tour vans lined the driveway of the stone buildings. Our faces were smeared with sweat, desert dirt, and grease. Brushing the hair from my face a shower of red dust fluttered down. My new amber necklace swept a clear path on my tee shirt as we walked through the glamorous gathering on the veranda, creased khaki suits fresh from the tourist shops, leopard print blouses, all eyes following us. The rustic lounge was filled with guests in smartly tailored safari suits sipping cocktails. There was one last cabin available, the clerk said, eyeing us slowly.

"We'll take it," we said in unison.

Standing tall we linked arms and walked across the veranda toward our cabin.

We called Kadzo. We had arrived safely. She was relieved but sounded alarmed at the same time. There was rioting in Nairobi over the elections. Authorities were trying to downplay it so tourists wouldn't run, but it was dangerous, she warned. They had shut down the university. The newspaper was expected to be next. The government was trying to block international news given their dependency on foreign aid and tourism. She feared our video equipment might make us look suspicious. Roadblocks were everywhere. They were stopping vehicles, doing searches. No one knew what was going to happen next. Stay where you are until this whole election mess is over. We looked around our room. This might be it for a while. Out our back window a dark mountain side and wide trout stream were visible under the half moon. The only good news from Kadzo was that the protests had distracted the government and squatters were beginning to reclaim some of the burned land in Mathare.

After a hot shower and shampoo that poured red foam from my head, I found a long wrap-around skirt and a simple top that set off the amber necklace – the last clean clothes in my bag.

The flagstone walkway was lit with low lights that cast an amber glow as we headed to dinner. The lodge had been built with a waist high circle of stone walls with massive poles rising to support a gigantic thatched roof. Right next to it was a lighted pond and saltlick viewing area. We were seated at a thickly planked round table, the chairs so deeply cushioned the comfort was almost startling as we sank in.

A man in a Save the Elephants tee shirt squeezed behind David's chair to get a better look.

"Hard to believe we're letting them go extinct. Look how close they are to us. Did you get a good look?" He looked at us as he swung his camera around.

We nodded.

"Such magnificent creatures. At least I got to take some pictures."

A blonde woman joined him. She was looking through a long lens and snapped several shots as an elephant calf squirmed on his back in the ooze. Voices around us cooed.

"Frankly when they're gone from this earth, it just won't be the same."

More tourists with the same tee shirt joined the group, cameras clicking, mumbled coos.

"Wine?" the waiter asked. He was holding up a bottle of papaya wine. David nodded.

The pop music that had been playing suddenly stopped and we heard a deep breathy chant coming from behind the stone wall. Slowly a line of Maasai dancers emerged from the shadows, their lean silhouettes casting thin reflections across the polished slate tiles from the light of the barbecue pit. The lead dancer looked exactly like Tipis. I gasped feeling my face flush, fearful he might see us, embarrassed for him, embarrassed for us being seen in this setting. As he drew closer, I realized it wasn't him, still in a sense it was. An overwhelming embarrassment lingered, being here, gawking at wild animals safely behind our stone barrier. All of it soon to go extinct so we gawked, at the wildlife, at the native people's lean bodies dancing for us, taking pictures so we could tell the tale before it was only the tale that was left. How different were we than those in their cleanly pressed safari outfits? Even if we were different, did it matter?

A waiter carrying a flaming sword of meat came over to the next table as the dancers passed one by one in single file. They held their heads gracefully high, winding their way among the tables, twisting and leaping through the maze of tourists seated at their elegant tables, mudded hair bobbing to the pulse of elegant bodies, eyes cast far beyond all of us.

The next morning we woke to the rushing sound of water, a beautiful stream rushing over rocks, flowing from the green mountains that wrapped around the resort. The view out our back window was breathtaking in the morning light. The refuge of this place was tempting but given the tight documenting schedule we were on we chose not to linger. We notified Kadzo. Despite the missing passenger window the truck was running. There was a women's group project on our list down the southern coast near the Tanzanian border and this was as good a time as any. Not knowing if there were disruptions in Mombasa, we could bypass it. Our only choice was to push on.

MAKWIRU AND SHIMONI

The air around us felt startlingly clear and cool — like a magnet the sea was pulling us to her shores away from the dust of the desert, hopefully away from the chaos of whatever was unfolding in Nairobi. Once again we were trying to process the startling changes of life in Africa. The desert had challenged us beyond our comfort zone and now heading to the coast felt like heading home. As the day rolled on the scenery was changing. We were breathing easier. The colorful Swahili culture began appearing, capturing our hearts once again, but we knew we were heading into new territory.

South of Mombasa the history of Arab trading ships seeking African tribal markets lingered everywhere. This was the birthing ground of Kiswahili as a language, the fusion of Arabic, Persian and Bantu languages growing out of the need for trading. It was the lingua franca of slavers, invaders, from all over Arabia, Portugal, and eventually the rest of the world. It also became the lingua franca between Kenyan tribes, since each had their own language and were reluctant to learn another tribe's words.

Traces of Arabia were everywhere, in the styles of clothing and jewelry, in the mosques and veils of Islam, and most distinctly in the food — fish and chicken cooked in tamarind juice, spices and coconut milk, rice *pilaus*, peanut sauces and curries, none of which were found in the inland tribes. Though every corner of Kenya had a unique spirit that captivated us, it was here on the coast we felt we could stay forever.

Makwiru Island was offshore of Shimoni where we would meet the women who would take us to their island. But first we were determined to explore the deep coral caves for which the coastal town was named. *Shimoni* means deep hole in Kiswahili, and it was here that slaves captured by opposing tribes inland were kept deep below the ground to await Arab ships that would take them away in shackles to unnamed destinations. From the indistinctive rocky area where we parked there was nothing to indicate what lay below ground.

Picking our way down a sloping path we found slabs of rock behind a clump of bushes, ancient steps descending unseen from the scrubby roadside. The chill of the upsweeping wind as we descended was a clue on how deep we were going. Bulging coral outcroppings framed the steps above and on the sides, here and there a hole in the rocks overhead let in a shaft of light. Stretching more than seventeen kilometers inland it was a highway of connecting caves serving as the holding pen for slaves brought in from across the continent. While under British colonial control with their efforts to put a halt to slaving, the hidden entry provided cover from the watchful British eyes while awaiting the ships.

The warmth and fragrance of the coastal air left us halfway down the steps. One more step and we were shivering in the dank sourness, whispering as though someone might hear us. We wanted to see it all, to walk farther into these caverns, film a bit more of this horrific part of African history, yet all the while we were memorizing each turn lest we get lost. The spirits of the past were tangibly present. The fear, pain, brutality of all that had happened here swept over us as though it was all still present, lingering in the rocks lest anyone forget. We didn't linger.

Sitting by the shore in the sun we tried to absorb it all, the stark contrast of the glaring white sand, the pale turquoise of the sea, the same colors slaves must have seen as they emerged from the caves headed toward their fate. And there, not that far offshore sat Makwiro Island.

The women's boat soon came into view, a bulky open skiff with a small noisy outboard engine we could hear from afar. I had the video camera already set up and filmed as they waved and landed. Animated voices, hearty greetings, laughter surrounded us as the women swooped down loading our cases onboard. How quickly the air changes in Africa.

A kindly social worker from the council was thankfully there to translate as the women overflowed in a chorus of chatter. Their eyes darted between us looking for some sign of recognition of what they were saying so we nodded, smiling broadly all around, the ever-present regret that we didn't know Kiswahili and our language training seemed to be getting pushed further and further away.

The island was home to over seven hundred people all basically living as one family. Everyone took care of each other's children, shared whatever they had, taught skills to the young as they grew. The men all fished together and shared the catch. No school, no clinic. The women operated as a family group and made the most exquisite grass mats and baskets we had ever seen. We sat under a thatched shade for tea, the women in a circle around us, babies on their backs, dyed grass strands tucked in their wraparound clothing, weaving and braiding grass as they chattered, their fingers never stopping. When we walked through the village to see the meeting house they had built together, they walked and talked, braiding grass without a glance at their fingers. Their exquisite baskets were sold at Tototo, a vibrant store in downtown Mombasa, a business project of the council working with artisans up and down the coast, selling their products to tourists and residents. Recognizing their skill, staff had taught the women how to dye grass with local plants, weaving items that could be sold in at Tototo or exported from there.

It seemed like paradise except for one major problem. The island had no fresh water. Every gallon of water had to be brought from the mainland by a fisherman with a boat costing them five shillings per jug. Their weaving success had enlivened the women's industrious instincts so they applied for a grant from the council to get their own boat and motor to ferry water from the mainland themselves. The boat we came out on was that boat and this was the very first trip it was making. Once again African women were amazing us and once again, seeing our cameras, they wanted to re-enact their story so other women could take courage and better their lives.

With no prompting they grabbed their *pangas* and started chopping firewood, stacking it in small piles re-enacting how they had cut and sold firewood as their first project. From firewood they had graduated to making and selling charcoal, finally building their own meetinghouse where they started weaving grass, each step depicted for us with animated movements and joyful celebrations at each milestone reached along the way. We struggled for words to express our admiration, our thanks for sharing their story.

I couldn't help wondering as we drove back up the coast if this small island community had found some marvelous secret to living together as a mutually supportive, caring society where no one was left out of the circle, at the same time worrying that they might be seeing us and our flashy gear as what they'd like to become.

The riots had not spread to Mombasa so we headed up the coast to Kanamai. A cluster of white cottages sat just back from the beach under tall coconut palms. Nearby, a large building with a thatched roof held a commanding presence as we drove in. Kanamai was a conference center of the council, a beautiful venue for meetings as well as an affordable place where staff with their families could enjoy the ocean just as tourists did at expensive hotels.

With little news of the riots in Nairobi our cottage became a welcome but bewildering retreat as we moved from one coastal project to the next, filming, learning. Women pounding metal into earrings and marvelous beads I purchased to add to my collection. A men's fishing project, smoking their catch on the beach for sale at roadside kiosks. One group was raising pigs on food scraps they collected from the beach lodges. They then smoked the meat selling bacon back to the same hotel.

Nearby we discovered Porini Village, hidden in the bush, wrapped in a coral rock wall with a barely distinguishable entry, a restaurant. Under its high peaked sprawling thatched roof one wall of coral rock held open fire ovens with huge pots hanging from chains over the red coals. The sweeping interior was wide open to the outdoors. A small adjoining village with families going about their daily tasks was part of the scenery. Huge tortoises brought in from the Seychelles, large enough for a child to ride, roamed the compound, visiting between the tables and the low sumptuous chairs. There was no menu. There was just dinner, Swahili tamarind chicken, beans and cassava all cooked in coconut milk. Waiters poured water over our hands so we could wash before eating African style with fingers. Water was again poured after eating. Sheer elegance in the bush.

But most evenings were spent writing, pulling notes together, trying to capture each detail, the desert trip, the slave caves, the women's groups, insights, the gift of it all, now listening to the surf crashing on the reef while wondering, given the riots, what would become of Kenya and whether our friends were safe. Often too tired to eat at day's end we'd sit on the thatched porch watching the moon rise over the Indian Ocean letting the day and our minds unwind.

What a comfort it is to share silence with someone you love. With thoughts and images colliding on where we had been and what might lie ahead it was hard to put words to any one thing. Only deep sleep could process it all.

BACK TO NAIROBI

Kadzo called, calm was returning to Nairobi. Few details were shared over the phone in the lobby of Kanamai's lodge. We headed back. The university had reopened but the government had apparently positioned an agent in every classroom. We were concerned for our Kenyan friends who were faculty there. We had been meeting with them as a peace group, cautious in where and when we met, not keeping notes since gatherings of five or more were illegal. Our discussions focused on strategies for establishing civil rights, valid elections, fighting corruption, probing what could be learned from African traditions that might work now. Within the tribe, elders had historically gathered to resolve differences, but between tribes the history was more of warfare, according to our African colleagues. With forty-two tribes, cultural norms varied widely especially on peace and justice. Kenya in many respects was the hope of the continent, the Switzerland of Africa as it was called. As a developing democracy, there were reportedly more than 400 NGOs making it their African headquarters given its relative stability, still the risk of sliding into a dictatorship required watchful eyes.

There was little information on how many had been detained this time, a subject never openly reported. Families were often fearful of inquiring about sons who had disappeared. In the government's eagerness in preserving tourism and foreign aid, the newspaper had reopened with highly restricted news.

We had taken some risks. A dear Kenyan colleague had come to us for help. He was a minister, outspoken on injustices, in imminent danger of being picked up. He desperately needed a passport to get out of the country. An "expert" could create one but it was very expensive and risky. We got the money to him in time and learned much later he had made it to Canada. We never felt sure who knew what in this process.

Life at the council had apparently gone on as usual except for the man sitting on a folding chair right outside our office door. Secret police was the whisper, taking notes on who came and went from our office. He nodded as we came in, was served tea at ten and three o'clock just as we were. Within a few days we became easy with his presence but watchful.

Everything had piled up in our absence, project leaders realizing we were wrapping up filming, last minute demands for their projects to be included. At last we drew a line in the sand and said the filming was done and sequestered ourselves at home.

Before we left for Africa we had been practicing what little Kiswahili we could learn from a small book, listening to tapes trying to at least master some greetings. Since arriving even small phrases had taken on new importance. *Jambo,* hello*, asante,* thank you. David was soon called *Daudi* by everyone, telling me Lani already sounded like an African name. We enjoyed the creative versions of English words turned into Kiswahili use, *baisikeli* for bicycle, *benki* for bank. But *habari* held the most meaning for me, the most common of greetings. What's the news? How is it on the path you've just walked? And every answer begins with *mzuri,* it's fine, things are good. That is what you say even when it's not so. Typically the greeting goes on and on depending how long it has been since last you met. *Habari za watoto?* How are your children? *Habari za nyumbani?* How are things at home? And after extended *mzuris* and nods the real news begins, the news of the path just traveled, the people seen, tales to be shared. The challenge for us at this point was deciding how to share the news of the path we had been on, how to share the tales that had been told and putting it all in this one film.

We did not look forward to framing the narrative much less editing. I stared blankly at the images racing past on the monitor, Mathare vegetable mamas selling their small stacks of tomatoes, women dancing to greet us, choirs stomping on stage, women raising honey bees and chickens in the hills. I felt a palpable loss that we had not filmed the children's home at Lake Turkana. Their story had been lingering with me, border wars killing off so many men and women, children left orphaned, sleeping on the floor of the famine relief station, then the children's home was built, but now too many problems, poor management, poorer communications. Many were calling for the home to be closed. Our trip up there had been repeatedly cancelled for logistical reasons and now it would be impossible to squeeze in such an ambitious trip with the little time we had left for editing. We would work with what we had, still there was this abiding determination to eventually see the children's home no matter what it took. It was difficult to stop my mind from trailing off with what we hadn't captured and focus on what we had.

We set up a studio in our spare bedroom darkening windows with blankets draped over the curtain rods. A *fundi* in the market built an eight-foot long table where we spread out our monitor, boxes stacked with tapes, my endless piles of notebooks and our small laptop computer. On the floor sat a monstrous surge protector guarding us against frequent power surges that ruthlessly scrambled or crashed anything plugged in. Of greatest concern was the safety of our long hoped for video editing system coming to us through colleagues at USAID. Most expats sent their footage back to the states for editing and production. We had neither the time nor the resources. They knew our situation and due to sheer magic they got us an editor. Now they inquired if using the footage we already had, could we create a separate film of the small business projects in the council that had been funded by USAID. They had an upcoming conference. Since there was no way to drag all of the conference attendees around Kenya to see projects whatever we could do would be appreciated.

We began by reviewing all of our footage. Our intent at this point was to provide not just a show and tell but to share lessons we learned from the people themselves. What worked and what didn't given the odds being faced by families living in squatter slums or poor rural villages? Were there patterns we could identify from projects that had really made an impact, what had endured over time? How much change can you hope for at the grassroots level before changes happened within the systems? I had annotated my notes almost beyond legibility in search of insights.

Often I wondered what good it all would do. What could I possibly communicate about Mathare Valley, about this mother in this place, me the outsider wandering through her life. I never doubted for one minute that I was living in two worlds, one foot firmly planted in each. What would I do if I were this woman, in this slum, with these children to feed? Regardless of the depths of my empathy or horror, to help change this woman's situation I had to insulate some place inside of me to make something happen. It would be too easy to get swallowed up in despair facing what she faced every day. She and I might both be walking through Mathare on the same day, stepping over the same trenches running with sewage, but our innermost thoughts and hopes were planets apart. I was here this day but I would be sleeping this night in a home with a deep bath and a clean bed and someday returning to a totally different life elsewhere. For her there was no clean bed, no elsewhere. She was surviving in what seemed an impossible situation and I was haunted by doubts that I could. You have to be very clever to survive life-threatening poverty, something I doubted could be communicated without being there.

While we had felt so wise saying feed a man a fish and you feed him for today, teach a man to fish and you feed him for a lifetime, I added my own queries. How do you teach people to fish when the government has made a deal with Japan to allow their factory ships into their waters in exchange for Mercedes for officials? How do you teach people to fish when textile factories are allowed to set up on the coast with no environmental regulations, dumping toxic chemicals that kill the fish in exchange for undisclosed payments? How do you teach people to fish when the shoreline has become a war zone? It was a theme I was to use often in speaking at conferences and presentations on various trips back to the US and a theme that ran through my conscience whenever I was asked what works at the grassroots level in poverty-stricken communities.

In trying to capture the spirit of the journey our cameras had suffered. On our last safari we had to solder a connection in the video camera using cables attached to our car battery all the while thinking our filming had at last come to an end. Miraculously the soldering worked like a charm and now we were hoping that charm would last.

Charm was hardly on our minds when we learned the video editor was held up in customs and required an exorbitant amount to bail it out, a total replay of our first days in Kenya. A week later when the editor was finally in our hands it was both heartbreaking and maddening realizing its limitations. This was no cut and paste as in today's electronic systems. This was physically cutting a tape and pressing tape on each end to join them. Clean cuts were not always possible and sound was totally out of our control. We took shifts reviewing the tapes in the editor, indexing places, projects, quality of the footage, stacking tapes into piles, each with taped lists, keeper piles, maybe piles, forget it piles. The limitations of what we could do haunted us. Cutting and shuffling scenes meant we were taking a picture of a picture making it a generation down from the original with an obvious loss in quality. Making copies from the final master would be another generation down.

The single soundtrack was a separate nightmare since cutting from singing choirs to Maasai cattle was fine but narrating the scene meant deleting the background sounds. Creating titles was reduced to a kindergarten exercise in cutting and pasting letters, laying them out on a banana fiber mat and filming them. We soon realized we needed to be minimalists in editing and reduce our expectations, which, while valid, added to our anxieties.

Our eyeballs started to noticeably swell. I stared in the mirror hoping the swelling was only temporary. It wasn't just puffy bags under our eyes, it was our eyeballs. We tried occasional ice packs. Late in the day Alice would find us with wet tea bags over our eyelids as she delivered a tray with cheese sandwiches and tea, muttering *"pole sana, pole sana"* so sorry.

One afternoon Kadzo stopped by.

"I tried calling. Your phone must be out."

We hadn't noticed. She looked around at the stacks of tapes, the editing gear, the heap of notebooks, then plopped down next to me on the couch. We leaned against each other. Words didn't seem necessary.

"Habari za video?" she asked.

She knew me too well.

"I just want to share something beyond what we see and it's not happening. The spirit of the people, the women dancing with the crowns of warthog teeth, fish on their heads, dancing themselves into a new determination, dancing into a hopeful space, but all anyone will see is women dancing with fish on their heads wondering how do they keep those fish balanced."

"You care too much." She squeezed my hand.

I held back the tears of frustration I'd been feeling.

"You do realize your skin is white, but your soul is black African?"

"Maybe. Maybe that's it."

We reminisced on our visit to her village near the coast when she took us to meet her family. She had wrapped a *kanga* around her city dress, swirling a wrap around her head, wrapping me in the same, joining her aunties and cousins in the kitchen to prepare our meal. We sat in the courtyard after dinner, listening to her tales, going to a school not far down the road run by Scottish missionaries, learning to read and write in English, learning to dance the Highland fling and the reel since her tribal dances were considered pagan. She later learned the reel was related to witchcraft and we both laughed at that. She had shared how while a student at the University of Pennsylvania for her master's degree in social work, she had carried grocery bags on her head with cars stopping, people gawking.

"Cultural roots run deep, without our even realizing it," she said.

I had to half laugh in agreement.

"So, the reason I came looking for you two is I'm moving into my new house. You must come. Help me cast out the bad spirits and welcome in the good ones. Part of my deep cultural roots." She was smiling broadly. "Tomorrow. You need the break. No excuses."

Laughter and chatter filled the air as friends bearing baskets of fruits and small fried curried dough balls gathered outside Kadzo's house. Herbs and incense were burning in shallow bowls which several guests carried as we followed her inside. With fragrant bowls held high so smoke reached every corner, the rooms were soon thickly clouded. Some guests were chanting as we moved from room to room, the rest of us waving our arms to waft the smoke higher, driving out evil spirits, inviting in the good. Kadzo placed dried pork bones over her top window ledges to deter *shifta* thieves since, we were told, Muslims shunned pork. Afterwards we gathered in the front rooms for wine, food and celebration, Kenyan academics, NGO colleagues, family friends, the African dance of cultural traditions and scientific minds. It was the perfect break we needed.

We charged on completing the small business film barely in time for the USAID conference. The feedback was heartening. Over beers afterwards at the Thorn Tree Hotel our colleagues reported the film was the centerpiece of the conference sparking discussions in every meeting. With irrational zeal we plunged back into editing the council's film. Days and nights ran together. Several weeks later after countless, sometimes mindless, reviews we declared it finished. We slept through the next few days reviving ourselves barely in time for the big event.

Memories blur over time, marching bands, flag bearers and choirs parading through the streets of Nairobi, crowds gathering at the

Kenyatta Conference Center to celebrate the 40th anniversary of the council, endless speeches. Our favorite was Bishop Tutu of South Africa bringing the crowd to their feet with his gift of humor and wisdom. Guest choirs from all over Africa dazzled the audience with one rousing song after another and once again I felt lifted into the sweeping excitement of clapping out the rhythm, hundreds of people dancing in place.

Even the afternoon opening of the conference meetings unfolded in high gear, as well as the showing of our film, and the enthusiastic reception it received. European and US donor groups were requesting copies of the film, asking what next steps we'd recommend, where was funding most needed. Several wondered if I would do evaluations of various programs, formalizing recommendations on what was working, changes needed, which needed more support. It was an alluring prospect. I had never thought I'd be returning to what I had been teaching. In one rush the compromises we had to make in editing, the sound track limitations, all seemed to dissolve in the response to the content of what we had filmed. It was the people and their compelling stories that had won the day. We were too tired to take it all in, already mentally moving on. We had to get home to finish packing. In the morning we were leaving for Lamu to at last study Kiswahili.

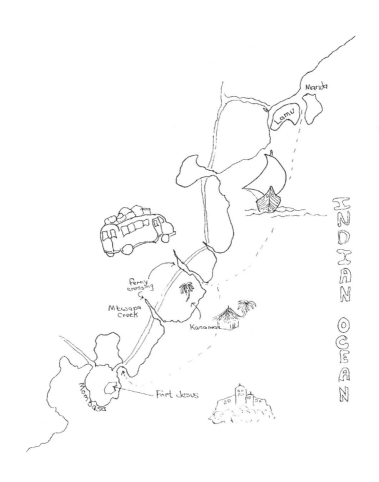

LAMU

In a state of near exhaustion and questionable satisfaction we plopped our luggage and our bodies on the bus for Mombasa and headed at last for our intensive course in Kiswahili on the island of Lamu. We had fumbled through nearly eight months in Kenya knowing only simple Kiswahili greetings and common phrases ever grateful for the grace of Kenyans who were thrilled at even small attempts to speak their language. Since early childhood I have been in awe of multilingual people thinking they must have some special blessing of the gods. Here in Kenya with more than forty tribal languages and dialects most Kenyans spoke their tribal language, plus Kiswahili and those who were educated also spoke English required in the schools making it easy to be complacent about our feeble language skills and remain in awe of theirs. Though young children can apparently learn more than one language with ease we had no illusions about becoming fluent in just six weeks at this stage in our lives.

The trip to the coast had become familiar scenery rolling down from Nairobi's mile high altitude of dark green blossoming hills to the drier bush country with scattered herds of zebra, wildebeest and gazelle grazing under the sprawling sparse branches of acacia, giraffe families

162

stretching necks high to study the intrusion of the highway's traffic, baboons lined up side-by-side perching on fence rails or rocks along the side of the road watching us pass as though we were the entertainment of the day.

Dinner at a small hotel in Mombasa, restless sleep, then before dawn we were climbing onto a country bus headed up the coast to the port where a boat would take us to the island of Lamu. A steady flow of people boarded with crates of chickens, chickens held in arms, bulging bundles and people-sized boxes. More bundles were tied on top than it seemed possible to fit. As we headed north people and their bundles got on and off the bus at random points. We kept our bags under our legs clutching our small backpacks on our laps. Soldiers with automatic rifles stood at the front of the bus chatting with the driver, there to protect us from *shifta* bandits along the way we were told, an element of the trip we had not considered. At each river to the sea we all piled out, boarded the ferry carrying our bus and helped pull on the rope that propelled us all across the river. Vendors selling tamarind juice and paper cups of cashews were everywhere. At various small villages children boarded the bus scrambling down the aisle, climbing over the squat baskets of chickens, selling frozen sticks of coconut milk dripping down their arms and sweet sesame seed bars.

At two o'clock we stopped in a roadside mosque so the men could wash their hands and feet at a spigot just outside the door and pray. How distinctly different these up-country tribes seemed than the coastal tribes near Mombasa where Arab features, flowing garb and mosques were everywhere. Here women walked the roadside, small colorful Muslim headscarves half hiding their hair, their breasts bare, the dichotomy of cultures. We continued north crossing the Tana River, enormous crocodiles sunning on the banks and by heat of midafternoon we had arrived at last at the end of the line.

Grungy and weary we dragged our luggage from the bus to the dock where we were hurried aboard the crowded boat to the island of Lamu. Peering over my lapful of bags I had to catch my breath at the sight. The crystal-clear turquoise of the Indian Ocean wrapped around us, fishing dhows coasted by, Lamu growing more distinct as we approached. Its stone seawall, white stucco structures and domed mosques seemed like an artist's romantic painting of an ancient Swahili island.

It was just that. With a documented history dating from the 12th century, actual history much earlier, its narrow streets, sequestered houses, numerous mosques and even its water-sewage system were still functioning much as they did centuries ago. I was mesmerized by the architectural distinction of the Swahili house from articles I had read. Now it was thrilling knowing I'd be seeing them apparently untouched by time.

At the Lamu dock swarms of local boys hassled to grab our luggage and guide us through the town. Due to the narrow streets, vehicles aren't allowed on the island except for a few military trucks, so pushcarts and donkeys do all the trucking. We decided to haul our own gear, fighting off the persistent mob, and trudged off to find Usama, our contact at Lamu Craft, a carving workshop. When Usama introduced himself, we were surprised to be facing a sandy haired American but decided not to express our surprise. Twisting down streets barely three feet wide he led us to our house, an authentic Swahili townhouse managed by the museum. Deeply carved doors led into a courtyard circled by porches, ten-foot deep rooms, fully furnished, the court side of each room wide open, a simple carved railing where a wall might have been. High thick walls with only peep holes to the street ensured total privacy. Heavily carved Swahili furniture crowded the rooms along with canopied beds too fragile to sleep in, stiff-backed wooden couches, heavy, tall back chairs with seats so shallow you could only perch on them. We looked around and wondered what you did when it rained with no walls on the courtyard side of every room. The kitchen looked unusable, a small kerosene stove against the rain-vulnerable railing to the courtyard, almost no counters, a few shelves with a solitary cup or soup bowl here and there. In back there was a more private harem room with a high stone wall covered with small arched niches carved out. Tall poster bed frames with thin mattresses that looked barely long enough for a child were bunched together looking as though this was a storage room for the museum. Behind the harem room was an exquisite private courtyard with frangipani, pomegranate, and coconut palms. The exposed stone stairway to the roof led to an incredible view of the harbor where dhows were ghosting in loaded with mangrove poles and fish.

It didn't take us long to realize that despite the view and the beauty of the courtyards the rooms were basically not usable spaces. Since we would be living in this ancient house for more than a month, we decided to drag our mattresses up to the roof, Arab style since the rainy season had not yet set in, creating a bedroom of sorts to catch the ocean breezes. By the time the sun was setting we were moved in and picking our way down the narrow streets to Suli-Suli, the house where the eleven younger students were staying, mainly college students. We were the elders of the group along with Ginna who had ventured to Kenya on her own planning to find volunteer work for the year and would become our life-long friend. By contrast to our museum house, Suli-Suli was stunning and comfortable, three levels of rooms facing its court and thatched huts scattered about its rooftop for sleeping. Here we met Rob, the director of Friends World College, a former linguistic professor from Columbia University who specialized in Kiswahili.

Usama, originally from New York, married to a Lamu woman, now called a born-again Muslim by the students, would be providing field trips to immerse us in the Swahili culture. Three or four times a week we each spent the afternoon with our assigned tutor walking through everyday activities around the island practicing our Kiswahili. The program was tightly organized and despite the laid-back setting the schedule was daunting.

The first few days of classes jarred us into a new routine. Despite a deluge of vocabulary lists, sixteen classes of nouns to wrestle with and verb structures with embedded objects, it felt refreshingly different than filming. Saturday there was no rest and we were off on a treasure hunt that lasted seven hours trudging about the island asking questions in Kiswahili trying to find obscure people and places, roaming the old dhow boat yards asking the *fundis* the names of different types of sailing vessels, plucking fruit from a grove and getting local people to identify it for us, recording all of our new words.

Early the next morning we climbed aboard Usama's dhow, about twenty-six feet long and very beamy, and sailed to Manda Island across the harbor to explore ancient ruins and swim on the white sand beaches. Fishermen were spreading freshly caught swordfish and stingray on the black rocks to dry in the sun. Dozens of dhows coasted elegantly between the islands, some carrying tourists out to the reefs and ruins, others going about their ancient business of fishing or cutting mangrove poles for shipment to Arabia.

We were struck by the constancy of the sea here. For six months of the year the winds blow *Kaskazi*, from the north with no storms, consistent steady breezes and no rain. In April there is a lull before the winds switch to *Kusi*, south, when the heavy rains and squalls roll in and dhows are beached for the season. For more than 2000 years these same dhows have sailed down from Arabia on the *Kaskazi*, traded their goods, and returned on the early *Kusi* winds before the storms. Countless smaller dhows were still trading between the islands of the Lamu archipelago stretching more than a hundred miles nearly to the border of Somalia.

Beyond the ancient streets of Lamu the Peponi Hotel sat regally facing the sea. Despite the touristy nature of the place it proved a great gathering spot at sunset for our classmates since unlike the traditionally Islamic cafes of Lamu town they sold beer and wine. One evening on the terrace we sat with a young man who pointed out the cargo dhows coming in from Arabia. That one is probably loaded with portable tape players, he told us, that one too. Sixty to eighty feet in length the dhows had beamy bulky hulls and a solitary lateen sail. He knew every vessel, when they had left Lamu carrying mangrove poles to Arabia and what they were probably carrying on their return trip.

The mangrove poles, *boriti*, were used in building houses, valuable in Arabia since they had few trees there. Typically used as beams, the limited length of a stout mangrove pole determined the width of the room, which is why flat-roofed Arab houses were usually built in long narrow sections with support pillars between. The young man was learning to be a navigator for the route to Arabia on just such a cargo dhow and he hoped when the winds shifted to the *Kaskazi* monsoon he would be helping to guide a dhow just like these.

As it grew dark, he pointed out the stars as they appeared. This one he would follow first sailing for three or four days depending on the angle of the waves, then he would follow a star that had not yet appeared but he would show us when it did and that star he would follow for more days, and so on. When we questioned him about charting a course to Mombasa or the Seychelles it was evident this was not part of his process. He was studying only how to sail to Arabia and back to Lamu, not how to sail between any other two points. Someone else might be studying the stars to the Seychelles.

The flash of excitement in his eyes and voice captivated us hearing him explain the pattern of waves you must watch for, cloud formations, the direction birds were flying during the day, the position of the stars at night. With our love of sailing we couldn't pull ourselves away, imagining what it might be like to sail on one of these magnificent dhows.

Other evenings we joined local residents watching a film from India projected onto the blank wall of a building on the outskirts of town. People dragged out old stuffed sofas and lounge chairs, bringing pots of mint tea to share, and squealed in delight at the romantic involvements dancing across the ancient plastered wall though none of us understood a word of Hindi.

With our heavy class schedule time was passing too quickly. Usama had arranged for us to attend the burning of the fields, a two thousand year old ceremony on Manda. We were off again sailing to Manda, then hiking inland to the village. For twenty-four hours before the burning, an *n'goma* had been held, people praying for hours, some studying the winds, sacrificing chickens, drinking potent ginger tea. Piles of grass had been strategically placed around the fields waiting to be burned.

We joined the tea drinkers on mats set back from the fields and watched as the fire starters solemnly took their places each standing with a flaming torch awaiting the signal. The elder in charge was still studying the winds. A few piles of brush needed to be changed. He shouted the command then walked the perimeter of the field checking once more the position of the piles, feeling the wind at different points, everyone awaiting his decision. The line of fire was shaped like a horseshoe to allow a path of escape for the firelighters. We clustered together behind a brick house for protection. When the call rang out and the grass piles were lighted in a strict sequence, each man signaling the next through a rhythmic chant that beat through the air. Flames shot skyward and in minutes thick billows of black smoke blocked out the sun. Women and children started shrieking, some crying out remembrances of years past when loved ones had been trapped and perished in the fires. One elder who lost a son in a burning collapsed near us reliving his grief. The anguish all around was palpable, the memories too painful to express mingled with what must have been the anticipation of a new crop, cassava, cabbages, food to sustain this island community through another season. With few tools available, much less tractors or plows, this was how they had prepared their fields for centuries. Little had changed.

We tried to capture some of the blaze on video but the heat dragged down our batteries. With amazing accuracy the flames broiled through the dry brush clearing the land for planting before the rains. Retreating further upwind we sheltered behind a larger stone building. Even a brief glance around the corner met us with a blast of heat and choking smoke yet somehow people were ready to celebrate. We were treated to a communal dish of *pilau* eaten Arab-style, people sitting around huge round platters on grass mats eating with the right hand only. The heat from the fire was still stifling as most left the tending of the fires to the firelighters and elders. David and I joined them but couldn't take our eyes off the fiery fields. As the celebrating rolled on through the long afternoon, more food, more ginger tea, the blaze slowly lost its energy burning down to a smoldering blanket of charred earth. Tenderly we picked our way along the edge of blackened smoking fields aghast at how much had been destroyed, wondering how traditions survive, these same charred fields being set afire for more than two millennia. In the broiling sun we trudged back the two kilometers to the shore and hailed a boat to take us back to Lamu.

Despite the class schedule, there was time to enjoy the beach, shopping in the countless shops for sarongs, wraps and baskets. We faithfully carried our word cards everywhere and local merchants and restaurant owners knowing we were students quizzed and drilled us, correcting our pronunciation while we sipped coconut water splashed with lemon. It seemed the entire community was committed to teaching us the language and pleased with whatever progress we made. One of our master teachers who became a dear friend was Sawiti, the cook who prepared authentic Swahili dishes for our class every other night at Suli-Suli. Poaching crab and fish in spicy coconut milk Sawiti was soon beloved by all. Other meals we ate at the many local tea kiosks where yogurt, fruit, curries and seafood were extremely reasonable.

During class breaks we walked through the town marveling at the ornately carved Swahili doors, visiting the many workshops where this centuries-old craft was still practiced. We ordered Swahili safari chairs from Said Mohamed at Lamu Craft who became our friend. He and David talked boats for hours trying to find a solution to the high cost of construction that was driving dhows into extinction. These boats were the lifeblood of all the coastal tribes and island communities who depended on fish, yet nearly half the cost of the dhow was in the iron nails that rusted out in two years. David suggested wooden pegs and suddenly there's a group gathering round ready to chat. Years ago dhows were built with wooden pegs so it was surprising that this seemed to be almost forgotten in favor of more modern nails and screws. We parked it in the back of our heads as a possible small economic development project reviving the ancient use of local woods for pegging.

Lunchtime found us with Ginna at our favorite café, laughing together at our rough Kiswahili as we ordered fish soup and paper-thin pancakes laced with tart lemon sauce while the younger students hiked to Peponi. Daily, fishermen walked past carrying huge fish strung on a pole between them, luminous rainbow-colored dolphin fish, the life and color fading out of them on the way to the kitchen behind us. The waiter quizzed us on the Kiswahili words for what we were eating, a delightful and usually humorous exchange but typically we couldn't linger as all shops closed promptly with every call to prayers five times a day.

About midway through the course Usama offered us a longer dhow trip, nearly a week visiting the northernmost islands of the coast archipelago stretching nearly to Somalia. We each bought a *fumba*, a grass mat shaped like an envelope to sleep in, and packed up. Late one night at high tide under a full moon we set sail coasting past the Lamu seafront toward the Manda channel. Around midnight we found ourselves sailing snuggly between the mainland and Manda Island when suddenly the captain ordered silence. We were all on high alert. It sounded as though we were approaching a huge waterfall reminiscent of that edge of the world painting that flashed through my mind's eye. One of the crew perched on the bow suddenly leapt backwards arms wide in alarm. Word whispered around. Elephants were crossing the channel just ahead.

We could only see the thrashing and churning of the water ahead but the whispered word was that a sizable herd was wading from the mainland to Manda Island. We slackened the sail to slow down, as colliding with elephants was not advisable sailing procedure. We all crouched down as the crew let out eerie cries to scare off strays we might not spot in time. The entire scene was surreal as we helped lower the sail as silently as possible. Word went round that if the elephants saw the tall sail looming over them they might charge the boat. We held our breath with each eerie cry listening to the wild churning of the water ahead, the parade of dark silhouettes growing more distinct in the moonlight as we drifted closer. Breathless silence then the sound of rushing water grew fainter. We watched in awe as the massive silhouettes rose onto the shore. We continued on in total silence.

Around two in the morning we glided to a stop, grounded on a sandbar. At last sliding into our *fumbas*, we all huddled together against the curved sides of the dhow dozing off as the crew set nets and built a fire on the bar. Each hour of the night brought its own dreamy confusion, first a small shark was caught in the nets, then a half dozen large crab. We half sat up to watch the night mirage of kettles over the fires as the catch was immediately boiled before it might spoil. In the morning we drifted off the sand bar with the tide rising with the sun and feasted on boiled crab for breakfast.

A brisk wind took us to Pate Island to explore ancient ruins and deliver fresh fish to cousins of one of the crew. By afternoon we were off to

Kiwaiyu the northernmost island of the chain. Here we anchored and waded ashore holding our packs over our heads. One side of this remote island faces a sheltered cove with protective trees just back from the beach so we strung makeshift tents under the wide branches. Almost immediately we were surrounded by children from the small island village wanting to trade seashells for our pens or pencils. There were none on the island and they badly need them for school. We all searched our pockets and packs and gathered whatever we could find. Instantly we had friends and realized we were functioning in Kiswahili. Sensing our eagerness, the children brought out their school readers and tried us out enjoying the role of teacher.

In the afternoon we hiked across the island and in the center found a landing strip, which seemed rather strange in such a remote place. When we reached the opposite side of the island, we saw the reason for it. Facing the open sea green Indian Ocean sat a small stark white hotel almost blinding in the tropical sun. Thatch covered verandas wrapped around it, bougainvillea blanketing the surrounding hill, lovely tables in the shade. A solitary waiter welcomed us as we approached so we decided to stop for a drink. The hotel was vacant except for one man sitting at the bar. He came over immediately to chat. A Brit, he had been living here for several years, purchasing lobsters from the local fishermen then storing them in a holding cage. When he had enough lobsters, he phoned and a plane flew in with ice to fly the crates back to Nairobi where a commercial plane took them to Germany. Everyone was fascinated as we learned of the rock stars and famous personalities who had been guests here, this tiny perfectly isolated Indian Ocean paradise. It was evident such guests were few and far between yet sufficient enough for this private hotel to survive. Before we departed the man at the bar was trying to convince us what a great job it was and would any of us want it. The German company pays all of your expenses, including your bar bill, you have a suite at this gorgeous hotel, an incredible salary. His voice began to sound desperate. The only clause in the contract that concerned some fellows in our group, keenly listening, was that you had to sign a legal agreement not to leave unless you found someone who would replace you. He had been trying to leave for quite some time and seemed overly anxious with his pitch as we departed.

Two days on Kiwaiyu and we felt we understood some of the paradoxes of paradise, the outrageous beauty of untouched tropical beaches, the restfulness of an unhurried community, the almost frantic friendliness of the children for news from beyond their shores, their anxious pursuit of small items we don't even notice we have, and the desperation of being stranded in one of the most beautiful settings we had ever seen.

Though we all joked about taking the lobster job and just staying here each of us decided it was time to push on; we had a mission on this voyage — to pick up a fighting cock for Usama on the Island of Faza. So we set sail through a rolling sea under the unending equatorial sun. We had to anchor far out in the bay of Faza in order not to be stranded by the tide so we waded in waist deep surf more than a kilometer balancing our day bags on our heads. Even older than Lamu, Faza was a living ancient town untouched by the Portuguese invasions. We were able to go about the town with our budding Kiswahili, buy fruit, chat with the children who followed us everywhere. Usama eventually returned with his cock. He was also leading a young goat.

Back onboard the goat took the bow and the cock was tethered to the stern perch as we set sail back to Lamu. At teatime the crew chopped firewood on the stern deck, built a fire in a small iron drum and provided a spiced tea, fish and rice, all while we sailed at a brisk angle, feet braced against the hull's side. Soon the sun dropped into the sea and the moon reappeared to guide us back to Lamu harbor just before midnight.

As our course was drawing to a close, the women in our Kiswahili class had been invited to a wedding party. Shela was getting married. None of us knew her but that didn't seem to matter. While there are Islamic traditions across the world as well as Swahili Islamic traditions along coastal Africa, Lamu's version of these traditions is distinctly unique. The street in front of Shela's house had been blocked off for the bride's party and large grass mats were draped in layers across the alley and windows blocking the view of any man who might try to peek. Women began arriving at the party around sunset spreading their mats out together on the street. They threw off their *bui buis* and admired each other's dresses, polyester prints in bold colors, layers of necklaces and beads. Some were chewing *mirrah* with bits of chocolate as they laughed and gossiped.

The only men allowed inside the cordoned off street were the musicians who set up their drums and sat on stools with brass horns. Their soft rolling wail of provocative melodies floated through the streets of the old city and one by one the women rose forming a long line holding onto each other's waist, swiveling their hips sensuously to the rhythm of the ancient Swahili music that sounded strangely like jazz.

I rolled out my mat and sat leaning against the cool plaster of the house, my kanga draped around my shoulders. Grandmothers paused from their dance to show the smallest girls how to bend their knees so that they could thrust and swing their hips in slow, seductive circles. Inching forward with the erotic rhythm the line worked its way to the front of the bride's door. Every now and then we caught a glimpse of her eyes, watching between the slats of her shutters. Though this party was to arouse her interest in her wifely role, this night she was not to be seen.

Ginger tea was set out with tiny fried curried puffs. Throughout the night the music went on without pausing. Quite literally the entire evening was one song with no ending, musicians taking a break individually while the others played on. Women swirled their hips, bumping, thrusting to the sultry wail of the horns. Those watching squealed, urging the dancers on to sensuous heights, pinning paper money to the dresses of the most seductive. As the evening grew in intensity, some dancers were so bedecked in notes covering their dresses they swayed like butterflies in a mating swarm.

Drums thudded in a slow persistent beat that drove through the darkness. The music pulled me into it with a sensuous power that was frighteningly hypnotic. Scenes of everything I had experienced in Africa were streaming through my head as the horns wailed, the small elephant wailing from the opposite side of the bank trumpeting his anguish, the anguish of Mathare's mothers, the joy of women dancing with glistening fish balanced on their heads, desert blossoms bursting open, women warbling, trilling, celebrating the life that continued, everything churning together in this primal music.

Women lying on their mats to rest from their dance writhed with the rhythm of the music, whispering secrets to one another, touching one another as if practicing for making love, then bursting out in laughter. Even girls who had come with no thoughts of marriage on their minds would think of nothing else as the evening wore on.

"Tomorrow," one of our tutors whispered, "The men will gather in the mosque to wash and pray. They will put on their long white *kangzus* — how pure they will look. And these women — they will paint their nails, henna their bodies and splash themselves in perfume, wear their finest jewelry, their boldest dress. Then there will be two lines, two processions, one on each side of the street, one line of praying men in pure white chanting from the Quran and the other of women, covering their seduction with their black *bui buis* of course, calling out their teasing prophecies on the sexual prowess of the groom as they made their way to the mosque. Lamu has its own ways."

Above the lanterns hanging overhead the stars still shone. Mingling with the sultry music of the horns, the mosque calls began to rise through the night, tumbling on top of one another, men of the island heading to prayers. The moon had slipped behind some clouds giving the stars their full brightness. I pulled my *kanga* close around me feeling totally absorbed by the music and dancing forms, but so totally the stranger.

JAHAZI LETTER HOME

Dear Family,

It is so hard to know where to begin except to say we are safely back in Nairobi trying to catch up on sleep and the realities of what lies ahead. Our last weeks on Lamu were a blur of conversational exercises, writing business letters in Kiswahili, writing short compositions on our trip, drills and lectures, one from a local *mufti* extolling the role of women in Muslim societies and their proper behavior. Of course I had to get into an argument with him, difficult since he basically looked through me, dismissing any questions a woman might have and simply told me to read the Quran four times back to back before questioning anything.

Despite that encounter, we are amazed to realize we have flown through what they say is two college semesters of Kiswahili in twenty-one class days. I strongly doubt that, as the brain needs time to let language percolate and get absorbed which our schedule didn't allow at all. They do not expect us to be proficient but we can almost function in markets and restaurants and carry on brief conversations. We're hoping we have enough structure of the language to improve on these basics.

But the time finally came for leaving. The two-day bus trip back to Nairobi looked dreary, especially since the rains had begun on the mainland and we were told the coast bus often gets stranded by washed out roads. Remembering the few villages much less anything that looked like a hotel we scratched that option off the list. Flying back on a hired bush plane was expensive so we inquired — are there any dhows that sail to Mombasa? We were led to a Swahili sea captain, a *nahotha*, who spoke no English and with our new, thin Kiswahili skills we found out he was willing to take us on his fifty-five foot *jahazi* — if we got official permission. Our newly polished letter writing skills sprang into action, and we quickly produced wondrous letters of introduction and intent on a borrowed typewriter sounding very official about researching coastal islands and customs, my credentials as a professor. To embellish the look, we headed to the market where a *fundi* carved pink school erasers into convincing looking stamps that resembled official seals, a worthy skill.

Armed with our officially stamped documents we presented them to the captain. After considerable study we were granted permission. On departure day, Sawiti walked with us to the docks, giving us two soup cans with mango plants bursting with glossy leaves as a gift. Plant them at your home in Nairobi, he said, and you will remember me. With final hugs we climbed aboard the *Nawalikher*, First Blessing.

Basically, an open hull, the ship was loaded with empty coke bottles, cases stacked upon cases from deep in her bilges to what would be the deck level, but there was no deck as such, only layers of grass mats flopped over the top layer of coke cases creating a lumpy surface. I couldn't help but remember the cokes we had bought in the desert and how I had wondered how the empties made it back and fresh bottles arrived in that last place and how in heaven you could still buy a coke for the equivalent of a dime. Now here we were with a full load of empty coke bottles in this ancient ship and it would undoubtedly come back with a new load of coca cola.

All fourteen crewmembers were needed to haul the immense lateen sail up with its heavy spar. The halyard lines were woven of bristly hemp, nearly three inches thick, and the crew lined up one behind the other chanting in rhythm, pulling together at one beat in their familiar cadence. The moment the wind filled the sail we were gliding past the

176

now familiar coastline, our bow to the open Indian Ocean, Lamu Island fading from view.

Shortly after we cleared the islands and were beyond the reef, our *nahotha* noticed the winds had already begun their seasonal shift, and despite the stiff breeze that had us clipping along it was no longer directly behind us. We would need to tack back and forth for the entire zig-zag voyage to Mombasa. Tacking with this huge lateen sail is a laborious maneuver at best since the heavy upper spar carrying the sail has to be flipped over the tip of the mast to the opposite side on each tack. We were aware this would add considerably to the length of this journey, which was not in the least a disappointment.

Food for all meals consisted of rice and whatever fish might be caught on the trailing lines, eaten communally from Arab platters. We had been advised to carry our own condiments, tamarind and spices, mainly red pepper, carefully wrapped in paper packets, each person seasoning the area of food on the platter from which they'd take their portion. Carefully observing others, I learned how to discreetly sprinkle my spices and tamarind over a small area of rice, then with my right hand scoop up a bit of fish from the center with my seasoned rice without disturbing the areas where others had seasoned.

The only "facility" was a perch sticking out over the aft rail. This meant you climbed over the rail onto two boards with a gap between. There you would squat with only a short grass mat skirting the perch giving a semblance of privacy. Being the only woman on board I had prepared for this by wearing a tent like sundress, but the proximity of the perch to the wheel which at all times had the captain or a crew member steering, was more of a cultural challenge than I had bargained for. Climbing over the rail at the angle we were sailing with the deep rocking swells of the sea was a feat in itself, much less planting my feet on the balancing boards and assuming a graceful squat. Images of the Indian Ocean's infamous great white sharks were inescapable as the vessel leaped and plunged in the heaving waves just below my bare bottom.

At night we slept on the grass mat deck in our beloved *fumbas* finding the least lumpy stretch we could. In the clear blackness of the ocean's night sky the brilliance of the stars made it difficult to sleep. We simply lay there, eyes fixed upward, too amazed to even feel tired until a light rain started falling. We folded our *fumba* flaps over our heads and stayed relatively dry, while still feeling the wonderful breezes. I was a bit taken back in the morning to see the wee mango trees plants Sawiti gave me on parting had been eaten off clean. Probably ship rats we were told. I shuddered thinking how soundly I had slept once I let go of the stars.

The crew was extremely polite, eager to chat in Kiswahili, pointing out leaping fish, sea birds, then hurrying off on the captain's call to come about, the laborious task of switching the sail to the opposite side taking all hands. By mid-day the winds had shifted growing decidedly stronger and the *nahotha* decided we had to pull into Kilifi harbor to anchor for the night. Kilifi is an extraordinary resort town with sleek yachts and weather worn dhows anchored side by side, its steep banks lined with baobab trees and monkeys squirreling around the shore. As the sun went down the *nahotha* called for prayers and the crew, all Muslim, stood by the mast facing Mecca, and prayed.

By four o'clock the next morning we were hauling anchor and setting out once more. We hugged the shore beating against the wind and at last around noon the wind shifted and we were clipping on a steady run for Mombasa. At sunset we passed under the old canons of Fort Jesus. Knowing that we hoped to make the night train for Nairobi, the *nahotha* ordered the crew to hurry with the anchoring and getting the boat lowered. We were rowed ashore, the *nahotha* calling out "*haraka, haraka*" to speed the rowers on. He carried half of our luggage as we climbed onto the dock, then ran ahead, his long white *kanzu* flapping around his legs, turbaned head held high, leading us through the winding streets of the old port. When we reached the main road we gasped as he jumped into the middle of the road, arms outstretched, and stopped a car. He threw our luggage in the back and commanded the driver to take us to the train station "*haraka, haraka*", which to our amazement the driver obligingly did.

Hardly believing what had happened we boarded the train five minutes before departure, and in full disbelief settled into a compartment. The railroad cars are old and elegantly paneled in mahogany, immaculately kept. There was a much needed sink, for after three days on a dhow we were rather ripe, clean clothes to slip into and a dining car out of the past with silver serving dishes and white table linens. We were in a different world. So much had unfolded since we left a lifetime ago.

Sorry we could only send postcards from Lamu. Each day was so full and mail from the island is a challenge. It is so easy to worry from a distance and so often I long for news, to hear the big thoughts, the small things happening in your lives. I will call the kids today, I need to hear their voices, to know what they're doing, thinking. Wondering how John is doing. This brings so much love to each one of you.

Lani

Elephant outside our tent. Kilimanjaro in the background.

Lioness with cubs walking ahead of us as we learn to drive on the left in Nairobi Game Park.

Bushbuck above, buffalo below.

Maasai leaping at circumcision celebration.

Maasai girls dressed for the celebration.

Joyce and Lani reviewing video.

Joyce with family. She built this home using mud and dung.

Filming approaching fishing boat as we enter Lake Victoria from the papyrus canal.

Fishing boat landing after all night casting nets.

Play staged to show how disputes are traditionally handled. Little fire for little problems.

Women's group down the road to welcome us with warbling songs and trills.

Council social worker massaging non-thriving infant in Mathare Valley, children watching.

Preparing daily meal for children in Mathare Valley.

David swinging from the trees and Lani with kissing camels.

Boran woman weaving new grass on her house at Rappu.

Lamu waterfront above. Lani and Ginna on Kiswahili class trip to Kiwaiyu Island.

David letting children see themselves on video.

One of many mosques on Lamu Island.

Hauling boat onto the deck before we set sail on the Jahazi.

Our *nahodha* at the wheel.

Catching dinner aboard jahazi as we sail to Mombasa.

Chasing the wind.

BACK HOME

Nairobi seemed as we had left it. Alice was a flutter with everything that had happened while we were away, monkeys raiding our mango and avocado trees, no water from the city for days and just when she had planted more *skumawiki* which was now growing dry, and one of our cats had disappeared. Two marmalade kittens were there when we moved in. We named the female Neblina and the male Paco and despite their similarities, it was easy to tell them apart. Neblina was smart and Paco was clueless. Feeding them was a scene, Neblina with one paw on Paco's head holding him back, Paco paddling the air trying to get to the bowl. Not trusting Neblina's cleverness we had left both outside when we left. They had beds in the greenhouse where Alice fed them. It was smart Neblina who had disappeared.

After a fruitless search we came back to the house. Later that evening I heard a faint meow. At first it sounded like it was coming from the fireplace in the living room. David got a flashlight and looked up the flue. Nothing. Then I heard it from the kitchen that backed the

193

fireplace. A soft meow was coming from inside the wall in between. When we opened a cabinet door, we noticed a circular plaster patch in the wall. I tapped the patch and the meowing grew louder, clearly coming from inside the wall behind the patch.

David ran for a chisel and hammer. It is not easy breaking through a thick concrete patch in a brick wall. When the hole grew to the size of an egg an oily black paw poked out. Chunk by chunk to the tune of anxious meows the hole grew and we extracted an oily, sooted black cat. At arm's length I delivered her to the sink and squirted her with shampoo head to tail. She foamed up into an enormous black blob. It took multiple shampoos and rinses before orange fur appeared.

The mystery was solved in the morning when we noticed two flues poking from the chimney on our tile roof. One flue led to the fireplace, we had checked that out, the other looked like it led to the cabinet where it appeared a hot water tank might have once been. Nablina had obviously been determined to get back in the house.

We called home tracking down family. I couldn't keep back tears hearing my children's voices, sounding more mature than I wanted to acknowledge, the sound of my parents' loneliness, yet their spirited encouragement poking through my abiding guilt as an only child.

News of John was disturbing, only that he hadn't been feeling well, but I couldn't set it aside. We sat every evening on the porch listening to BBC news. All eyes were on Eastern Europe as one drama after another was unfolding. The Soviet Union was teetering, refugees were fleeing across borders, the archenemy of the free world was in chaos as the world watched breathlessly, focused on little else. We were torn between jubilation for the freedom this would mean for millions in Eastern Europe and the inevitable shifting away of concern for Africa. We were already experiencing the results of what many called compassion fatigue, or more explicitly Africa fatigue. How many starving children can one see on nightly news clips and still care? Are these the same images from last year or is this something new? How many droughts, how many corrupt leaders in Mercedes eliminating their political opposition while we provided famine relief? How many tribal wars that never seem to end? It was onto this stage that the collapse of the Soviet Union entered, and the world's eyes, hearts and charitable pocketbooks were shifting.

Friends at the council offices were swamped. There had been little progress on getting aid for Mathare Valley families following the fire since we left. Bulldozers had cleared large parts of the damaged area undoubtedly awaiting new construction. The drought in the north was growing and families were pouring into the city with nothing to eat. The problem didn't seem to be lack of resources as much as the pace of making things happen. Critical urgencies were handled as everyday tasks and our American sense of managing crises with a make-it-happen-now and whatever-it-takes approach was totally foreign. It was hard to accept how accustomed our Kenyan colleagues had become to life-threatening events, how unbelievably patient they were with dysfunctional systems such as rice getting held up in the port of Mombasa waiting for bribes, more land being given as loyalty rewards to the army.

Funding had come through for building the solar powered electric fence in Rapsu, so David made a quick trip there to work on preparations while I began assembling a team for the evaluations. Over the next month we lived in a whirlwind mode grappling with logjams and catching up on everything that had happened while we were in Lamu. There were encouraging responses to our preliminary proposals for upgrading squatter settlements, follow-ups on the documentary and the drought crisis. We were in the midst of pinning a patchwork of notes to our office wall when we got a call from the Mathare Valley clinic. Please come as soon as possible.

Theresa, the lead nurse at the clinic, met us at the feeding station there, her face drawn. Mwangi, the *askari* or night guard, had been killed. She had arrived at work that morning and found him. The police had come and he was in the morgue. People said a gang of men had come in the night and Mwangi, undoubtedly drunk, had gotten into a scuffle with them. No one of course admitted to seeing anything or knowing whether Mwangi knew the men and had been drinking with them or whether they were trying to steal grain from the feeding station and he had encountered them in the act. All possibilities were discussed.

195

Theresa knew Mwangi's only relatives were back in his village so there was no one to claim the body much less transport it back home to be buried. She had called the head of the council first but he would not release a car or driver. They would pay for a simple coffin, but couldn't transport him home, it would be a bad precedent. Everyone would want transportation to carry the deceased back to their villages. Not to be stymied, the clinic nurses knew the council had a station wagon that probably could hold a simple coffin. They also knew we had priority in requesting vehicles for our work. Of course the nurses all wanted to accompany Wangi home too. We listened, waiting for the request to be spoken, could we get a vehicle, but the words never really came. So much of what happens in Africa is between the lines.

For vaguely stated purposes, we secured a station wagon, a staff driver volunteered and somehow we even obtained a second vehicle that David would drive for the nurses. The next morning the nurses were waiting in somber church attire bearing armloads of flowers and we all crammed in the cars. Our two-vehicle procession, the station wagon and coffin in the lead, wound its way out of Nairobi into the foothills of Mt. Kenya towards Mwangi's village. Roads slipped from tarmac to gravel to dirt, then to barely distinguishable ruts as the climb got steeper and the switchbacks more severe. This obviously was a footpath only occasionally used by vehicles but none of the nurses seemed concerned, chatting away retelling Mwangi stories and the endless troubles that had befallen him throughout his life.

David followed the station wagon at a safe distance, down-shifting with the climb, through a fast-moving stream that felt more like a river, then back onto the dusty ruts, shimmying around sharp mountain turns. It was evident the station wagon with Mwangi was struggling even more, its wheels spinning as we climbed higher. Someone announced from the back seat that we were almost there. A steep incline with a sharp switchback turn lay just ahead edging a dramatic drop off into the valley below. I held my breath. The station wagon driver paused, backed up towards us, then revved his engine and shot forward up the hill in a burst of dust. With the jolt, the back door of the station wagon flew open and Mwangi's coffin skidded backwards towards us. A chorus of screams rose up from the nurses. One corner of the coffin caught on the edge of the door frame, just enough to keep it from launching over the cliff at the sharp turn. With the coffin hanging, cantilevered over the bumper, the driver continued his charge up the remaining stretch ricocheting between boulders into the midst of the gathering of villagers watching in astonishment. In retrospect, it was a fitting end for Mwangi's journey home and a fitting start to his funeral.

There was no time to catch our breath or remark on our dramatic arrival as everyone was aware that with the heat they had to get that box in the ground without haste. Solemn greetings went all around, the coffin was un-wedged from its miraculous position, possibly the only miracle in Mwangi's life, and lowered into the hole. An elderly man, apparently acting as minister of the day held a microphone plugged into a small boom box and began. It was immediately evident bass sounds were not coming through the mike only an ominous shrill over the whole scene which no one seemed to notice.

"Blessings to these kind people from Nairobi who brought poor Mwangi home. We who are his family and friends have gathered. We all knew him well, dear God, and we all know Mwangi was not a good man."

A chorus of amens murmured around.

"We all know he will probably not go to heaven."

Another chorus of amens.

"So, Lord, we have gathered here today simply to pray for his soul."

Everyone was nodding.

"We all knew Mwangi drank too much."

"Amen."

"He beat his wife and didn't support his children."

"Lord, save his soul."

Mwangi's widow was stoic, nodding, several small children hanging onto her legs, women with their arms around her.

"He never brought a blanket back home to his mother when it was cold."

Even the nurses, arms bearing flowers, were nodding now.

The minister looked around approvingly and went on. "He had shillings to spare from his work in Nairobi, but never sent anything back home for his family, this we know to be true. But dear, *Bwana Mungu*," he looked up to heaven at this point. "In your infinite goodness may you look down kindly on his family standing here today and bless them. Now let us all say, amen."

We all responded, "Amen."

Hymns rang out as the mourners threw handfuls of dirt on Mwangi's box. Several men with shovels completed the task while women fetched kettles from a nearby fire and served tea all around. Simple metal plates of *ugali* and *skumawiki* were passed around which we felt awkward accepting but couldn't refuse. Though there were chickens running around it was evident none had been butchered for Mwangi's wake.

Back in Nairobi we were never openly confronted on having commandeered two vehicles for Mwangi's journey home but there was a chill from the head of the council that couldn't be disguised. As for the staff and especially the nurses our bonding had been sealed.

LETTER TO DAVID'S MOTHER

Dear Mary Sue,

For so long now I have wanted to write to you about David. I think we don't often take the time to say what we may feel is the obvious, or we feel too embarrassed or awkward, so we leave many things unsaid. But I don't want to let David go unsaid.

I truly salute your motherhood in having raised a very special person. When I think of how difficult it must have been to raise a son like David after his father passed on I truly am in admiration. He tells me about his wild youth, jalopies without brakes, teenage drinking and partying, and his half-hearted attempts at one college after another. Then I stop and wonder what was in a mother's heart. But somehow you must have seen through it all and knew what lay beneath! I'm sure a lot of faith and praying went into those years. I can appreciate it all the more having raised three sons and a daughter myself. But then mothers always do seem to have special strength, don't they?

There are so many places that your spirit glows through David — in his sincere love of people, his hopeful caring for the powerless, in his love of life. Amongst our African friends he is a marvel to behold. Everyone loves 'Daudi' — the way he plunges into stalled cars, broken water pumps, charcoal ovens that won't work, and windmills that died long ago. He gives a spark of hope and humor in often the strangest places and offsets the formality or many pompous occasions with his relaxed manner. In so many ways I think I never could have come to Africa with anyone else. His spirit, his ability to fix anything that breaks and his ability to make you feel good about yourself no matter what is going on in your life, all create a most exciting and comforting life place.

I know long ago you must have come to grips with David the minister who doesn't like church. I don't think that part of him will ever change but who knows. I do know his spiritual beliefs are part of the way he lives and isolating them into ceremonies is not this man's style. He is always insightful when I am probing into my own cosmic inquiries and it is so rewarding being with someone who will wonder with you and come up with a fresh viewpoint. I find that is one of the most exciting things about life with David! We think a lot together, philosophizing out loud on our front porch in the evenings. That will always be one of my fondest memories of Africa, the richness of life we've experienced on so many different planes.

So, dear mother-in-law, I toast you. I'm sure your love and your enduring prayers carried David through many a bumpy beginning, and though he will never tell you — I will. You did a good job and I for one am grateful. Thank you.

Love always,

Lani

THE ELEPHANT FENCE

Solar panels, wiring, the batteries were all in the back so we expected to be riding a bit low. A few cases of battery acid were tied onto the roof of the red Suzuki we had signed out from the council's vehicle pool. Our own bags were stuffed wherever they fit. We were at last on our way to rig up the solar panels that would charge the electric fence in Rapsu. Our friend Ginna from our Lamu classes was with us eager to experience whatever she could of our latest adventure. By mid-afternoon we were skirting the base of Mount Kenya heading north when our vehicle lurched awkwardly to one side. David coasted to the edge of the road and jumped out.

"I don't believe it!" His muffled shout came from under the hood. "The engine's no longer connected to the frame of the car! This beats everything."

I stuck my head under the hood to stare at the dangling, mangled braces that were supposed to hold the engine to the frame. The engine looked suspended in midair. Obviously, we couldn't move until it got welded and how far it was to the nearest welding shop was something neither of us wanted to contemplate much less how we'd move to get there.

We cast our eyes across the landscape. The forest sloped toward a heavy line of brush that ran along the edge of the road. There wasn't so much as a hut in sight. A warm wind was blowing briskly. With all of our cameras onboard plus solar equipment there was no way we could leave the vehicle. Ginna and I sat on the running board staring down the empty road wondering what would befall us next. David was still under the hood assessing the situation when we saw a shadow emerge in the distant bush. A young man with a sprightly step was heading toward us.

I called to David. He hit his head on the hood as he looked up.

The young man greeted us with a wide smile. *"Pole sana, bwana."*

David explained the problem. We needed a welder. A welder? His smile broadened. He had a cousin. Just over there. He pointed with puckered lips toward the forest. Just wait. He would be right back with his cousin.

We shared some cheese and bread while we waited, staring at the place in the brush where the young man had disappeared. We tried not to think about the stories we had heard of people stranded, offers to help, then a gang comes back and robs the travelers. Still, we had little choice. None of us put our worries to words.

Before we had finished eating, the young man reappeared. Behind him was an even lankier man pushing an iron handcart with a pair of welding tanks strapped to it.

"I don't believe my eyes," we all whispered almost simultaneously.

David jumped up literally throwing his sandwich in my direction and rushed over to greet them with unabashed hoots.

Within a half hour the welding was done, a pittance of a fee requested, we paid more and were on our way again, wondering what had just happened. We never got used to this part of Africa where all seems lost, no solution in sight, and miraculously pieces fall together and no one is surprised except us. There were also times with the simplest situations when everything falls apart and everyone accepts it without complaint except us.

The sun was casting low amber light on the mud houses of a small village as we turned off the main road onto a rutted road. We still had to get through the game park to reach Rapsu. No one was admitted into the park after dark, which didn't give us much time. I waved to a cluster of village children standing by the side of the road. A young woman with a baby on her back waved from a doorway, then looking startled, waved both arms frantically running towards us. Children were racing from every direction, stooping to pick up things as they ran. David slammed on the brakes and we heard a tumble of gear fall from the roof rack. He leaped out waving his arms. The children were retrieving bottles of battery acid that had been rolling out of the boxes strapped to the top.

"*Iko mbaya*! (It's bad.) "We were both shouting.

It was then we saw smoke pouring from under the hood. David threw open his door. Ginna in the back seat flew over us scrambling to get out as I jumped out the front with the camera bag. A mushroom of dark smoke belched out when David threw open the hood. He tossed his jacket over the flames and soon only wispy gray streams were left. Inspection showed electrical wires had melted, undoubtedly during the welding, and now a mass of charred, smelly wires remained. We couldn't speak.

We quietly collected the plastic bottles of acid from the children. "*Asante sana, asante sana.*" Thankfully none of them was leaking. Mothers stood by with wide smiles as we climbed up the back of the vehicle to inspect the damage on top. Evidently one acid bottle still inside the box had leaked eating through the cardboard and rope. A waterfall pattern of acid had drizzled down the side of the Suzuki leaving a trail of shiny bare metal. We tied the boxes with what rope we had left. One more round of thanks to the onlookers and we got back in the car hardly daring to hope.

We held our breath. David tried the key. Impossibly, the engine started. No gauges, no lights, but we were running. Taking deep breaths, we smiled and waved to the women and children as we pulled away.

It was dusk with no pink left in the sky when we reached the gate at the game park. Sorry, only guests with reservations at the lodge can enter after dark, the attendant said.

"Thank goodness we have reservations," I said with all of the enthusiasm I could muster. "We were so afraid we'd be late for dinner."

David was trying not to smile. I could almost feel Ginna's eyes rolling behind my head. The guard waved us through all the while staring at our lopsided load. He never mentioned we were driving without lights.

Dusk turned to night before we had gone a mile. It was impossible to see anything on the narrow park road. We crept slowly straining our eyes, whispering when we thought we saw something as though the darkness demanded silence. I found an old flashlight under the seat and hung out the window pointing it at the road ahead. The thin yellow beam barely etched the boulders ahead at the side of the road. In the few minutes since we left the gate the forest around us had grown inky black with huge boxy shadows.

David hit the brakes pointing ahead. Barely visible black mounds in the black night. Elephants, the boxy shadows, loomed around us. We didn't dare spook them. Slowly more black mounds emerged from the darkness on either side of us. We were completely surrounded by elephants quietly munching the dry shrubbery. Silently we waited until the herd moved on, then inch by inch we crept on, sweeping the road with the dimming beam of the flashlight. It seemed forever before amber lights flickered in the distance, the lodge. Feeling we had used up our allocation of good fortune we had little hope but went in to inquire. They had only one room, a large suite available. Despite the price we took it.

The next morning, we drove to the edge of the park in the full light of day, crossed the now familiar narrow bridge, two broad planks barely wide enough for our tires. Rapsu stretched just beyond. It felt like coming home.

After a full day of greetings, walking the line where the fence would go, admiring the post holes that had been dug, and figuring out how we'd repair the Suzuki's wiring, we ate dinner on the porch of the old missionary house listening to BBC on the small radio we brought. The main focus was again Eastern Europe, the collapse of the Soviet

Union. There was nothing about the drought and famine, the wars in Sudan, the tense elections. It was as though we were living on another planet that wasn't even in sight of the rest of the world.

Early the next morning women were carrying rolls of wire, some cutting the long grass with *pangas*, all chattering with rippling tones that rang through the morning air. Along the river's edge groups of people were digging more deep holes, dragging long fence posts through the dirt. Children danced in front of me waving at my camera lens shouting, "Photo me, photo me."

The village worked through the heat of the day and by evening David and a few men had the panels firmly attached to the roof of the missionary house. The sturdy corner fence post next to the house had been set with massive supports bracing it on all sides. The lead wires were strung from the battery bank and regulator in the house through the open window frame to the corner post wire. In addition to all of the technical information David had to gather on amps per elephant, we also had to calculate how high an elephant's trunk was when swinging ahead to feel its way, as that would be the height of the fence wire.

By day's end the villagers had completed a half-kilometer of fencing and we turned on the system to make it hot and test it. Of course, David had to demonstrate to everyone how touching the wire would give you a shock but it wouldn't harm you. The children were so delighted to see him jump as he zapped himself that they clapped and shouted for him to do it again. Realizing he was the evening entertainment he did it again and finally said enough. Tomorrow the post digging and fencing would take up where we left off, but this night at least a section of the fence would be turned on.

Women walked by pointing out this first stretch to one another, babies strapped to their breasts, balancing clay jugs of water on their heads, animatedly chatting with one another while young children darted around them kicking a ball of wadded plastic bags tied with string. I had created a small booklet about the fence drawing illustrations and made copies for the children. Now I could only watch as teachers gathered a group around them, booklets in hand, pointing out the wires and solar panels, explaining everything. Beyond the river a few elephants had gathered, waiting the setting sun, surveying the stretch of fencing that had just been completed.

It was the middle of the night when I woke with a start. Dogs were barking, cries rang out from the village, men's voices, shouting something together. Clanging noises shot through the air with a tinny rhythm. We sat up. We were suddenly aware of people rushing about in the darkness of the village. Peering out through the stick slats in our window, charcoal shadows stretched long and low across the blackness of the fields as the invisible clanging drew closer. Slowly forms emerged from the void. The eerie glow of flickering torches drew yellow streaks across the acacia trees giving form to the shapes in the darkness. There was an abstractness to it all that made everything seem unreal. Suddenly an unearthly scream shattered the silence and a massive dark form loomed directly in front of our house. Men with spears clustered around it their shapes suddenly standing out in the half-light of the torches as a hail of rocks came down on the back of the huge bull elephant bellowing just in front of our door.

I gasped pulling back from the window. The elephant reeled around hitting the section of electric fence that had been strung from the house to the corner post. The momentary zap sent him into a roar. We threw open the front door. More rocks were flying through the air, thumping like a dull drum against his massive body. Small boys ran back and forth at the edge of the grouping, banging spoons against metal pots sending up a blaring cloud of confusion around the frightened beast. From the midst of the din a spear shot out glancing off the side of the elephant, but not before it had sliced a gash.

The elephant loomed high in front of the crowd, enormous tusks, one of them broken, pointed straight at the group, swinging his massive body wildly from side to side. Slowly some men were walking backwards while others rushed forward banging pots, throwing stones. The poor elephant was frantic. He had managed to pull up the corner post with all of its huge supports creating a snarl of wire and long fence posts. With an ear-piercing shriek he jolted in one direction than another and finally, free of the snare, ran toward the river. Within moments he was lost in the blackness of the water.

Aman stepped forward. "It was Gogi," he said. "The one who stands and waits. He is the one."

We surveyed the damage from the porch as people began returning silently into the darkness of the village. They had almost killed him. I found it impossible to utter the words. My heart was pounding, I had been too terrified to scream out, to stop them from hurting this magnificent animal. We looked at the pile of rubble that hours earlier had been the corner fence post, the supporting framework, everything leading to our roof. With a little more thrashing about our house might have collapsed.

The dark brush around us was still. The moon sent pale fingers of light through the stick lattice of the windows. The night returned to its peaceful sounds, a few squawking night birds, the cry of a bush baby somewhere in the distance, and now and then the lone barking of a village dog announcing his suspicions in the shadows.

The fence was repaired the next day, the solar panels reconnected, and the next stretch of fencing had begun. That next night Gogi led his females in their evening parade across the river. Men with stones and boys with kettles stood ready to send out a din of confusion around them if any should break through the fence, but the elephants simply continued their march along the fence, never touching it, grazing on the field grass, returning to the river.

Each night the scene repeated itself, the parade of elephants along the fence searching for its endpoint before they would graze. On our last night there with nearly three kilometers of fence completed, we watched from the rickety porch as Gogi led a herd of females across the river. They walked in a heavy, slow line circling the settlement keeping a distance away. Not one elephant had touched the fence since that first night. We wondered how they all knew. Gogi must have communicated something. Habari, what's your news? How is it on the path where you've been? And he had told them.

EASTER SUNDAY

The air is hot and windy at Rapsu. I sit in the relative coolness of the old missionary house once again and stare through the rusted ragged screen at the river with its thick palm shrubs. Beyond the river the hot, dry bush land of the game park stretches out, the massive Baobab tree standing sentinel. Last night some Somali herdsman broke through the elephant fence in eight places. They had wandered far from their northern homelands with their camels in hopes of finding water and grazing areas. Apparently, the fence blocked their path and they learned quickly how to smash the wire between two stones to cut it without getting a shock. But it is Sunday, Easter, and it was clear the project staff does not want to work on repairs. Staff at the council had all left for their home villages for an extended holiday which is why we are here in Rapsu. In some sense we feel more at home here than in Nairobi.

We prepare a small breakfast and almost finish our tea when a young boy, rushes in. He is Hassan. Will I come to see his mother, she is very ill with fever and covered with sores. The dispensary gave her some medication. It did not cure her, he says. He went to the nurse, but the nurse was not quite awake. He just mumbled something through the crack in his door. He would not come.

David heads off to try the nurse again. I find some towels and give Hassan a bucket of water to carry and follow him. We weave through the settlement of shaggy grass bearded domes toward the manyatta where his mother lays. A boma of thick thorn bush surrounds the woman's compound with a collapsed granary that once stood on stilt legs to keep animals from the food and cotton. Now there is neither food nor cotton so the collapsed heap seems of little consequence.

Hassan's mother is sitting inside her home on a few palm fronds, her legs straight out in front of her. The tightly plaited mats lining the interior undoubtedly hold out the rain quite well, but also hold out any breeze. She does not look up but moans softly, rocking back and forth. Her head is hot and clammy, her body covered with shriveled skin patches.

"Pole sana, Mama," I whisper.

She speaks only Kiboran so Hassan translates. She is very hot. Her skin pinches her too much, he says. I soak the towels in the bucket of water, wringing one out placing it across her legs. I ask Hassan to make a palette to carry her out into some shade. He brings a cowhide and helps her lie down. As I lay a cool towel across her brow I see her face, a mass of lines and furrows, her eyes glazed with the milky film of cataracts. She is thirty-eight, Hassan says when I ask. I drape the other towel across the back of her neck.

A pretty young woman comes in and squats beside me. She is scrubbing her teeth with a small stick. She stares at the sick woman and says something. Hassan translates. "This is her stepmother. She has just born a new one. A male. My father is very happy. He is a soldier, you know. He works here at the post. Just here." Hassan is smiling.

The young woman twists a *kanga* around her head and walks back to her hut. She is willowy and graceful, but there is a resigned coolness in her face.

209

"Ah, there is the man." Hassan stands up and points as I wring out the towels once more.

"What man?" I ask without looking up.

"The one they caught cutting the fence wire. He has been punished."

"Punished?"

"The soldiers have beaten him, here, and here, and here," he smiles pointing to his feet, his knees, his crotch as the Somali man limps slowly towards the forest.

My stomach lurches. The sick woman moans and stretches out her scaly thin arms, her nails digging into the painful skin as though she were trying to pull it from her body. I hold her hands to quiet her.

"It's wrong to beat people," I whisper to Hassan. Then I remember his father is undoubtedly one of the soldiers.

He smiles.

Some women with sharp *pangas* swung over their shoulders approach. They all greet me, watching as I repeat rinsing and wringing the towels and draping them over the woman's legs.

"Tell them I am trying to cool her fever."

One woman stares at me intently. Her face is strong and confident as she lifts up the *kangaa* covering the sick woman's legs, kneels beside her, and asks her something.

Hassan whispers to me that this is a very powerful woman. She circumcises all of the girls in the village. Then he asks, still in a whisper, "If the nurse cannot cure my mother, if he doesn't know this disease, will you take my mother in your vehicle to hospital?"

"We should first see what the nurse says."

"Yes, but if he doesn't know..." There is an urgency in his young voice.

"Yes, we'll make some kind of arrangements."

Hassan looks pleased.

A tall man smartly dressed in khakis and a pale green sport shirt walks toward us. He shakes my hand and looks down at the woman. He asks her something in a strong voice. She mumbles something, pulling her *kangaa* over her face. Her sores seem to be a great embarrassment to her as she is huddling shyly.

"This is my father," Hassan whispers proudly.

Behind us a tiny baby cries, the newborn. The young mother crawls out of a nearby hut, the baby strapped to her breast. She squats nearby. She is still picking her teeth with the stick. They gleam brightly against her tawny skin. Her eyes are deeply fringed with heavy lashes, her high cheekbones and narrow carriage all flow together in her startling beauty. My mind is whirling. These two women, the strong smartly dressed man. He says something to Hassan and walks on without looking at his new son. Just beyond the boma he greets two other men warmly and with loud chattering voices they head down the trail to the soldiers post.

I cry inside for this woman. I do not even know her name. I lay the cool wet towels over her once more. Her body seems limp. I wonder if she will die soon. She mumbles something.

"My mother says she feels better now. Her head is not so painful and her skin doesn't pinch so much."

Just beyond the *boma* I see David coming with a tall husky man, apparently the nurse. David has succeeded.

"The nurse was very happy to come," David blurts out before I can say a word, obviously knowing my frustration with the nurse's initial reluctance might burst forth.

The nurse knees down, looks at the sores on the woman's back, arms, legs, checks her pulse. "It's malaria," he declares. "I'll give her another injection, but she will have to come to the dispensary."

"But the sores?" I ask.

"It's another disease." He's turning to leave.

"What's the name of the disease?"

"It's called skin disease."

I nod.

"From the dirty water. I have tried to tell them, they must filter this water, but they do not listen. There is even a big filtration pipe here, but it's not working. We are asking -- who knows how to fix it? But nobody knows."

I wonder who started that project. Now no one knows how to fix the filtration pump.

They lift Hassan's mother off the cowhide. She struggles to stand and they half carry her to the dispensary.

"I'd like to look at that filtration system," David calls out to the nurse as they leave.

"We shall do that," the nurse calls back.

We are aware as we walk back to the house that people are standing in groups, talking, glancing at us. Some wave cautiously.

TURKANA SAFARI LETTER

Salama Sana!

At last a small rain is falling and we have a Sunday afternoon without obligations. Our newsy letters have not been flowing as they should have this summer due to many factors. During our work with the video documentary, we felt overflowing with visual and emotional experiences to share. Now we're in the nitty-gritty intricacies of development work involving just as much adventurous travel, but perhaps harder to share inner experiences.

Last Sunday we said *kwa heri* to Gregg after a most wonderful visit. His friend Whitney had left three weeks prior after sharing a week on the coast visiting projects plus a week around Lake Victoria — all while we conducted interviews with staff and clients for the evaluation. With only a few days in Nairobi to reshuffle papers, laundry and gear, the three of us packed up for our long trip North towards the Ethiopian border to Lake Turkana — formerly Lake Rudolf. We had missed this area in our documentary travels as it was so remote, but a wonderful tarmac road was just completed that goes almost as far as the lake. Our task this time was to evaluate the Turkana Children's Home that the council established more than ten years ago. At that time constant borders wars and cattle raids had wiped out numerous nomad communities. Many of the adults had been killed. Simultaneously an extended drought coupled with freak flash floods had killed countless other families and cattle leaving numerous children alone. Those adults that remained were unable to care for their own children much less these wandering orphans. When relief food arrived, the lost children slept each night near the emergency kitchen. The council eventually found sponsors to build a home for approximately eighty children. Now with funding cuts, the home and another similar home built in Garba Tula are in desperate straits. The homes are so remote that adequate supervision from Nairobi is impossible.

We had long looked forward to seeing this corner of Kenya and the exquisite lake that is known as the Jade Sea. Once part of the Nile, it is rich with ancient species of fish and wildlife unknown in other areas. Over the centuries it became cut off from the Nile and is now an ecological entity of its own. Lake Turkana is a full two days drive from Nairobi and though the final last stretch being tarmac is eagerly awaited we have hours of "deviation" — roads under repair section after section that make it an endurance test through steep hills and mountains along the Rift's edge. Forests thin to scrub trees, then to bush country with herds of camel roaming the hot, caked soil looking for thorn bush. Baboon families perch by the roadside and tiny naked herder boys keep track of a long line of camels crossing the road. At noon we find a small village with one solitary sprawling tree so we stop and sleep in the shade for a few hours to pass the equatorial noon. The tarmac ends here. The remainder of the road is deep loose rock and gravel but at last we arrive at Kalokol, a small dessert village not far from the lake. We stop at a small shop and ask directions. The home is not far. Across the road we are startled to see an immense modern building looking like a small football stadium. We learn that it is an ice making plant, built by the Norwegians for the local Turkana fishing coop, a group the council started but had by now attracted its own donor support. It seems the ice plant and super tarmac road were part of a plan to help fishermen get their catch to markets down country as well as over to Uganda. A quiet, gentle young man explains that the plant was completed, operated for one day and the foreign consultants discovered that the ice cost one dollar per kilo to produce given the cost of fuel to run the plant. The cost of producing ice was greater than what the fish could sell for so the plant was immediately closed. Now all of the equipment was sitting here with sales tags on each piece while just outside the building goats and camels grazed on the scrub grass as they had for countless centuries.

We find the children's home, a cluster of small concrete buildings. The warden takes us on a brief tour and we meet the fifty-four children who live here. Most have few clothes on, the younger ones are totally naked. They sleep on the concrete floors – no mattresses, sheets or blankets for the cold desert nights. We try not to be amazed any more. There are so few plates and cups that two or three children must share a dish at mealtime. There are only enough benches and tables for a few of the oldest ones, the younger ones eat on the bare floor. The children are excited to have visitors and eagerly take our hands to lead us around. It is evident that clothing is a huge problem. There are no toys, no books, no balls. The older boys have wadded plastic bags, binding them together in twine to make a soccer ball that almost works. A few chickens and goats scamper around the compound where the children are building playhouses with palm fronds. Inside the older girls are weaving baskets they hope to sell. It is school holiday so even the secondary students who go away to the closest town with a secondary school, are now back at the home.

We are led to a vacated old missionary house nearby where we will stay. At night we pull our thin mats onto the flat roof to escape the heat. From here we can see a great distance over the flat land. Just next to us we look across to a Turkana village with small domed grass huts clustered together, grain sheds, and storage huts nearby made of twigs and brush. As the sun goes down fires are lit and singing and drumming fill the air, first from one settlement, then from another a bit further away. Like the Maasai, the Turkana are a very traditional people little changed over the years. As nomads they have been completely dependent on their cattle but border wars and cattle raids coupled with the drought have killed off most of their cattle. Many have learned to fish and perhaps those will survive. For others it seems questionable.

We are just about asleep under a spectacular spread of stars when the wind comes up. We had been warned that every night the wind sweeps in out of the East across the lake at a ferocious velocity. Soon we are clutching blankets, covering our heads against the blow, finally cocooning ourselves huddled against the wall of the flat roof, and somehow eventually drifting off to sleep.

In the morning Gregg wanders off with some local children to explore the land and find the lake's shore several kilometers away. The home had originally been built on the edge of the lake but over the ten years since then the lake had shrunk dramatically with various reasons being offered, some blaming Ethiopia for damming rivers flowing into it, the start of what many called the water wars, others claiming evaporation. That such a huge body of water could shrink several kilometers in so short a time seemed nearly unbelievable. Like a pied piper, Gregg and his troop of wee followers came across a man half-sheltered by what Gregg takes to be his house, a bush whose bare branches hold up a bit of palm thatch shaping a roof of sorts. He is chiseling away at a stone, making a point for his spear. Gregg engages the man in conversation with hand signs and the help of the children to learn what he can about the spear he is making, an almost prehistoric scene in essence, hard to fathom.

We begin interviewing the staff and then find time with the children alone to learn about their feelings and needs. Field programs are never simple. It is always so simple on paper to design a project, even relatively simple to get it funded, but to make it work in the field – ah, therein lies the crux, the human limit. Theory is always so much safer and clearer than application for reality comes in with its blunt paradoxes and human limitations. Here local churches were squabbling over control of the home, an untrained warden wandered around seemingly unaware that most of the children were night-blind due to vitamin deficiency, a fact we had discovered walking around with them at dusk. There is a budget for vegetables and fruit that hasn't been used in two years. Also. no milk has been purchased in two years despite available funding. Broken windows, beds in a storage room awaiting simple repairs while children are sleeping on concrete floors, and regulations imposed by the warden that isolate the children from the village since no children are allowed off the compound. We are sickened. We make a list of needs and try not to let emotions influence our task.

A previous report on the home had suggested that it be closed and foster homes be sought in the local community. We decide we must evaluate the capacity of the community to consider this so the next day we set off for the shores of the Jade Sea. Here fishermen straddling three palm logs bound together with sisal are poling out to spear Nile perch of enormous proportion. Along the sand spits huge crocodiles laze in the sun, most over fifteen feet long. Hippos glisten like black boulders in the green water. We take a boat out to a nearby island where there are numerous fishing settlements as well as a luxury lodge for tourists — hard to fathom given all we have seen. Landing on the island we walk down the beach where families are busy with their catch, mending nets, sharpening spears. We greet the fishermen, a few know Kiswahili. Women and children rush over to us wanting to sell necklaces of fish bone, pieces of crocodile skin, beads carved from bone which I can't resist, sewn leather bottles holding fish oil and their exquisite Turkana baskets. They are traditionally dressed, women with shaved heads except for one central band of hair, each with a majestic bib of beads that climbs up her neck elongating it dramatically. One woman approaches me holding up high a beautiful baby, see — he's a boy, she says, only one shilling. I ask her to repeat what she has just said, feeling certain I have misunderstood. Her daughter who speaks Kiswahili confirms the offer. Somehow I can find nothing to say except to tell her that her baby is beautiful. Before our walk is finished, we have been offered three more babies for sale. Our Western model of foster homes seems a bit out of step with these Turkana. Later in interviewing educated villagers we ask, long ago what did people do with orphans. The answer is as quiet and unsentimental as the dessert. Orphaned children were left to die, sometimes killed to save them the suffering. It was felt that if the mother died the child should die too. Many of the home's children had been untied from the backs of their dead mothers just prior to burial. Fathers left the family if the mother died, though no one explained when we asked why this was so. The fact that it was taken for granted was painfully real. Relatives, who were barely surviving themselves, never stepped in. Today things have changed little. If anything, life is even harder with the drought and loss of cattle.

It has been an intensive week here so we decide to take an afternoon to tour the lake. Armed with fishing rods we set off with a guide and a boat. The mystical green of the water is due to rich algae and as we skim across the choppy sea, we are surrounded by leaping fish, diving birds, shimmering patches of silver schools of fingerlings. In an hour we reach a large island set like a prehistoric landscape of volcanic rock. Crocodiles and pelican share the beach peacefully. Before the day ends Gregg has landed two whoppers each about twenty pounds. We give the fish to the cook at the children's home together with a sack of vegetables we have purchased, feeling at least this evening dinner may be more nutritious.

Our last day has been set aside for photo work leaving us feeling near despair at the thought of leaving this situation unchanged. But leave we must if we are to make anything happen. After saying good-bye to the children, we circle round to a village where we've been told a women's group is making finely woven, tough hassocks of remarkable quality, and our presence there makes baskets appear from nearly every hut. Gregg and the chief strike up a marvelous communication and soon it seems the whole village is around us. We buy far more baskets than we know what to do with and reluctantly say goodbye.

Back in Nairobi it is a matter of paperwork, reports and drafting a new working plan for the children's home evolving it into a child development center for the entire community's benefit – training in nutrition, cooking, early learning, sewing, family planning and health care. The new program will undoubtedly get funded. Thinking of making it actually happen leaves us with a sinking feeling in our stomachs. Few people with experience or training to run such a center want to live in faraway Turkana. We can't change geography any more than we can change history.

Sorry this is so long and without the resolution we'd like to be sharing. Anxious to hear any news from home. We treasure even the smallest detail of what's happening there. Hug each other for us.

Lani

PASTOR HUMPHREY

A slight man in a thin brown suit peered around the doorway of our office at the council, eyes smiling as wide as his mouth. "I have come to see you" was the simple beginning of what was to become an enduring friendship. Humphrey had heard about the Trickle Up program we had taken on, started by Glen and Millie Leet, Americans with long standing ties to the United Nations. Fed up with big money for developing countries going to big people, the Leets based Trickle Up on one hundred-dollar grants given to groups of five or more who wanted to start a small business. If the group provided a one-page plan for their business promising to share profits according to who did the work, they would receive fifty dollars to launch their business and three months later when they filed a report, the second fifty dollars.

Humphrey had heard about it. It sounded like the answer to a prayer. He needed yarn.

"Yarn?" We invited him to sit down. Philip brought in a tray of tea.

"Mmm, yarn. It is not for me, but for this women's group. You see, I was in seminary for three years and went out searching for forgotten people I could serve. That is when I came upon Ruai, just on the edge of Nairobi, a ranch, it spread so far in every direction but now it is very small, most of the workers lost their jobs when the ranch became small but they had nowhere else to go so they stayed, squatting there, and when I came with my pamphlets speaking of hope and being loved they were most welcoming so that is where I started my church."

He paused for a sip of tea.

"But I want to share a story to explain to you why it is we need yarn. You see the people were all illiterate and they were being tricked and cheated by so many so I began teaching this group of women to read. That is how it started."

We pulled our chairs together.

"These women were very excited knowing how to read you see, that is when they confided in me about this woman. She sold these, these fetishes."

His eyes shot from mine to David's, perhaps expecting a reaction. Evidently seeing none he continued. "You see, she was destroying so many poor people with fear. They went to her thinking they had been hexed by their enemies, believing some horrible thing was about to happen to them. She had amazing power over them, listening to their stories then selling them her prophecies and warnings for a few shillings, don't go near the road, stay far from the river, that is where these women fetch their water, and if you remove this fetish some terrible evil will find you in the dark.

"The women of the village were all very worried about this one family. This evil woman had told them they must not let the sun shine on their youngest son until the next moon was full or something dreadful would happen, so believing her, they locked their son in a small basket granary and only opened the lid at night to feed him. The other women all feared the child would go mad in there but even the father, he would not listen. So many were suffering because of this woman. Even our own believers. They took their last shilling to buy a fetish. That is what these parents did, even their parents before them."

He took a deep breath searching our faces as he continued.

"We had to do something so we prayed together. Some had been released from her power. Still — seeing the terror that lingered in the eyes of others — knowing how many more would fall prey to her — we could avoid it no longer."

"That's when we decided. We must go to her ourselves. It was very brave of these women to agree for you see this woman, Ndege, that is her name, she was a witch.

I took a deep breath, bracing myself, hoping Humphrey did not notice the skepticism in my eyes.

"It was almost evening when we arrived at the small cluster of huts, the part of the village where she lived. Women were outside their doors nearby, cooking the evening meal. One man was standing outside his door and watched us, it was as if he knew we were coming, me with this group of women. His eyes were so hollow, like black pools sunken in his face. Muffled words came from his mouth like too much *ugali*. I could tell in his eyes he knew why we had come. His wife was inside, he said before we asked. Then he was gone.

"I went to the door and called her name. There was only one small candle burning inside. It was like entering a cave of shadows. The women were hanging onto each other, right behind me, I could feel them, peeking around to see. Ndege sat on a low bed huddled like an animal, glaring at us. Strings of leather pouches hung around her neck. Gourds were everywhere, across the floor, large ones, very small ones, the whole room, small sacks of herbs, old whiskey bottles filled with different colored liquids. Something dark was filling the room as she looked at us, her eyes wild, flashing first from one face, then another, words coming out none of us could understand, her jaw shaking back and forth in this twitch.

"Ndege, we have come to pray for you," I said as softly as I could, though inside I was terrified, I am not embarrassed to tell you. Ndege let out this loud scream in a man's voice, like low thunder in the clouds. My hands became so cold and sweaty. These women behind me, they pulled back toward the wall, holding each other's hands so tightly so I stood in front of them as strong as I could be for it was me who had convinced them we should come."

"Ndege hung her head down almost into her lap. It was then she began speaking in this squealing voice of a small child in pain. The words cut the air, like a knife cutting through us. It was too loud for our ears. It was too loud, unnatural for this bone thin woman, but before we could speak this voice changed again, now it was a man speaking in slow deep moans. We were all silent. Fear can make you hardly breathe. Prayers were stuck on our lips so we couldn't push them out. But then the grace of courage came to us. Sounds escaped into that darkness like steam rising up from us, louder and louder we prayed over the demons. It felt as though the darkness itself was swaying as Ndege screamed, the voice of the old man, then the voice of a child."

"We sang every song we knew. Between our songs we prayed, begging her to pray along with us. That is when she threw herself down on the ground, twisting, raving. Suddenly two voices were speaking from her at once. Two! I was shaking so hard inside myself, feeling like I must run very fast. That is when my legs started to move but instead of running I went forward and touched her. Those brave women with tears flooding their faces were watching me, their eyes so wide, wondering what would befall us, but they had faith and slowly we were all with her. They knew Jesus had healed by touching and they must do the same that *Mwalimu* had done. First one woman then another reached out with a shaking hand, as though they were each putting their fingers into a burning flame. Their eyes puckered shut, still singing, each woman there was touching her, then laying hands on her. Ndege's body convulsed and this agonizing scream went through her into the night, even beyond the village, but those women never stopped singing, soft endless singing. Then as if she was choking on her own breath, Ndege sucked in a gulp of the thick air. Her sobs became soft gasps, short, like trying to swallow the air."

"Speak to us," the women pleaded. "Speak to us as yourself. We are your sisters. We have come to pray with you."

222

"We could see the darkness swim above her, hovering close, but the faces of those women were closer, their hands solid, pressing against her. We felt the power so we didn't let our song end. Ndege's voice was weak as she whispered some words no one of us could understand."

"I knelt down next to her. 'Take off the fetishes, sister. Take them off. This evil will leave you,' I said, though I do not know where those words came from." Humphrey's forehead was sweating now as he spoke.

"Ndege pulled back from me, clutching her strings and pouches to her breast. 'God will protect you! His power is greater than all other powers! But you must be the one to cast off this evil!' I said those words again wondering where this courage was coming from. Ndege cried, curled up like a baby on the floor, her voice growing weaker and weaker, then her hand moved slowly toward her neck. We dared not breathe. She pulled one fetish off waiting for death to strike. Our hymn grew softer as our hearts were all pounding so, our eyes fixed, unable to blink. Nothing happened. The air inside the hut was so still. The one poor candle had burned very low. I feared it would go out. Then one by one, Ndege pulled off the other pouches, strips of leather, each one a separate struggle, curses of the past. We smelled fear, burning bones, ravings echoing somewhere in her cave. She was too weak to speak more than a whisper by then, but there was this one last fetish. She pushed her face into the ground smearing mud across her wet cheeks. Two women picked her up and held her in their arms like a baby for she had grown so very thin you see. She opened her eyes. Silence, her voices were still. She pinched her eyes shut as though she knew death was near and pulled the last fetish off expecting the world to disappear but the singing of those women filled the shadows of the little hut. Ndege's eyes were glazed, rolled back. We had all sung ourselves out of the land of fear and pain into the realm beyond and she had come with us."

"The blackness of night had swallowed the compound, I could tell this, for neighbors drew closer, but not too close, listening and watching. The women came out from the doorway and rekindled the fire in front of her house. Some carried the fetishes on the end of sticks so their fingers would not touch them and threw them into the flames, others helped their dear sister Ndege to a blanket beside the fire."

"*Mungu yuko* — God is. *Mungu yuko* — there is a God."

"Her husband came back from the shadows and just stood there, watching with the neighbors, smelling the smoke, the burning fetishes. We all sang *Karibu na Wewe, Bwana Mungu* — Nearer My God to Thee. The air was very thin and so clear so we were sure our voices had reached all the way to heaven."

I felt frozen to my chair, unsure of my own thoughts, how I was going to respond, just studying Humphrey's face as he spoke, hoping he wasn't studying mine.

"You see, that was how it started. These women had gained great courage. It was this same group of women who then began going with me to visit the sick and searching for a way to earn a few shillings to buy medicine and feed their children. One of the women knew how to knit and taught the others so they began showing their sweaters to people and that is when the blessing came, just this week — a large order for school sweaters, but of course they do not have enough funds to purchase the yarn. So this is why I have come. We need yarn."

Yarn. I'm not sure how long I sat there. Where does one belief end before another takes over? How different is calling out the confusion of a dark mind from chanting to the drones of long horns or from stomping feet and clanging symbols singing familiar hymns in native tongues. How different is it from dancing with a fish on your head to transport you into the joy you need to carry on? Or from going home and meditating so I can find myself once again?

LETTER HOME: RUAI

Salama from Kenya,

Life has taken another unexpected turn, which seems to be our way of life in Africa. Too much has happened in such a short time it is hard to know where to begin. We had given Humphrey, a young pastor, a small check for a group to buy yarn for knitting school sweaters and they were so proud of what they had accomplished they came to our office bearing a box of green beans begging us to visit them. We felt compelled to go to Ruai. Despite the mud huts and meager diets, the group's vitality gave us a spurt of renewed determination. That vitality also inspired other Ruai groups to launch projects that we were able to fund through this program and now there are groups doing charcoal, sewing school uniforms, a men's group smoking fish, a youth group selling bananas. We passed on a five-hundred-dollar donation from a church in the US that helped Humphrey launch a nutrition project, four young women are now being trained by the council's nurses to set up a demonstration kitchen for teaching mothers while feeding fifty children daily.

Housing was obviously another critical need. Ruai is located within the city of Nairobi so structures have to be permanent which means

225

stone or concrete. People were fearful their huts would soon be demolished by the city council. We brainstormed with the youth group on what was available for building. Broken rock from a nearby quarry was free for the hauling. Sisal poles and fiber from the sisal leaves were free for the taking from the abandoned fields of the ranch. The land also had *muram* soil that when wet packs down hard as concrete. The idea emerged to build a double wall of cut saplings, load it with broken rock, then plaster everything with *muram* adding a finishing plaster of concrete. Everyone turned out for wall day — women carried five-gallon jugs of water on their heads for mixing *muram*, children wallowed in the mud pits to churn it into a smooth slurry and the older youth slung the mud filling the gaps in the walls. Roofs always present a dilemma due to the outrageous cost of corrugated iron.

I noticed strong basket domes to house chickens overnight and asked if there were people who knew how to weave these baskets. In a rush of excited ideas the group decided to build a basket roof. Weekends found us with fifteen youth slinging mud into walls, mixing concrete with sisal fiber for plastering walls, and together figuring out how to weave a basket dome to fit over our four meter by four-meter house. The day the group carried the finished basket and hoisted it over the walls the whole community turned out to cheer them on. Layer after layer of sisal was woven in next before the entire dome was plastered with the concrete sisal mixture. The entire structure was completed for one hundred and eighty dollars US and quickly became a symbol for the community and more ideas spread.

Women wanted a daycare center. The few remaining fields of the ranch were devoted to growing miniature vegetables for export. To keep his women workers in the field, the new ranch manager agreed to pay four women to run the center so more women could work. It didn't take long to transform the plywood church and I found myself coaching the four new teachers in Montessori methods and making learning materials, counting sets from bottle caps, scraps of fabric for matching, corn husk dolls. Fifty children rushed in when we opened the doors though nearly two hundred wanted to attend. I was embarrassed to learn they had named the center the Lani Nursery School.

There are always more needs. Within days women were asking me if I knew how to bake bread, a growing favorite food but expensive. David began welding steel drums for ovens and since none of the women had ever used an oven much less baked bread my bread baking workshops began. Within weeks a functioning bakery was running, selling to neighboring communities with more profits than the women could have dreamed possible. It is humbling to realize how sharing such small skills can have such an impact and at other times the simplest things are impossible to change.

With this I'll close, hoping you know how much we wish you were all here experiencing this with us.

Love, Lani

APPENDICITIS LETTER HOME

Dear family all,

Sorry our phone call lost its connection. This is just a note to say I am fine, didn't want you to worry. It just all happened so fast. We were asked to accompany a visitor to Tanzania and Zanzibar to see some innovative projects. It would have been our first time there so we were very excited. We packed up Ange Ove the night before and were just loading the water jugs in the morning when I felt a distinct pain in my belly. I sat down waiting for it to go away but it was constant and in a spot so specific I could put my finger on, nothing I had experienced before, so we took off for the hospital. They whisked me in and within minutes this very British doctor was telling me it was appendicitis and they were taking me straight into surgery. When I woke up I was surrounded by nurses, a blur of stiff white bonnets, striped gowns starched so stiff they looked like a choir of cardboard cutouts circling my bed. The anesthesiologist came in, a young Indian doctor, reassuring me all went well. The bonneted starched choir buzzing about me were student nurses, four of them giving me a bath, others bringing a pitcher of water, a tray of tea, checking my temperature, obviously practicing their skills on me. Then came the surgeon, the appendix hadn't burst, we caught it in time. If this had happened while on safari to Tanzania it would have been a different story. This Nairobi hospital is the only one with Western standards in the entire region. Government hospitals are overflowing and apparently disastrous. All to assure you I am feeling fine and very grateful. Will try to call again soon.

Love to all,

Lani

SHARING KENYA

Life in our African universe was shifting gears. The heavy push on program proposals slowed to a doable pace and we were actually going to the office every day like normal people. Life in Kenya was now familiar. David came home one day with a phone number on a scrap of paper.

"Puppies. Cairn terriers. What do you think?"

A few days later we were having dinner at the home of a Canadian woman who was interviewing us on our acceptability for purchasing one of her Cairn terrier puppies. Over a plate of braised beef tongue and lima beans we were queried and didn't even pause when she stated that of course we'd have to agree to show the dog when it was old enough. She was trying to introduce the breed to Kenya and would guide us through the process when the time came. An adorable ball of fur had already captured our hearts so the words just spilled out, "Of course. We'd be delighted."

So it was that Stadi entered our lives, looking so much like our beloved Kimmer when she was a pup. Alice seemed surprised when we gave him a name, Stadi, meaning old man of the sea in Kiswahili. She was even more surprised when we talked to him and he responded, sit, stay, come. Over the next months the cats eventually adopted him, but not the monkeys. As he grew, he loved to chase them and they'd scamper up a tree and glare down at him. Then one day he grabbed one by the tail. The monkey spun around and slugged him with his fist sending poor Stadi rolling backwards. Lesson learned.

When we got the call months later from the breeder telling us Stadi was eligible for his first show in a few months it shouldn't have been a surprise. She showed me how to groom him, plucking his ears, between his toes, and how to prance him in circles. I did my best practicing in our yard quite aware of the monkeys' watchful eyes glaring curiously down on us.

The show was held at the polo grounds. Looking around we felt dreadfully unprepared. Judges had been flown in from England and Australia, and there we were in the midst of men in pith helmets and knee socks and women in long floral dresses and hairdos, all sipping glasses of Pimms on the well-mown lawns. Cages of elegantly groomed dogs sat on an open shelter at the edge of the showing ring. The pomp of it might have been amusing had it not stood in such stark contrast to everything else in our lives. A promise made was a promise kept, however, and we carried through. Stadi won a blue ribbon for best in breed in his age group and blue ribbons in the next two shows each under different judges, earning him his championship status. His silver cup became our ticket out of the polo grounds.

Megan arrived for a visit in the fall and pitched in sorting my stacks of papers and countless notebooks so we set up a spot in the office for her. On weekends David took her tenting in Amboseli and touring various projects, father sharing with daughter what this venture in Africa meant. It was around Christmas when I flew back to the states, our second African Christmas, just as the jacaranda trees were in full lavender bloom, just as everyone was heading back to their village for family time, so was I. Garrett and Mary Beth were getting married. Being with my kids really spun me around, seeing them more as adults, each off on their own life path. My dad had marked his atlas map with every trip we took, ever the navigator. My mom kept repeating how relieved she was, so relieved to see me. The jolt back into American culture was more abrupt than I expected. The small luxuries of everyday life stuck out, the ease of systems working. In our house in Nairobi we joked that if the water was running and the electricity was on, the phone certainly wouldn't be working, and now I was back in the land where everything worked and everyone took everything for granted.

After the wedding, Garrett and Mary Beth followed me back to Kenya for their honeymoon and together we set out an ambitious agenda. Somehow the four of us packed into our wee VW bug with tents and gear and headed to Amboseli National Park. Park rangers came out of their fenced-in compound and guided us to the camping area in the open savannah. That should have been our first clue. Picking out a spot to pitch our tents we kicked aside a number of dried elephant patties. That should have been our next clue. We had already learned that African elephants are much larger than the more docile Asian elephants. We knew all too well that they will readily attack when they feel threatened, but the excitement of the moment prevailed.

After a full day of driving through the park and a campfire dinner, we crawled into our tents. It was a strange rumbling that woke me up, a low gurgling sound. I woke up David. We poked our heads out of our tent. Elephants, one right outside. We were peering between elephant legs at the moonlit peak of Kilimanjaro. We were later told it was the churning of their stomachs we had heard. When they had moved on all four of us crept as quickly and quietly as we could for the relative safety of our VW bug. David and Garrett threw more wood on our campfire until the flames shot up, an extra precaution for the remainder of that sleepless night. Later we were able to laugh about it together. Sitting on our porch sharing experiences felt like home had come to Africa.

LATRINES FOR MATHARE

There was a cholera outbreak in Mathare Valley. The word came like a lightning strike yet no one was surprised. The newspaper article blamed the goat butchers dumping waste in the river where so many fetched their water. Everyone knew it went beyond that. The lack of latrines meant people were dealing with human waste any way they could and the consequences were inevitable. Nurses at the clinic were swamped with sick children dehydrating before their eyes. Outraged at shouldering the blame the goat butchers called a community meeting at the clinic and staff asked us to accompany them.

The clinic was full when we arrived. We listened. The city had never been willing to fund latrines for Mathare Valley, still the publicity of cholera in Nairobi was a major threat to tourism. One nurse spoke up. The city might grant permission to build a latrine if someone else paid for it. It would have to meet their criteria of course. More people were going to die if we don't do something. Heads were nodding. Where do we get the money? We charge people to use the latrine, someone suggested. A great mumble and chatter buzzed around, people circulating, voices rising and falling. We had no clue what was happening until the room finally quieted down. The leader of the meeting clapped his hands to gain attention then read the decision off his notebook. Someone would have to be hired to keep the latrine clean, guard it at night. Only those who paid the fee could use it. Fees for goat butchers selling meat would be one hundred shillings, goat butchers selling guts fifty shillings, vegetable mamas twenty-five shillings, renting out a bed twenty shillings, selling home brewed beer fifty shillings, bottled beer one hundred shillings. We looked around. All heads were nodding in agreement, no questions raised.

We looked at each other in disbelief. Friends at the university had been trying for years to determine how the economy of Mathare functioned, how it was stratified. Now here it was all clearly laid out.

Someone suggested the name of a young Kenyan engineer searching for a job. He had the necessary qualifications to design and oversee construction but would need a modest salary. Obviously outside funds would be needed for the completion beyond what Mathare residents could raise. I started contacting donors while David worked with council staff in Mathare getting the permits. Within a few weeks Mathare families were digging a deep pit for a six-hole latrine under the watchful eye of the young engineer. They had collected funds sufficient to pay for two courses of concrete blocks for the foundation. We had secured some outside funding, but were awaiting more responses. Every shilling would be needed.

There was never just one thing happening at the council. I was studying the calendar on our office wall, almost unreadable with crossed out appointments and overlapping commitments when David returned from Mathare. They were going to need more funding sooner than expected. They were almost ready for the corrugated iron roofing panels and there were no funds left. He didn't want the work to slow down waiting for materials or people might get discouraged and drift away.

Phillip brought in tea and set two cups down amidst the clutter on my desk and handed me the mail. I shuffled through it and handed David a well-stamped envelope from the states with his name on it settling

233

back with my cup of tea. If there's one piece of British colonial history I appreciated it was a well-brewed cup of tea and the uninterrupted tradition of tea time twice a day.

"Oh my god!" David plopped down in his chair, letter in hand, head thrown back. "I don't believe it." He was laughing, waving the letter in the air. "I don't believe it."

"I'm too tired to guess."

"Old Jeep."

"What about Old Jeep?"

"Five thousand. The guy who drove off without paying? Remember how duped I felt? Told Jim about it as we were leaving. Apparently, he contacted a lawyer, tracked the guy down. Told him to pay up or he'd report it to the police."

"That was a lifetime ago," I said.

"It's a check."

We stared at the check then laughed in disbelief. Five thousand dollars. It was enough to buy the corrugated iron for the roof of the latrine, a gift from Old Jeep with its own metal roof sawed off.

When the roof was completed David headed to Mathare to check on final details. He found volunteers painting the structure. Five-gallon buckets of paint had apparently appeared out of thin air. He decided not to ask. Brilliant blue, yellow, red, was being creatively painted on walls, doors, around vents.

A crowd gathered for the opening ceremony of the latrines. Men in three-piece suits stood on the steps making speeches interrupted by outbursts of clapping and cheers. Over the following weeks and months, we got regular reports from Mathare staff. The latrines were working well, the committee was meeting regularly, inspecting the cleaning, seeing that fees were collected. We also got word about another organization. Seeing the success of the latrine they contracted a professional construction firm to build another latrine in Mathare, red brick, real glass windows, smooth concrete floors. It stood like a gem in the mud, but within a month it became so filthy gangs started trashing it and it was eventually locked by the city. We weren't surprised.

Little in Kenya surprised us anymore. The stream of requests coming in for small business grants was overwhelming. Humphrey was coordinating more than a dozen groups selling everything from bread to wire fencing churned out by a youth group. He had spread the word beyond Ruai and now Peace Corps Volunteers and NGO workers were stopping by offering to be coordinators for small communities across Kenya. The number of groups had reached more than 400 when Ford Foundation contacted me. They had been searching for what worked in development assistance for the lowest grassroots level and were curious about this direct-grants program. Would I be interested in doing an evaluation of what profit these businesses were actually making, what was the impact on the lives of the recipients of such a small grant? My own curiosity had been growing on these same questions. Within weeks they approved the evaluation design I submitted and we would be on safari across Kenya once again.

LETTER: JEANNIE'S VISIT

Jambo!

What an amazing month since Jeannie arrived. I am really saddened to think she is leaving tomorrow; it hardly seems possible four weeks have gone by so quickly. Sharing Kenya with my daughter takes more than this little slot of time, still we are all catching our breath at the pace of all we've done and seen. It was so special going back to Lamu with Jeannie, this time by small bush plane. Seeing the coast from the air for the first time was beautiful and alarming. From every creek and inlet fingers of red silt were flowing for miles into the deep turquoise of the Indian Ocean swirling in spider web patterns. It looked like the continent was bleeding its precious soil into the sea. We landed on Manda Island across from Lamu at the "international airport." The sign was posted on a tiny hut next to the single sand landing strip. Then to the ferry taking us to Lamu. Walking the streets was a joy showing Jeannie the house where we lived, our favorite wood carving shops, kiosks for lunch, this time seeing it through new eyes. Three full days went too fast.

Luckily we had a break from work so we were able to stay on the coast another week. We had never taken time to experience Fort Jesus, built by the Portuguese in the late 1500s, a massive stone structure jutting out from Mombasa harbor serving as a slave trading funnel to Arabia and the Persian Gulf and a gateway to India. While we had a growing familiarity with today's Kenya, this was stepping back into its history of invaders. The remarkable design of this fort had canons pointing in every possible direction of attack from the sea, others pointed inland to forestall local uprisings. We hadn't expected to be this emotionally hit seeing such a massive operation, slave-holding cells much as they had been. Having seen the caves of Shimoni, this fortress filled in another part of the history few wanted to remember.

Back in Nairobi we were due to check on projects in Ruai. Jeannie mastered the video camera and filmed as we went. Then we were off to Maasai Mara Game Park — rhinos, lions, giraffes stretching out their legs to drink, zebras everywhere. A new experience, staying in tent cabins like tourists. From there we set out on a three-day trip around Mount Kenya checking out potential village improvement sites. It's been a whirlwind.

Thanks for sending the videotapes with Jeannie. We have been memorizing lines from African Queen – "Human nature, Mr. Allnut, is what we've been put on earth to rise above." Sends us into howls every time. Also loving Casablanca, "Looks like this is the beginning of a beautiful friendship." Alice watched the tape of Ringling Brothers circus with us, exclaiming, "hakuna nguo!" no clothes, over and over seeing the trapeze artists. When the elephants danced, she kept whispering, "ona, ona," look at that, shaking her head in disbelief.

These past few days we've been scouring the markets with Jeannie in search of treasures to bring back, stopping for a cold beer at the Norfolk Hotel where Hemingway supposedly hung out, a fitting closure to her visit. She will have so much more to share with you. Over the past ten months we've had the joy of almost back-to-back visits from our children. With Chris in college in Alaska and Becca a new mom, sadly both are unable to come, so this may be our last visit from family. All the sadder to see her go.

Love you all so much,

Lani

EVALUATING LIFE

"Tell me about your business."

"We sell beans, rice, maize. See these cabbages, and *skumawiki*. We sell also *mboga*, these vegetables." The group leader was pointing to their wooden stand set back from the road as the other women crowded around her. "Each week we buy these great sacks."

"How much profit do you make?"

The leader bent towards the women, most likely explaining my question. We waited.

"We don't make profits."

"No profits?"

"Then," I was hesitant. "Why do you keep working?"

They all laughed. "But how would we live?"

Thinking they had not understood my question I took another approach. "Tell me what happens when you buy these great sacks of beans."

The leader didn't hesitate. "We sell one tin of beans for two shillings. Same for maize. Same for rice. The women who worked that day take home the wilted outside cabbage leaves or too soft tomatoes that can't sell tomorrow. At end of week we each take home a kilo of beans, a kilo of maize, a kilo of rice." They were all nodding, smiling.

"And then you buy more beans, maize, rice?"

"Yes." There was a pause as they whispered to one another. "And other things, sometimes."

"Other things?"

"Sometimes we buy *sufarias*, new pots for cooking, one for each of us, though we say to our husbands 'this belongs to my group, I can use it for now, but the group wants it back,' for you see the husband might sell it to buy beer. Sometimes we buy blankets, sometimes we buy soap. We decide together."

Hesitantly I asked if they kept a record, wrote down numbers, how many shillings for the bag of beans, how many to buy the *sufarias*?

They were all shaking their heads. They did not write down numbers. Even if they knew how to write down numbers it would not be wise. The men might see how many shillings they had.

I tried not to react to the picture that was emerging, looking down at my carefully crafted questionnaire I flipped it over to the blank side to take notes.

"Do you spend group shillings on other things?"

They began chattering among themselves again before the leader spoke up. "School fees. We pay school fees."

"Ah, school fees. For each woman's family?"

They were all nodding.

"But what if one woman has six children in school and another has only two?"

They looked puzzled at the question.

"We pay school fees. For children to learn. Also *dawa*, medicine, if someone is sick, family members," the leader explained.

Heads were bobbing, back and forth passing comments on to the leader.

"And weddings. We cook for weddings if someone in one of our family marries, we all cook."

"Does anyone write any of this on a piece of paper?"

Heads were shaking.

I was restructuring my questions as I went. "Since you started this business how has your life changed?"

A chorus of voices burst out at once, hands waving, some laughter. The leader listened all around, hushed the group then spoke.

"They say now their children are all going to school, not just the boys, even the girls. Also they say their *sufari* is full every night."

A woman came up and whispered in her ear.

"Oh, yes. We are also learning to read. The kind social worker, from the council, she is stopping by. She has given us some of these old school books. She teaches us the words. Perhaps next time you come we will even be able to write down numbers for you."

David had been taking pictures, shooting video, women filling tins of beans, peeling wilted outer leaves of cabbage, dancing in celebration at day's end, both of us wondering as we drove off with all the blanks on my questionnaire still blank, how could any picture or questionnaire capture what had just unfolded. Indeed, what had just unfolded?

Traveling from group to group, women raising chickens, selling eggs or honey, raising rabbits, weaving baskets woven from sisal or beach grass, it didn't seem to matter. Every session began with a welcoming song, women beating out the melody with clapping hands and hoots. Every session ended with a dance, pulling me into their midst. Lifting up each other's spirits seemed an essential part of every gathering. The story was the same with groups everywhere we went. The added boost of the small grant had enabled them to buy wholesale, or buy tools that helped the business take off. All hopes of analyzing real data, however, had drifted away in the wind. What I came away with were dozens of stories with a similar thread. Women were devising mutual support societies providing each other with healthcare, education, nutrition and obviously emotional support. By any human development index, it was amazing.

My questions had to change. Tell me the story of your group before you got the grant. Tell me the story of what you did with the funds. Tell me the story of your group now. The storytellers needed to be unleashed. The teacher had to become the learner.

Our final lap of group visits for the evaluation was flying by, my notebooks were piling up but there was one woman I had to visit before I could write my report. It was walking through Mathare we first met Imani, mother of ten children selling small packets of charcoal, scooping the black lumps from giant burlap bags into newspaper cones, a day's worth of fuel for one woman to cook, costing a few shillings. She had built a cardboard lean-to and it was here she and her children slept on top of the sacks, cardboard protecting them from the rain, they in turn protecting the precious sacks from those who might try to snitch some coals in the night. This was home, no room to stand up, a bit of shelter, three stones outside the blanket flap where they cooked, no furniture except sacks arranged as beds under a cardboard roof.

Imani was measuring out the coal, her older children folding newspaper cones, younger ones scratching pictures with sticks in the sooty charcoal dirt that first day when we stopped. It was evident the children were not in school. We stopped to greet her, introduced ourselves, asked how her family was doing, how her charcoal business was doing. Listening, to the acceptance, to the hope. With a bit of help how would she make her business better. She was quick to reply. Kerosene for lanterns, that's what she would sell, as well as charcoal of course, but there was much more profit in kerosene, she had seen it with her own eyes, she poked a finger to her eye in emphasis. You would not believe how well the kerosene sellers were doing, also those selling soda water, yes, the water here was not to be trusted, people wanted soda water. Her eyes glistened when we spoke of the small grant. With her plan she and her older children more than qualified.

Now almost a year later we were headed down the same road where we had first met her in Mathare. She spotted us before we recognized her. There she was, boards spread across boxes forming a long counter, children at one end filling tins of kerosene, others wrapping cones of charcoal, at the far end the tallest daughter selling soda. With squeals she pulled us over, a tumble of words flying through the air.

"*Nyumbani yangu, nyumbani yangu,*" my house, my house, she kept repeating pointing toward a mud and wattle hut behind the counter. See my daughter, the one selling soda water, she goes to school, she even knows numbers, she writes down everything now so we are not cheated anymore.

Before I could catch my breath much less pull out a notebook she was pulling us inside her small hut. Look at this. She stretched out to her full height. I am so blessed as you can see. I now have a house where I can stand up.

I realized in that moment I was no longer horrified at Mathare. I was seeing beyond the squalor, this real face, this real woman, her bed made of sticks, a mattress of poly sacks and blanket fluff, a crate with tins of meal and beans next to a stove, a metal grate perched on stones.

Sit, sit she insisted leading us to the bed. We squeezed together and hesitantly sat down. By now we had learned that to sit down is to accept the hospitality offered. She rushed out. Children took turns poking their heads through the doorway, giggling at us. She came back bearing two bottles of orange soda.

Now, she said, I have the greatest gift of all. I have enough that I can give to others. She handed us each an orange soda. I could feel my heart sink into the blanket fluff. Words totally failed us. She watched as we drank the sweet orange soda, nodding and smiling at our every swallow.

Back home attempting to type what had happened on our feeble laptop felt impossible. Written words could never paint a picture of Imani. We humans are ingenious problem solvers. We are also storytellers, even when we tell our stories with waving hands and the generosity of warm soda. If we are to learn we must listen to each other's stories. If we are to teach, we must tell one another the stories we have learned from.

The opportunity to hear even more stories was suddenly upon us. More than four thousand women were converging on Nairobi. Women in colorful Latin American shawls, veiled women peeking through eye slots, black *bui-buis* covering them from head to toe, being followed by male chaperones, women in jeans, tee-shirts and backpacks arriving like swarms in pollinating season, which is essentially what the Decade for Women in Development gathering was. Ten years prior women from around the globe had gathered in Mexico City to lay out an ambitious ten-year plan to improve the role of women in development. Now they were gathering to share their results.

We had been planning our humble workshop for weeks and now we were bringing women from several of our business groups to Nairobi, most for the first time in their lives seeing the city, its tall elegant buildings, sidewalk cafes serving food they had never seen, sleeping at the YMCA with flush toilets, hot showers. They were there to share their stories of success at our workshop, one of several hundred alongside major meetings, Gloria Steinem moderating panels on women's rights, US Congresswoman Bella Abzug speaking on women and the environment, and Kenyan activist Wangari Maathai sharing her Green Belt Movement. The air was electric with ideas, groups gathering in the shade of sprawling trees in the parks between events, the hum of women's animated voices permeating the air.

The pollen I personally collected was hearing the first woman attorney in Korea telling her story, organizing other women attorneys as they emerged with law degrees in hand, identifying every law on the books that was unjust for women and setting out to change those laws. They became a force to be reckoned with besieging the males in their lives, leaders local and national, to change legislation as well as how laws were applied. Simultaneously they organized brigades of village women who set out on bicycles, advising women on their rights of inheritance, protection from domestic abuse, spreading the word about laws already in place but not adhered to at the village level. Now, ten years later, she was presenting their accomplishments. They had reversed 95% of the laws they had identified as adverse to women. Cheers went up in explosive waves, rising and falling as women translated for one another.

Under every shade tree, across grassy parks, women gathered after the sessions, famous women who had just given presentation to mass audiences now sitting in the grass with village women, NGO leaders, women sharing ideas, communicating anyway possible, hands waving in the air, hugging, laughing when they couldn't understand each other's words, hearing the spirit in each other's voices.

Our workshop went well. I was humbled, seeing village women we had worked with stand in front of women from other lands they couldn't have imagined, sharing their stories. As they boarded their buses on the final day it was hard to tell what impact the entire event had on them, heading back to their villages, back to their lives, wondering what stories they would be telling other women when they got home.

JOHN

John called. There were long pauses. He wanted to tell me himself. He just got the diagnosis. It was HIV.

I couldn't find words. Everything that finally came out of my mouth sounded so meaningless, so hollow. He had told the kids. He wasn't sure how they were taking it. Here he was, head of the statistics and biostatistics department, his own pattern recognition models were being successfully used by cardiologists to diagnose heart disease. He was an authority on toxicity and survival rates, a member of the Environmental Protection Agency's science review panel. He knew the odds better than anyone. He spoke of experimental drugs for HIV-AIDS. I tried to hear hope in his voice. I felt a profound silence settling inside of me.

"Medical science owes me one," he said quietly, humbly. I knew he meant to comfort me.

Those words never left me.

It was months later when David and I were collecting avocados and mangoes from under our trees, tossing the ones that monkeys had bitten into, filling baskets with the ripe fruit when the call came. It was Gregg. They had just taken John to the hospital. He wasn't sure how much time he had left.

"Start packing, I'll get the ticket." David was out the door before we could even discuss a plan. We had a contact via friends for getting last minute business class tickets at such low cost we were questioned checking in at the airport. I was on the plane that night.

The children and I converged in John's condo near the university, the anguish of grief needing few words, seeking respite in hugging each other, staring out at the Hudson River, barges heading to unknown places, water shuttles carrying people from shore to shore. We were rotating watches at the hospital. John was not expecting me. We hugged finding it hard to let go. I sat beside his bedside as we held hands, sharing long ago memories of silly things. He was alert at times, then drifting into deep sleep. Graduate students flowed in and out throughout each day. Respects paid to their advisor triggered his sudden alertness, questioning cach one on progress in their dissertation research, zeroing in on their problems, hurdles they faced, throwing out suggestions for alternative approaches, his mind clear and vibrant, eager students taking notes on scraps of paper and the backs of hospital menus. One after the other they came. Day after long day.

Flags flew at half-mast across the campus of Columbia University. The chapel was overflowing as tributes were spoken, accomplishments I never knew about spoken by people I had never met, the John I knew, the John I never knew, an endowment in his name created by the university in his honor.

In the months I was away, HIV-AIDS had been rapidly spreading across the African continent. In Uganda churches were inserting informational pamphlets in choir hymnals. In Kenya it hovered as the new plague, the unspoken fear over every community. Meanwhile the drought was still swallowing the green edges of the desert, Mathare was still growing with families fleeing rural hunger, women were still averaging seven children each, tourists were still flowing in to see the real Africa. I spent my grieving time at home with David, taking solace in my notebooks and writing.

FINDING MYSELF

If I find myself in the desert, let me not dwell on the burning sun or the parched earth,

Let me stand sleek and light like the solitary blade of grass, straining not to block the scorching winds, but bending with them gracefully,

Let me take my sustenance from far beneath the sands where treasures have been laid, if only I grow roots to reach them.

If I find myself in the deepest forest, let me be as the fawn, grazing where I might,

Sleeping where the grass is willing, listening to the wisdom of the trees in the stillness of the night,

Seeing not the dark loneliness but only the glint of moonlight silvery on a single patch of leaves,

Slowly brushing me with the gift of hidden light.

If I find myself in faraway lands, let me be with simple people, eating as they eat, sleeping as they sleep,

Listening to their lives when I do not know their words,

Counting not the differences but seeing the self in each face, the flicker of shared soul in even the strangest heart,

The holiness of eternal wisdom in one whose robes are different than mine.

If I find myself on an ocean of uncertainty, let me sail with what wind comes,

Gliding as the gull caught in sun drenched drops, held by the warmth rising up from the sea,

Rushing with a breeze cooled from somewhere else to take me on,

Mingling as a droplet within the wave, unaware of where I stop and others begin,

Only aware of the ocean we are, the effortless flow that sings through us as we try to reflect the light from above,

Striving to be crystal.

COAST COLONIALS

While driving continued to be wild and crazy we had been noticing a definite escalation. Cars were revving up then bursting into roundabouts, squealing around curves, racing down dirt roads side by side. Safari Rally Fever we were told. Africa's version of the Grand Prix. Drivers came from around the world to speed their way through Kenya's hills, savannahs and villages, engines blasting, pedestrians and animals scattering when they heard the roar of the engines. Said to be the most challenging of the world's car races, the excitement was palpable everywhere we went. Tales of Safari Rallies past filled the air, the car that was airborne hitting a bump, coming down so hard it split in two, both drivers walking away unharmed, villagers lining up so thickly along roads there was barely room for a car to pass, approaching drivers snaking widely from one side of the road to the other to clear the crowd ahead. In the weeks prior to the invasion, Kenyan drivers caught the spirit, screeching around corners, challenging lorries and zebra striped tourist vans regardless of what lay ahead. Nairobi traffic became untenable. The coast seemed gratefully spared from this year's rally route so we packed up and headed out.

The drive to the coast was a string of familiar images, shifting beauty that constantly stunned us. From an altitude of more than a mile high the air changed from crisp to muggy, deep greens faded into paler shades, pines gave way to acacia. Then came baobab trees, the upside-down trees of mythology, some living for three thousand years, hollowed out trunks, some with girths over a hundred feet around, spacious enough to live in, doorways carved out by time, limbs dropping seed pods beloved by baboons. When we spotted the baobabs we knew we'd soon be seeing baboons. They were there in numbers, lining the roadside, perched on rocks or guardrails watching cars and trucks passing by. I was fond of waving to them as we passed, hoping to see a change in their grumpy gaze but never did.

We skirted Mombasa and headed up the coast. Kanamai would once again be our base, our home away from home.

Traffic was backed up at the toll bridge near the creek. A pushcart loaded with green coconuts had lost a wheel spilling its contents across the road. A few small boys scurried to retrieve the load and the wheel while horns blared. Traffic started up again.

The road was clogged with cars, buses, overloaded *matatus*, people hanging on the sides and rear, and pushcarts, none of them moving very fast. There was a funeral ahead. Mourners walking two abreast in the road, each carrying a branch of red bougainvillea, singing softly as they followed a crude wooden coffin in a pick-up truck. One by one vehicles pulled out to pass the procession.

The ferry was loading when we got to the next creek. The stubby barge had its own tempo. We leaned over the rail and watched the waters froth and foam around the heavy vessel. The creek cut inland from the Indian Ocean turning a deep turquoise with here and there a patch of silvered gold reflecting the long rays of the sun. Across the creek red tile roofs swept broadly over the startlingly white plastered walls of elegant houses embedded in the soft green fringe of palm shrubs above the cliffs. Further up this coastal road lay Kanamai, our home away from home.

A few kilometers beyond the ferry a lorry was stopped at an angle in the road ahead blocking traffic from both directions. People stood in the tall grass along the side of the road in silent rows. A zebra striped tourist van lay on its side like a beast that had lost the chase and now stiff and alone awaited its fate. Sunburned tourists huddled together in silence staring at the blanket spread over the lifeless form in the road. It was hot in the sun, the sticky heat hanging like a wet shroud over the road. Cars and vans had backed up in both directions. Someone began directing traffic around the lorry. Vehicles thumped along the rutted ditch in a slow parade past the circle of onlookers. I couldn't take my eyes off the figure lying in the road. How many times had we escaped that fate, how many head-on collisions, how many lorry's barely missing us, squeezing us off the road, spirit woman arms stretched wide.

"Heard about it. A German woman," Harry said when we arrived at his house. We had met Harry through friends on previous trips to the coast, an elderly Brit confined to his lounge chair due to diabetes and leg problems, welcoming all and sundry to his house perched high on the shores of Mtwapa Creek north of Mombasa. If Harry didn't know where some place or person was or the history of something, no one did.

"A *matatu,* racing down the wrong side of the road, as usual. The tour driver swerved and they flipped. Doesn't take much to flip."

As usual he had a cold supper and drinks ready to welcome us. His leg was propped up on a stool near the screening where he could spend the afternoon watching the creek.

"When the police finally arrived, someone told them there was a coffin nearby — at Mrs. Cummings' place. She's the woman who's been wanting you to stop by, always looking for new faces. Of course, I told her about you. Loves some company — tea and a chat sort of thing. Not sure what happened next, with the accident and all. You might want to pay her a call tomorrow. If you have time. Lovely woman. Lonely. But aren't we all."

He poured glasses of lemonade all around. "I should warn you, Jane is coming. I told you about Jane, didn't I? Half crazy, really pathetic. Her husband was in the colonial service, years older. I'm not sure what happened, but eventually they divorced. I think he died of booze somewhere up in Turkana trying to run camel safaris. She was never allowed to get a work permit, though I'm not sure what she'd do if she ever got one. Born here, like the rest of us, but her parents died early and she couldn't hold onto a scrap of their land at independence. No smarts, no education, really. She's just been drifting around all these years. Anyway, every now and then she calls me up, says she can't pay the rent for the night at the flop house where she stays and needs to wash her dress and get a good meal."

"I can tell it's me you're all talkin' about." A woman peered around the corner, a stuffed market basket in hand. She was painfully thin, legs like sticks, arms weak and colorless. "Speaking of which, a guy at the bar gave me twenty shillings this afternoon. And coming here on the *matatu* a guy actually got up and gave me his seat. Can you beat that? In Kenya? Now I need a beer."

She sat down and looked around the room.

"I really don't care if you all was talkin' about me. I'm a character. Harry knows, don't you, Harry?"

She walked into the kitchen and popped open a bottle of beer. Standing in front of the open refrigerator she ate cheese and cold meatloaf out of hand then returned to the veranda.

"Hey, I heard your fancy pants neighbors having a big shindig. Some bloody healer is coming from England and they've got all these tents set up like it was the queen's wedding. They're bringing in Gilmore by bush plane from Naivasha. He can't even sit up now, I hear. Cancer. I won't live long enough to die of anything like that."

She drank half a bottle of beer without pausing, then retreated to the kitchen.

"A healing session?" I looked at Harry.

"Quite a big deal here. Last time this bloke came, they had nearly a hundred people show up – came from all over Kenya. Expect it will be more this time. He's got a worldwide reputation, you know. At least that's what some say. One young girl came, leukemia. Now apparently there's not a trace. They discovered him in London, cockney chap, psychic too. They bring him back every year or so, figure there's enough old settlers here who'll chip in for his airfare.

"Hard to really say what got healed, due to the bloke, I mean. You never hear the full story. One woman said he talks to you real soft, tells you to relax, think of white light, he passes his hands over you, your head goes sort of fuzzy, and then his hands settle on the sick part of you — all without you telling him what's wrong or where it hurts."

Jane stuck her head through the kitchen door, sandwich in her hand. "As for me, I don't go for any of that religious stuff. Spooks me out."

"It isn't religious," Harry burst in. "He's just a gifted man, that's all. And it so happens a lot of people were cured of some pretty dreadful diseases without a prayer being said, so there!"

"Then you should go and get that leg healed, not like any of us have money buried somewhere for doctors - or medical insurance — ha. Hell, we'll probably end up in some government hospital like Africans."

It was another one of those moments when remaining silent felt so wrong. We both got up, ready to excuse ourselves as Jane rolled on without a pause.

"Sidney's got a fat job with that new beach hotel. With those Italians, Mafia probably, but they pay well. He gets a house right on the beach. So, I say, what's wrong with Mafia, anyway? I'd work for them if they'd give me a house on the beach."

Harry let out a bellowing laugh as Jane disappeared down the hall toward the spare bedroom. It was getting late. Our cottage was waiting for us at Kanamai, which gave us the excuse to be on our way. Harry pleaded with us to stay for supper, Jane would be sleeping it off, his eyes were almost desperate, but somehow we had to get out of there.

Once again the Indian Ocean became our solace that evening. I wrote on the terrace listening to the waves wash over the reef until it was too dark to see. In the morning a note from Harry was delivered to our door. He had called Mrs. Cummings. She was delighted we were in the area, how dreadful that we had passed the scene of the accident, really hoping we could visit this time. Though we had wanted to spend more time pulling notes together her invitation was so compelling we couldn't say no.

An elderly man opened the gate outside her property and nodded as we drove through. Two peacocks stretched their necks as we pulled up the driveway, then pecked their way across the scrubby yard thankfully content to ignore us. Almost hidden by an overgrown cascade of bougainvillea the modest house sat on a slight rise overlooking the sea, wraparound porches giving it a quaint, comfortable look.

Mrs. Cummings welcomed us at the door. A petite woman with a thin smile, she led us into a screened section of the porch with overstuffed wicker furniture and a small table set for three. We had barely introduced ourselves and sat down where she indicated when she began.

"It took a lot of effort, mind you, to get people to put in a few shillings each for that simple wooden coffin. But what could I do? She was a white woman after all. Goodness. We must have a cup of tea and think what to do. Jacob! *Lete chai sasa!*"

She settled back in her chair, her white hair fluffed about her face like a furry halo, her deep-set eyes looking suddenly intense.

"Just like that. After all the work I went through to have things ready. Well, it's gone, can you imagine?"

Jacob set down a large tray with an ornate cracked teapot, and three small cups. Beaded nets covered the milk pitcher and the sugar bowl. Mrs. Cummings poured the tea and took a deep breath.

"You know this whole coffin business started last year. Just after old Milton died a few of us girls got talking, with so many of us getting on in years around here, and what with the roads being what they are and the ferry sometimes not working, well, it could take a long time, that is if someone did pass away, to get a body into Mombasa to a decent funeral home. And what with the heat and all, well you can just imagine. You've just seen for yourselves, there's not even someone around here who can pick up a body decently. What with our younger generation off and gone, no one left to bury us but each other. Like a bunch of British elephants gathering at the graveyard, waiting our turn, just waiting — that's what my husband always said when he'd had a few. Though Lord only knows what anyone does, when it does happen that is, except I suppose get some neighbors to help load you into a station wagon or something. Like this poor tourist.

"That's when we all agreed to start freezing tins of ice. You know, sticking small tins in the freezer whenever we could. Lord knows in this heat how much ice you'd need to get a poor soul into Mombasa from here. Especially if the ferry was out and you had to wait a day. Heaven forbid. So we all agreed to have that coffin built, just a simple one, by a local *fundi*. We all pitched in to pay for it of course, and they moved it to my shed. Well, we've felt splendidly prepared mind you, and to tell the truth I haven't thought about it much since, except now and then when I freeze a new tin of ice. Until today." She paused and looked suddenly startled.

"Dearie me, I wonder if we shouldn't have sent some ice along."

She took a long slow sip of her tea. "Of course now we must begin again, to take up another collection for a coffin. Poor Mrs. Reynolds, dear soul. I know she'll be shocked to hear we've lost that box. Mind you, it was nothing fancy, but at least it was a proper box."

"Now tell me, what do you Americans think about all of this mess in Nairobi, these students parading around, and this whole election business, just a sham for the fat pockets to do as they always do, having these poor illiterate people line up behind photos of their candidates to vote mind you, no more secret ballots, calling it the African way, and with the army counting who's in what line, just a sham, don't you think?"

We both started to respond at once, but the phone was ringing. Jacob came in with a fresh pot of tea as she left to take the call. We quietly agreed we would leave as soon as she came back.

"Well if we survived the *Mau Mau* we can survive this," she said returning quickly to the room and immediately pouring us another cup or tea. "At least Brewster is close enough to help me, just up the road, that is if anything boils over. But goodness, all he has to deal with. His son, not sure if Harry told you. A real Kenya cowboy, hasn't earned a shilling of his own since he grew whiskers and causing no end of turmoil with all of his African girlfriends. Fancies himself a real safari rally type, racing cars around the countryside. Of course, his whole generation never expected they'd have to earn a living now, did they? With land that stretched beyond eyesight, who'd have suspected it would come to this? Grew up snapping their fingers for servants, and never set a potato to boil in their entire lives. I'm sure poor Brewster is beside himself. All those wild car races and beaded women, and what with the rest of that land probably going to be taken away from him by the government if he doesn't cultivate it – that's the new law, you know. But of course he never says a thing. A real gentleman of the old school, Harry's oldest friend, but I'm sure he must have told you that."

I shook my head. She offered us some biscuits and suddenly changed the subject.

"Will you be settling here? I mean permanently?"

"No, we have family —."

"Worth considering as you grow older, dear, though I've never been to America. I mean where else in the world could we be sitting as we are now – in the dead of winter! I mean, with flowers all about us, and of course the birds. Some days I go down to the shore and just stare at that ocean. Here we sit — and with people to fetch our tea and wash up after us. Now mind you what my sister in England is putting up with at her age. She could never afford to live like this, just a Common Council flat if that. No, I've thought of going back, but then I just look around at my flowers and my birds."

"Harry tells me you're filming all of these projects around Kenya. Really quite an eyeful, I imagine, I mean with all of the corruption and bureaucracy, trying to get anything done that matters must be frustrating."

David was already standing up to leave and given the look on his face he was struggling to remain silent.

"We have met amazing people everywhere we've been," I said. "Struggling against so much history, so many impossible situations, and yet … ."

Mrs. Cummings was rising in an obvious acknowledgement of our imminent departure, smiling broadly, reaching for my hand. "It's wonderful what you're doing, my dear. Truly wonderful. I'd love to hear more about it sometime."

A large African gray parrot squawked from a perch in the archway of the veranda as we left. Mrs. Cummings patted its head, cooing to it. A gentle breeze stirred in the coleus plants that almost blocked the view of the garden beyond as we drove away.

I felt so depressed that evening back at Kanamai, wondering if we were part of another wave of outsiders who had descended upon Africa. How many Mrs. Cummings were there here? The coast seemed to attract them, or so we had heard. We had friends, several British families who had made commitments to Kenya's independence as a new nation recovering from colonialism, becoming citizens at a time when others were fleeing, spending their lives in education or medicine, quietly, respectfully supporting those around them. Still, the lingering shadow of colonialism was everywhere, and neo-colonialism was growing.

Back at Kanamai we sat on the veranda of our small cottage watching the waves as they crested over the reef. Coconut trees rimmed the shoreline, our collection of coconuts lay on the small wooden bench where we had cracked open some to nibble the sweet meat. The moon was rising casting glittery streaks over the water. The allure was strong. This truly was paradise. For some.

When the dust from the Safari Rally was finally settling across Kenya we headed back to Nairobi. Ange Ove coughed and quit about halfway. We pulled over and got out. David's head was under the hooded wrestling with the air filter when I saw them approaching. Baboons. They were lumbering towards us from their roadside perches, five or six of them casually swaggering, fanning out. They had always looked fairly harmless as we whizzed by from the safety of our car, but seeing them at ground level, heads about my shoulder height, massive chests, long teeth protruding from their grumpy lips, all painted another picture.

"Baboons!" I yelled to warn David then scrambled into the back seat and emerged with a metal cookie tin and a flashlight, the only loose things I could grab. I started banging on my tin drum, shouting at them. The baboons paused, probably amused, then, broadening their circle of approach came closer. With no food to throw at them the only thing I could do was up my volume and my antics. Arms spread wide I began leaping around as best I could, trying out a lion's roar, banging on the tin. David kept glancing up while he stuck to his task. When he swung down the hood with a bang, we both made a dash, jumping back in the car, slamming our doors behind us. The baboons sat down and watched as we pulled away.

"Just another day in Africa," David said smiling.

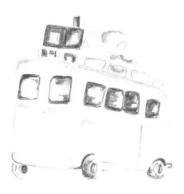

KWAHERI, ALICE

In a sense we began to leave Africa the day we arrived. Promises to family, storing the stuff of a life we'd eventually return to, it was inevitable this safari would ultimately lead us home. All of this danced in and out of the background of our thoughts despite the compelling beat of African drums. Some expats made a life commitment to stay, to work with the most needy in the world, others with few ties back home escaping into another culture was what they came for. We didn't seem to fit in either category.

Word reached us from Rapsu. Someone had cut the wires on the elephant fence. Before the fence was built they had been skimming bags of relief food, selling them in the market, no secret to the community. When the fence went up, and the shambas grew back, the relief food stopped. The guilty man expected relief would begin again if he cut the fence but the elephants didn't forget. Even with the wires cut, they no longer raided the fields and relief food was no longer needed.

The latrine project in Mathare was doing well, various groups now seeking to construct more like it. In Ruai, the nursery school, bread-baking and house-building projects were thriving under Humphrey's guidance. The city council's decision to deem the basket roof houses permanent meant more could be built launching the youth group into a profitable enterprise making concrete-sisal roof tiles. A young

American couple had moved into the squatter settlement, Quaker volunteers, making a long-term commitment to the community.

There is a time for accompanying others along the path, sharing the challenges, offering what you can. There is also a time for quietly walking backwards out of the scene so others hardly notice you are no longer there. Home was beckoning.

Alice's face sank then she broke into tears when we told her our plans. We would be leaving in a few months. We weren't sure we'd be coming back after our furlough so we were giving up the house. She had known from the start we wouldn't be in Kenya forever, but despite the nearly five years, maybe because of them, time didn't matter in that moment. I put my arms around her enormous shoulders as she sobbed, holding back my own tears. Long ago she had made the decision to eventually return to her village beyond Lake Victoria. Now she didn't know how she was going to support herself if she did. She had children there, other family, but everyone was struggling. Perhaps selling vegetables like so many other women, she sobbed out the words. We all knew vegetable mamas could barely feed themselves. What about bread, I asked. When I was teaching the Ruai women's groups to make bread Alice had followed along and while her general culinary skills remained dismal, she had taken to pounding and kneading bread dough like an athlete.

She twisted her lips from side to side, something she was prone to do while thinking.

"*Labda.*" Perhaps. A long pause. "*Labda mkate.*" Perhaps bread.

We extended our bread baking sessions beyond kneading. Alice made jots in the small notebook I had given her despite knowing she couldn't read, trusting her own memory system, proportions of ingredients, rising time, baking heat. She was not exuding confidence. Every time a golden-brown loaf emerged from the oven she raised her arms up in astonishment beholding a miracle.

"*Ona!*" Look at that, she'd exclaim sucking in her breath in disbelief.

Over the next months we followed a determined course in miracles. David tracked down a prison project where inmates were fabricating wood-burning ovens out of heavy sheet metal. On Alice's departure day it took several men at the prison to help lift her new oven onto Ange Ove. As Alice stared up at the hulk of black metal tied down with a bale of rope, we tried to read her eyes, hoping beyond hope she would be able to turn out her own miraculous loaves.

The bus station at the edge of Nairobi was a mass of humanity, dozens of colorful buses surrounded by people lugging impossibly bulky bags, baskets of chickens, babies strapped to backs and breasts, everyone scrambling to find the right bus since few were marked. Floating departure times were the order of the day. Buses broke down. Needed a part. People sat by the side of the lot, waiting. It was the kind of scene we saw as total chaos when we first arrived in Kenya, wondering where the signs were, where were the arrows pointing to which line to wait in. Our left-brained systems, were so orderly, so logical compared to what we saw as chaos. Now, seeing the swarming crowds weaving through each other, elderly mamas getting helped onto buses, people pitching in to hoist bulky bags on top of the bus, calling out the names of destinations to each other, spreading the word as departure times changed, it all seemed normal.

Alice jabbered away in frustration as we picked our way through the crowded lot then burst into excitement pointing to a mustard colored country bus. It took David, the bus driver and several other men to hoist the heavy oven onto the top amidst the sacks of beans and chicken baskets. In all the years we had spent here we never did understand why chickens were always traveling from one place to the next across Kenya. The driver promised he would help Alice unload her oven.

With everyone rushing onboard to grab a seat there was only time for a quick last hug. We didn't even try holding back tears as we watched the bus with Alice's oven perched on top waddle out of the bus station. So much of Africa as we knew it was wrapped up in that one amazing woman and now she was leaving us.

TUTAONANA

Our cameras and film, my notebooks and sketchbooks would travel with us. Stadi was in his wooden crate made by a *fundi* in Mathare Valley. I took down the card I had pinned to the wall in our workroom and tucked it into my bag, my own wording from a Lau Tsu quote.

Start with what the people know, work with what the people have, teach by showing, learn by doing, and with the best of leaders, when the task is done, the people will say we have done this ourselves.

Kadzo drove us to the airport through now familiar roundabouts, lorries still bearing down on everything in their way, goats and people still scattering, bougainvillea in pinks and crimson still climbing over stalls stacked with tomatoes and squashes, the mauve of the Ngong Hills still guarding the outskirts of Nairobi.

"*Tutaonana,*" we shall see each other again, I said.

"*Uso kwa uso.*" face to face, Kadzo responded

Other parting words and promises had already been spoken.

Zebra striped buses were lined up at the airport waiting to load tourists bound for swank hotels and wildlife resorts, setting off on their own safaris to see the real Africa. We worked our way through the crowd of new arrivals, the waving signs of tour leaders gathering their flocks eager to embark on their safaris, the buzz of excitement filling the air as we boarded our plane.

I reached for David's hand as we took off, gaining altitude. The African landscape was growing smaller looking more like a make-believe world, something we might have imagined but now knew, purple hills ringing a city of now familiar streets, the highway of baboons and baobabs sloping to the turquoise sea, another ribbon of road leading to the far north, the game reserve where we learned to drive on the left. Just as we spotted the icy peaks of Kilimanjaro on one side of the plane and Mount Kenya on the other, we rose through the clouds and Africa disappeared. On the final day in one moment the mandala was ceremoniously brushed away as scattered sand. Nothing in this life is permanent. We are all on the path to somewhere. We were on our safari home. Just another day in Africa had lasted five and a half years.

AFTERWORD

Africa still had its hold on us from the moment we arrived home. Famine was devastating southern Sudan so after six months of long-awaited family time, absorbing our children, our parents, we accepted the request to return for one year to manage relief efforts for Church World Service in Nairobi. Dealing with the logistics of getting lorries of relief food through the Congo and Uganda, tracking assistance to refugee camps along the Sudan border with Ethiopia, dealing with recipient countries charging cargo fees for offloading famine food for their own people, all presented different challenges. During that year we also conducted a needs evaluation of the island nations of the Indian Ocean, Seychelles, Madagascar, Mauritius, and Reunion and coordinated a conference in Mauritius to share the results.

When we finally returned to the States after that final year, David became Executive Director of the Trickle Up program, and I worked with the United Nations Development Program developing a training manual for semi-literate grassroots business groups using storytelling as a planning process, returning to Africa once more to field test the training in various countries. When I later became Executive Director of Church World Service, I returned to Kenya once more on a very special trip to welcome the Lost Boys of Sudan as they crossed the border into Kenya having walked more than 1200 mile across the desert fleeing war. Later I served with the Peace Corps as Director of the Center for Field Assistance and Applied Research until my retirement.

Eventually we found that long longed for sailboat, sailed to the Bahamas and lived aboard Ishmael for two years before building a family compound with the help of our kids and grandkids on a small island in Maine. Life has many stories to be lived through, told and remembered, each a lesson of the heart.

ABOUT THE AUTHOR

In the 1980's author Leilani van Ryzin Havens sets off with her husband David for Kenya to document, film, and evaluate life at the grassroots level. From the Indian Ocean to Lake Victoria, Lamu Island and across the desert to the far North, they are pulled into the lives of Maasai youth, nomadic tribal leaders, squatter slum families, women's groups, and aging British colonials. Listening to their stories, the rhythm of their words, the depth of meaning they reveal is spellbinding but there is no one face of Africa, no one story to be told. In long letters to family back home, she shares her five and a half year journey. Painting with richly evocative words her vivid descriptions of the people and places of Kenya are brought tangibly to life as her own safari of personal discovery and healing unfolds. Sharing insights of what it means to cross into another culture, the reader is drawn into an intertwining of treacherous adventures, humorous encounters and personal discovery, realizing that by walking with others on a piece of their path, it is possible to find oneself.

ACKNOWLEDGMENTS

With special thanks to Marla Akin for her insightful suggestions and enthusiastic encouragement that came like a burst of new energy in bringing the pieces of this memoir together. Newly retired as assistant director of the University of Texas Michener Center for Writers for over two decades, her generosity of time, talent, and excitement for this book was a true gift.

My enduring thanks to Bill Perry, linguist, cross-cultural trainer, Peace Corps colleague, and true friend, for his depth of insight, his sense of delight in reading and rereading this manuscript and his persistent encouragement and technical expertise, all essential in making this book happen.

Made in the USA
Monee, IL
11 May 2022